Sisters of Notre Dame
1520 Ralston Ave.
Belmont, CA 94002

P9-CAF-626

Tolkien and C. S. Lewis

Those are the golden sessions . . . when our slippers are on, our feet spread out towards the blaze and our drinks at our elbows; when the whole world, and something beyond the world, opens itself to our minds as we talk; and no one has any claim on or any responsibility for another, but all are freemen and equals as if we had first met an hour ago, while at the same time an Affection mellowed by the years enfolds us. Life — natural life — has no better gift to give. Who could have deserved it?

—C. S. Lewis, "Friendship," The Four Loves

Also by Colin Duriez

TOLKIEN AND THE LORD OF THE RINGS:
A GUIDE TO MIDDLE-EARTH
(HiddenSpring)

THE C. S. LEWIS ENCYCLOPEDIA

THE INKLINGS HANDBOOK
(with David Porter)

Tolkien and C. S. Lewis

The Gift of Friendship

Colin Duriez

HiddenSpring

Copyright © 2003 by Colin Duriez

All rights reserved. No part of this book may be reproduced or transmitted in any form or by any means, electronic or mechanical, including photocopying, recording, or by any information storage and retrieval system without permission in writing from the Publisher.

Cover design by Stefan Killen Design
Cover photos courtesy of Getty Images

Library of Congress Cataloging-in-Publication Data

Duriez, Colin.
    Tolkien and C. S. Lewis : the gift of friendship / Colin Duriez.
       p.   cm.
    Includes bibliographical references and index.
    ISBN 1-58768-026-2 (alk. paper)
    1. Tolkien, J. R. R. (John Ronald Reuel), 1892-1973. 2. Lewis, C. S. (Clive Staples), 1898-1963. 3. Tolkien, J. R. R. (John Ronald Reuel), 1892-1973 – Friends and associates. 4. Lewis, C. S. (Clive Staples), 1898-1963 – Friends and associates. 5. Oxford (England) – Intellectual life – 20th century. 6. Fantasy literature, English – History and criticism. 7. Authors, English – 20th century – Biography. 8. University of Oxford – Biography. 9. Oxford (England) – Biography. 10. Inklings (Group of writers) I. Title.
PR6039.032 Z639 2003
820.9′00912 – dc21

                                                                        2003009013

Published in North America by

HiddenSpring

An imprint of Paulist Press
997 Macarthur Boulevard
Mahwah, New Jersey 07430
www.hiddenspringbooks.com
Printed and bound in the
United States of America

To the siblings

Ian, Barbara, Stephen,
Elizabeth, Paul, Julian

Contents

Preface   ix

1   The Formative Years (1892–1925)   1

2   Meeting of Minds and Imaginations:
"Tolkien and I were talking of dragons...." (1926–1929)   24

3   A Story-Shaped World: "Mythopoeia" (1929–1931)   45

4   The Thirties: The Context of Imaginative Orthodoxy   60

5   The Inklings Begin: Friendship Shared? (1933–1939)   77

6   Two Journeys There and Back Again:
The Pilgrim's Regress and *The Hobbit* (1930–1937)   88

7   Space, Time, and the "New Hobbit" (1936–1939)   99

8   World War II and After:
Charles Williams Comes to Oxford (1939–1949)   112

9   A Professor's Wardrobe and Magic Rings (1949–1954)   130

10   Surprised by Cambridge and Disappointed by Joy (1954–1963)   146

11   A Farewell to Shadowlands (1963–1973)   166

12   The Gift of Friendship: "Who could have deserved it?"   174

Appendix A: A Brief Chronology of J. R. R. Tolkien and C. S. Lewis   189
Appendix B: The Enduring Popularity of J. R. R. Tolkien and C. S. Lewis   198
Notes   205
The Writings of C. S. Lewis and J. R. R. Tolkien   221
Bibliography   227
Acknowledgments   233
Index   235

Preface

I have been aware of the friendship between J. R. R. Tolkien and C. S. Lewis for a long time, since first reading the latter's autobiography as a student, but in writing this book I have been surprised to discover how very strong and persistent it was, despite frictions and troughs that, perhaps, one should expect to occur over nearly forty years. As far as I know, this is the first book that has focused primarily upon their remarkable literary as well as personal association.

J. R. R. Tolkien is, of course, a well-known name around the world, because of the phenomenal popularity of his book *The Lord of the Rings*, and especially since the trilogy of films by Peter Jackson. Indeed, a whole country, New Zealand, where the films were shot, has become "Middle-earth." Hobbits, orcs, Mordor, and a magic ring need little explanation in many pubs, schools, and campuses around the globe.

What is less well known is Tolkien's important and complex friendship with fellow Oxford academic C. S. Lewis. Without the persistent encouragement of his friend, Tolkien acknowledged, he would never have completed *The Lord of the Rings*. This great tale, along with the connected matter of *The Silmarillion*, would have remained merely a private hobby. The quality of their literary friendship invites comparisons with those of William Wordsworth and Samuel Taylor Coleridge, William Cowper and John Newton, and G. K. Chesterton and Hilaire Belloc. Tolkien's Tree-beard, his Ent creation, was inspired by Lewis, especially his sometimes emphatic deep voice — *Brm, hoom!*

C. S. Lewis also has great popularity throughout the world, particularly through his series of children's books, *The Chronicles of Narnia*. As the series title highlights, the focus of these stories is upon an imagined, other world. In creating this world for children, he was steeped in the unfolding events of Middle-earth, which Tolkien read to him as the chapters of *The Lord of the Rings* were being composed. His first Narnian story, *The Lion, the Witch and the Wardrobe*, is set to become a major film, directed by Andrew Adamson, whose previous work includes *Shrek*.

Not only was Tolkien's debt to Lewis enormous. All of Lewis's fiction, after the two met at Oxford University in 1926, bears the mark of Tolkien's influence, whether in names he used or in the creation of convincing fantasy worlds. Tolkien himself is recognizable in the central character of Lewis's science-fiction stories, Dr. Elwin Ransom. It was Tolkien who helped to persuade Lewis, for many years an atheist, that the claims of the Christian story, in its humble setting in first-century Palestine, should not be ignored, appealing both to the intellect and the imagination. It was Tolkien also who later persuaded Lewis to accept a Chair offered to him by Cambridge University after initially turning it down not once, but twice. Lewis had taught at Oxford for nearly thirty years but had been passed over for a Chair there on three occasions.

The friendship between Tolkien and Lewis lasted from soon after their first meeting in 1926 until Lewis's death in 1963. Like all friendships, especially those lasting over such an extended period, there were ups and downs. With Lewis and Tolkien, a distinct cooling took place in the final years, though the similarities that united them were always stronger than the differences that separated them.

Tolkien and Lewis have, quite rightly, individually been the subjects of major biographies. In composing this study of their relationship I owe an enormous debt to the main biographers — Humphrey Carpenter, Walter Hooper, the late Roger Lancelyn Green, George Sayer, and Andrew Wilson. There are also many significant studies of facets of their lives and work, including the account of Lewis's early life by David C. Downing and Tom Shippey's study of Tolkien as a philologist. The length of my bibliography gives an indication of the sheer wealth of scholarship available, providing fascinating insights into aspects of their professional work and writings, and their fiction. To try to capture the elusive and complex friendship — spanning so many years of their lives — has imposed a necessity of selection. As part of this process I have created vignettes at the beginning of most chapters and occasionally elsewhere. These are brief imaginary reconstructions of central moments in the story of their lives and their friendship, based upon those facts that are documented. The living pulse of the friendship, in fact, comes through as much in their fictional output as in passing references in diaries, letters, and the reminiscences of friends. Any account of the friendship must keep a wide eye on their writings as well as on the events and main relationships of their lives. In writing this book, and attempting such a wide-angle approach, I have been astonished at some of the misleading statements that have been made authoritatively, statements that should not go unchallenged. To quote from a leading dictionary of twentieth-century literature (I shall spare blushes, and not name it): "Lewis was . . . a misogynist, of the opinion that women's minds are intrinsically inferior to men's. Not surprisingly, his relationships with women were mostly fraught." The writer of the entry obviously was unaware of Lewis's kindness to children evacuated to his home in wartime, his care for his adopted mother for over thirty years, his taking on two stepchildren, his painstaking replies to those who wrote to him with their struggles, his giving to charity — the examples could go on. As for his view of women's minds, one has only to read what he says about Joy Davidman's brilliance; to notice his friendship with Dorothy L. Sayers, one of the best theological minds of her generation; or to observe how he modified his argument against naturalism after debating with philosopher Elizabeth Anscombe, to realize that the statement is seriously misleading. A further error occurs later in the same dictionary article: "Lewis and Tolkien, despite their friendship, despised each other's writings for children." Tolkien disliked the Narnian Chronicles (he felt that they were tainted with allegory), but he did not despise the stories. As for Lewis, he never failed to praise *The Hobbit*, recognizing, soon after its publication, that it was likely to become a classic of children's literature.

I have mentioned my enormous debt to the thorough work of the major biographers of Lewis and Tolkien. There are, of course, many other debts to acknowledge, not least the many individuals — too many to name — who have encouraged me to continue to explore this unique friendship. These people belong to several countries — England, Ireland, the United States, Spain, Italy, Sweden, and Poland. Particularly important to me have been The Tolkien Society in the United Kingdom; The Wade Center and its ever-helpful staff, and the hospitality of Mrs. Mary Bechtel, in Wheaton, Illinois; the Oxford University C. S. Lewis Society; and friends at St. Luke's in Thurnby. Thank you, Lyn Hamilton, for driving me around the chaotic urban-scape of Birmingham on a wet, blustery day, as we sought the vestiges of Tolkien's childhood places — and for reading the manuscript. Likewise thank you, David C. Downing, whose insights are always illuminating, for reading it. Walter Hooper, thank you for your encouragement in the project (though, characteristically, you are probably unaware of how helpful you have been). I hasten to add that any errors that still remain are my own. With writers like Lewis and Tolkien, of course, there is a formidable knowledge of their work among ordinary readers, so I ask you to be patient with my shortcomings. Sometimes what might seem a baffling omission is simply the necessity of not over-burdening my book with details that properly belong in a more specialist study. (I still do not know whether Balrogs have wings, despite the excellent visualization in the film, *The Fellowship of the Ring*, though I think I have worked out why hobbits eat fish and chips. Similarly, I am not completely sure why Lewis did not tell Tolkien about his marriage to Joy Davidman, though I give the best reasons I can discover, and I simply do not know whether Lewis was physically intimate with his adopted mother, though I doubt it.) Thank you to The Leicester Writers Club, for stimulus and good fellowship. Thank you, too, Jan-Erik Guerth, my editor, for helping me continue the journey, and for your encouragement and always wise counsel.

Colin Duriez
Leicester, February 2003

1

The Formative Years

(1892–1925)

Two boys crouch on the edge of a Birmingham railway embankment, half hidden in the wild plenty of its flowers and grasses. The taller is about nine years of age, and his brother, Hilary, two years younger. It is a drowsy day in midsummer, 1901, when time itself is on vacation. The only sounds are an occasional tram in the semi-urban sprawl behind them in which they live, or the squeal of coal wagons being shunted in the coal-yard near King's Heath railway station. The older is pointing out to his brother some tiny colorful plant he has discovered in a tangle of undergrowth. Then comes the augury they have been waiting for: the slow, rhythmic bursts of a steam train pulling towards them from the south. They stand up for a better view as the shining black engine emerges from the slight heat haze, the curve of its many coal wagons behind it. This train has come from the mining valleys of South Wales over a hundred miles away bearing rich, wet coal, to feed the fires of industrial revolution that has already expanded Birmingham to four or five times its size in the previous ninety years, and which will soon expand it twice larger again. As the coal wagons rumble past very close to them, making the ground tremble, the older boy looks intently at the names on their sides, just as he has many times before, stirred by the numinous beauty of place names he cannot yet pronounce, names like *Blaen-Rhondda, Maerdy, Senghenydd, Nantyglo,* and

Tredegar. The boy's name is John Ronald Reuel Tolkien, and he is known to family and friends as Ronald or John Ronald.

Almost seventy years later, in 1970, J. R. R. Tolkien will reveal something of the significance of this encounter with Welsh place names in an interview he gives to the BBC. In many ways, this boyhood epiphany marks the birth of the tales of his invented world of Middle-earth, a world of hobbits, elves, and darker beings like orcs and dragons. In that interview Tolkien explains his fascination with the place names: "Welsh has always attracted me by its style and sound more than any other; even though I first only saw it on coal trucks, I always wanted to know what it was about." He elaborates that his writing invariably begins with a name. "Give me a name and it produces a story, not the other way about normally." He says that of modern languages Welsh, and later Finnish, have been the greatest inspiration for his writing, including *The Lord of the Rings.* Welsh, in fact, is to inspire one of the two main branches of his invented Elven languages and many of the names in his mythology, such as Arwen, Anduin, Rohirrim, and Gwaihir.

We leave the brothers on that railway bank, their futures before them, and quickly soar like a bird high above Birmingham. Now we see the city's vast encroachment on the small green fields and woodlands of West Midland England — Tolkien's Shire. We see as only an occasional balloonist has seen: dusty roads radiating and rippling out from the city and through the varied hues of the intricate patchwork of rural England. Streams and canals cut through mild hills and gentle undulations to the River Severn to the south. Even in the summer's heat this greenery is refreshing to the eye. We fly across the crowded city's heart and then follow the main railway line north, ignoring its many branches, and eventually reach Crewe, then the Mersey Canal and the bustle of Liverpool port, and the green Irish Sea. Venturing westward the Isle of Man passes below us, and then, soon, the Ards Peninsula of the north of Ireland, the Mourne Mountains on our horizon to the south. This is the country of Lewis's Narnia, the world he will invent in later years, inspired by Tolkien's Middle-earth. Like Ulster moving below us, this world of Narnia will have an eastern coastline, and, inland, a landscape like County Down, with fens and moors to the north, and mountains to the south. We follow the peninsula round into Belfast Lough, full of shipping as usual, with the city bright in the distance. The great gantries of the Harland and Wolfe docks — at that time the largest shipyards in the world — are now visible, as proud ships such as the *Olympic* and later the *Titanic* take shape under the toil of skilled and inventive engineers.

About the same time that Tolkien is fascinated by the Welsh place names on coal wagons, a much younger Clive Staples Lewis has his own epiphany. His six-year-old brother Warren Lewis runs into the nursery at Dundela Villas, a robust house quite near the shores of Belfast Lough and not far from the Harland and Wolfe docks. He carries the lid of a biscuit tin filled with moss, flowers, and sticks to proudly show his younger brother. This is the earliest encounter with beauty that Lewis will later recall, a raw and "incurably romantic" experience. It allows him, not yet three years of age, to see in a new way the garden outside in which he and his brother "Warnie" play. For Warren has made the lid into a miniature pretend garden by carefully lining it with moss, artfully pushing flowers and twigs into the mold. Hitherto he and his brother have played in their real garden oblivious even to the shape of leaves. Now Lewis sees his garden, and the natural world within his infant reach, through Warren's creation. "It made me aware of nature," he later recalls in *Surprised by Joy*, "not indeed, as a storehouse of forms and colours but as something cool, dewy, fresh, exuberant." Its importance will increase even more in memory, becoming an image of unobtainable paradise, a means for capturing an inconsolable longing he is to call "joy" or *sehnsucht* and which becomes a distinct thread running throughout his writings. His brother's toy garden in fact contributes to his imagination of Paradise ever after. Lewis's epiphany marks the beginning of a habitual process of "seeing from" — looking from memories, literature, or any other lens to catch the ever elusive but unmistakable quality of joy and beauty he endlessly seeks. It will be many years — almost half his life, in fact — before he finds anything concrete and satisfying enough truly to look *at* through these experiences that engender joy. This is when he reluctantly admits he has been wrong to believe that God does not exist, or to believe that he is merely a force manifest in nature. He discovers that God is the very source of our existence. As Lewis will put it: "He is the opaque centre of all existences, the thing that simply and entirely *is*, the fountain of facthood."

Tolkien and Lewis will continue to have childhoods strikingly dominated by their imaginations. Lewis in Belfast will create (with Warren, his brother) a world of talking animals called Boxen and Animal Land while Tolkien in the English Midlands will invent languages, and fall under the spell of existing languages like Welsh and Finnish and, later, ancient Gothic. Significantly, both will lose their mothers, Lewis at the age of nine, Tolkien when he is twelve. Tolkien has already lost his father; this was at an age when memories were only just beginning to be organized enough to remember; Lewis will become alienated from his father by his mother's death and what he will feel at the time is a banishment to England, to an unhappy boarding school. Both Tolkien and Lewis will start writing seriously during World War I, in which Lewis will be wounded and Tolkien will lose two of his closest friends.

Tolkien was born on January 3, 1892, in Bloemfontein, South Africa, the first son of English citizens Arthur Reuel Tolkien and Mabel, née Suffield. Arthur Tolkien had been born in Birmingham in 1857 and had traveled to South Africa, to join the Bank of Africa in a career move, eventually ending up in an important branch in Bloemfontein, seven hundred miles from Cape Town. Mabel was also born in Birmingham, but thirteen years later, in 1870. Her family originally came from Evesham, Worcestershire, where Hilary, Tolkien's younger brother, eventually made his home as a market gardener. Tolkien was to identify with the rural West Midlands, particularly Worcestershire, and with his mother's family, the Suffields, more than with the city-dwelling Tolkiens. In Bloemfontein the family lived "over the bank in Maitland Street: beyond were the dusty, treeless plains of the veldt." A letter from Mabel Tolkien to her in-laws describes baby Tolkien as looking "such a fairy" when dressed up in white frills and shoes and pinafores. She also describes him in the same letter as looking "more of an elf still" when undressed. On February 17, 1894, Hilary Arthur Reuel was born, providing a companion for Tolkien who remained after the death of their parents, a parallel in the early years to the companionship of Lewis and his brother Warnie.

In April 1895 Mabel Tolkien and her sons sailed for England, in consideration of Tolkien's health. The infant was coping badly with the heat of Bloemfontein. Arthur Tolkien remained, absorbed in his work responsibilities. The three stayed with Mabel's parents and sister, Jane, in their tiny family villa in Ashfield Road, King's Heath, Birmingham. Tolkien was confused by the change and sometimes expected to see the veranda of Bank House in Bloemfontein protruding from the Suffield home. Many years later he recalled, "I can still remember going down the road in Birmingham and wondering what had happened to the big gallery, what happened to the balcony." Also novel and strange was seeing for the first time a Christmas tree after the "barren, arid heat."

Then came news that changed the family more than geography and was, as a consequence, to plunge them into poverty. On February 15, 1896, Arthur Tolkien was carried away after a short illness from rheumatic fever and severe hemorrhaging. Aged only thirty-nine, he was buried in the old cemetery on the corner of St. George's and Church Street in Bloemfontein. The funeral had taken place by the time Mabel received the information which filled out the stark words of the initial telegram. The family did not have the money even to consider visiting his grave thousands of miles away.

That summer the heartbroken family moved to 5 Gracewell, a smart and good-sized semi-detached cottage almost opposite the pond side of Sarehole Mill, then about a mile outside the city of Birmingham. Though near to the city they were in the very heart of rural Warwickshire. With only horses and carts, it was "long ago in the quiet of the world, when there was less noise and more green." For Tolkien it became his home, associated with memories of the mother he was so soon to lose: "The Shire is very like the kind of world in which I first became aware of things. . . . If your first Christmas tree is a wilting eucalyptus and if you're normally troubled by heat and sand — then . . . just at the age when imagination is opening out, suddenly [to] find yourself in a quiet Warwickshire village, I think it engenders a particular love of what you might call central Midlands English countryside, based on good water stones and elm trees and small quiet rivers and so on, and of course rustic people about." Sarehole Mill (still conserved in Birmingham today) made a particular impression on his imagination: "There was an old mill that really did grind corn with two millers, a great big pond with swans on it, a sandpit, a wonderful dell with flowers, a few old-fashioned village houses and, further away, a stream with another mill." Tolkien nicknamed the terrifying miller's son "The White Ogre." The local children, suspicious of their long hair (the custom for middle-class little boys) derisively called Tolkien and Hilary "wenches." (Typically Tolkien was fascinated by the label.) In a letter Tolkien speaks of the old miller and his son bringing terror and wonder to him as a little child. In another letter he wrote of living for his early years "in 'The Shire' in a premechanical age." He added that he was a hobbit in fact, though not in size. Like hobbits he relished gardens, trees, and farmlands that were not mechanized. He too smoked a pipe and liked his food plain. In the drab mid-century he dared to wear ornamental waistcoats. He was fond of mushrooms fresh from the field and liked expressing his very basic sense of humor, which some found tiresome. He also recorded that he went to bed late and, if he could, got up late. Like hobbits, he traveled little. In *The Lord of the Rings* he wrote of a mill in Hobbiton, located on the Water, which was torn down and replaced by a brick building that polluted both the air and water.

It may have been around this time when another important feature of his imagination started: his recurring dream of a great flood, a green wave. Eventually, after a long gestation, this part of his memory was incorporated into the same imagined world in which The Shire lay, Middle-earth. The dream became Tolkien's fictional account of the destruction of Númenor, his Atlantis myth.

In 1900 Tolkien entered King Edward's School, a grammar school then located near New Street Station, Birmingham, his fees paid by an uncle. At this time Mabel Tolkien and her sister May were received into the Roman Catholic Church, despite painful opposition from her Protestant family and Tolkien in-laws, resulting in an anxious poverty Mabel was unused to. They moved from their rural setting to just inside the city, to Moseley, somewhat nearer to The Birmingham Oratory. Founded by Cardinal Newman in 1859, this had become Mabel's spiritual home. The visionary John Henry Newman (1801–90) had done much to revitalize Roman Catholicism, bringing his Oxford learning, imagination, and independence into the life of that church. Moseley was on the tram route to the city center, making it easier for Tolkien to commute to school. The next year they had to move again, to a nearby terrace backing on to a railway line near King's Heath station, and it was here Tolkien discovered the coal trains bearing Welsh names. Later they moved to a run-down house in Oliver Road (now demolished as part of inner-city improvements) in the Edgbaston district, a short walk from The Oratory and close by the reservoir. The skyline was dominated by two towers which still remain. Local historians claim them as the inspiration for the towers of Gondor in Tolkien's Middle-earth, Minas Morgul and Minas Tirith, but they bear no resemblance to them. One is Perrott's Folly, ninety-six feet high and perhaps Birmingham's oddest building, erected in 1756. The other is the Victorian Waterworks tower. For a time the Tolkien brothers left King Edward's School and enrolled at The Oratory's own school, St. Philip's, where fees were less. In 1903, however, Tolkien gained a scholarship for King Edward's, just two miles away from his Edgbaston home, and resumed study there in the autumn. Tolkien took his first communion that year, marking his devotion to his mother's Roman Catholic faith.

Through their contact with St. Philip's School, Mabel and her sons met Father Francis Xavier Morgan, who was to pass on to Tolkien some of Cardinal Newman's ideals of education. Francis Morgan was a parish priest attached to The Oratory, and he had served under Newman. Father Morgan provided friendship, counsel, and money for the fatherless family. With the boys often ill and the mother developing diabetes, he enabled them to move to the pretty Oratory cottage, close by the Oratory's rural retreat in nearby Rednal village, deep in the Worcestershire countryside, for the summer of 1904. The rural atmosphere there was like that of Sarehole. Mabel died here some months later, and Father Morgan, who was now their guardian, took on the responsibility of the boys. He helped them financially, found them lodgings in Birmingham, and took them on vacations. At first, the Tolkien brothers moved to board and lodge with their Aunt Beatrice, Mabel's sister, in Stirling Road, Edgbaston. They shared the top-floor bedroom in her gloomy house, which had an expansive view of myriads of rooftops, with factory chimneys in the distance.

Tolkien remembered his mother as a woman of great gifts, beauty, and wit. She was deeply acquainted, he perceived, with suffering and grief. He believed implicitly that her young death, at thirty-four, was precipitated by "persecution" of her Roman Catholic faith by nonconformist relatives. The impact of her death on the brothers on top of the earlier loss of their father can only be imagined. "It is to my mother," wrote Tolkien, "who taught me (until I obtained a scholarship) that I owe my tastes for philology, especially of Germanic languages, and for romance." By "romance" Tolkien meant stories and poetry that gave a glimpse of other worlds, and which made a direct appeal to the imagination in their strangeness and wonder.

Mabel Tolkien was buried in the churchyard at St. Peter's Roman Catholic Church at Bromsgrove, not far from Rednal. Tolkien remembered: "I witnessed (half-comprehending) the heroic sufferings and early death in extreme poverty of my mother who brought me into the Church; and received the astonishing charity of Francis Morgan. But I fell in love with the Blessed Sacrament from the beginning. . . . "

❧

Clive Staples Lewis was born on November 29, 1898, on the wealthy fringes of Belfast, in the north of Ireland, to Albert J. Lewis (1863–1929), a senior solicitor employed by Belfast City Council and other bodies, and Florence (Flora) Augusta, née Hamilton (1862–1908). Both parents liked writing stories, and Flora had one published in *The Household Journal* of 1889, entitled "The Princess Rosetta." His brother Warren Hamilton Lewis had been born on June 16, 1895. Soon after becoming vocative, the young Lewis insisted that he was to be called "Jacksie" — and "Jack" he remained to close friends and family for the rest of his life (though, as was the custom, Oxford friends of Lewis usually called each other by their surnames, or by nicknames. Lewis was simply called "Lewis"; Tolkien often "Tollers"). The story of his early life, his conversion from atheism to Christianity, and his awareness of joy and longing for a fulfillment outside of his own self is told in his autobiography *Surprised by Joy* (1955) and his allegory *The Pilgrim's Regress* (1933). The Lewis family attended the Anglican Church of St. Mark's, Dundela, where Flora's father, Thomas Hamilton, was rector. Albert's father, Richard Lewis, was partner in a

Belfast ship-building company, and an evangelical concerned with the social conditions of the working class.

In 1905 the Lewis family moved to their newly built home, "Little Lea," on the outskirts of Belfast. The house became an important part of Lewis's early life.

> The New House is almost a major character in my story. I am a product of long corridors, empty sunlit rooms, upstair indoor silences, attics explored in solitude, distant noises of gurgling cisterns and pipes, and the noise of wind under the tiles. Also, of endless books... There were books in the study, books in the drawing-room, books in the cloakroom, books (two deep) in the great bookcase on the landing, books in a bedroom, books piled high as my shoulder in the cistern attic, books of all kinds reflecting every transient stage of my parents' interests, books readable and unreadable, books suitable for a child and books most emphatically not.... I had always the same certainty of finding a book that was new to me as a man who walks into a field has of finding a new blade of grass.

Lewis has provided us with a portrait of himself in the period before his mother died. Written in his diary in December 1907, it is recorded in the *Lewis Family Papers*, painstakingly compiled in the 1930s by Warren Lewis, and entitled *My Life, By Jacks Lewis*. There he writes of "Papy" being, naturally, the master of the house. In his father, he recorded, the Lewis features were strongly marked — these were a bad temper, and a sensible nature. His mother was like most women of her age, he noted, "stout, brown hair, spectaciles, knitting her chief industry." He himself, he thought, was similar to most boys of his age, and admitted: "I am like Papy, bad temper, thick lips, thin, and generaly wearing a jersy" (*sic*).

Less than two months later Flora Lewis had major surgery for cancer. In May 1908 she took Lewis with her to Larne Harbour for a convalescent visit. But the surgery failed to stop the invasion of cancer, and she succumbed on August 23, Albert Lewis's birthday. Albert had lost his father earlier in the year, and his brother Joseph died two weeks later. Adding to his grief was the burden of looking after his two sons alone. Lewis spoke of the loss in *Surprised by Joy:* "With my mother's death all settled happiness, all that was tranquil and reliable, disappeared from my life. There was to be much fun, many pleasures, many stabs of joy; but no more of the old security. It was sea and islands now; the great continent had sunk like Atlantis."

❧

Just under three years before Tolkien's birth, on January 21, 1889, his future wife, Edith Bratt, had been born in Gloucester. Her mother Frances then returned with Edith to the Birmingham area, settling in Handsworth as a single parent. Edith was brought up by her mother and her mother's cousin Jennie Grove. Her mother never revealed the name of Edith's father. It was because of the misfortunes of her early life, and those of Tolkien's, that the two would meet, fall in love, and eventually marry, even though these same circumstances inevitably brought stresses and strains into their romance and entwined lives.

In 1903, the year that Tolkien gained his scholarship to King Edward's School, Edith Bratt's mother, Frances, died. Edith was sent away to Dresden House School in Evesham where she received a musical education and developed her love and talent for the piano. Some years passed before she returned to Birmingham.

By 1907 Edith had completed boarding school. Her legal guardian, Stephen Gateley, found her lodgings at 37 Duchess Road, Birmingham, the home of the Faulkner family. Mrs. Faulkner was active in the Oratory parish and known to Father Morgan. The next year he looked for more suitable lodgings than Aunt Beatrice could provide for the orphaned Tolkien brothers and decided that Mrs. Faulkner was the answer. Thus sixteen-year-old Tolkien met nineteen-year-old Edith Bratt, and they became friends and allies against "The Old Lady." Soon he was in love. Edith was attractive, small, and slender, with gray eyes. Father Morgan (like King Thingol in Tolkien's tale of Beren and Lúthien, in "The Silmarillion") disapproved of their love upon discovering it. He was fearful that Tolkien would be distracted from his studies, and worried because Edith was not a Roman Catholic. He ordered his charge not to see Edith until he was twenty-one. Edith eventually moved to Cheltenham, near her mother's original home, to stay with elderly family friends, "Uncle and Auntie Jessop." During this period she eventually became engaged to George Field, a Warwickshire farmer.

❦

A few weeks after his mother's death, in September 1908 Lewis was enrolled at Wynyard School, Watford, Hertfordshire. His brother had entered there in May 1905. Lewis found the regime at Wynyard difficult to endure, learning little to satisfy his hungry mind. "The only stimulating element in the teaching," he records in *Surprised by Joy*, "consisted of a few well-used canes which hung on the green iron chimney-piece of the single schoolroom." Like the loss of their mother, the suffering caused by a headmaster on the verge of insanity (he was later certified) brought the two brothers even closer together.

Mercifully the school closed in the summer term of 1910, and by September Lewis was enrolled back home at Campbell College, just one mile from "Little Lea," where he remained until November, when he was withdrawn upon developing serious respiratory difficulties. These difficulties were not eased by the fact that Lewis by now, like his brother, was a confirmed and secret smoker. In fact, in spring of 1911 Warren gathered his courage and asked his father's permission to smoke. After the failure of the Campbell College experiment Lewis, in Warren's footsteps, was sent to Malvern, in the English midlands, which was famous as a health resort, especially for those with lung problems. He was enrolled as a student at Cherbourg House (which he referred to in *Surprised by Joy* as "Chartres," to hide its identity), a preparatory school close by Malvern College where Warnie was enrolled as a student. Lewis remained there until June 1913. During this time he abandoned his childhood Christian faith in favor of materialism (which he later, in his book *Miracles*, called "naturalism") and sought solace in his imaginative life.

❦

While Tolkien attended King Edward's School, he formed a discussion club with literary interests in the summer of 1910 with several friends, the key members aside from Tolkien being Geoffrey Bach Smith, Robert Quilter

"Rob" Gilson (the son of the head teacher at King Edward's School), and Christopher Wiseman. The group called itself the Tea Club (T.C.) at first, and then later the Barrovian Society (B.S.), because the tearoom in Barrow's Stores on Corporation Street, near the school, became a favorite place to meet. This was combined into the initials T.C.B.S. G. B. Smith commented on some of Tolkien's early poems, including his original verses about Earendil (then written "Earendel"). Around the time the club was formed Tolkien began inventing what he called "private" languages and was already able in Latin and Greek. Tolkien's friends enjoyed his interest in Norse sagas and medieval English literature.

According to Tolkien's authorized biographer, Humphrey Carpenter, Christopher Wiseman and Tolkien shared an interest in Latin and Greek, Rugby football, and a zest for discussing anything under the sun. Wiseman was also sympathetic to Tolkien's experiments in invented language, as he himself was studying the hieroglyphics and language of ancient Egypt.

After Tolkien left school for Oxford in 1911 the four continued to meet, and to write to each other, until the war destroyed their association. The T.C.B.S. left a permanent mark on Tolkien's character, which he captured in the idea of "fellowship," as in the fellowship of the Ring. Later the friendship with C. S. Lewis was to help satisfy this important side of his nature.

In October 1911 Tolkien entered Exeter College, Oxford, to read classics. By the next year he was socializing boisterously and he also started his own undergraduate club, the Apolausticks, committed to "self-indulgence" (which, at that time, meant little more than youthful high spirits). At this time Joseph Wright began tutoring Tolkien. While still at King Edward's School Tolkien had been delighted to acquire a secondhand copy of Wright's *Primer of the Gothic Language*. This Yorkshireman of humble origins (he started as a wool-mill worker when he was only six years old and taught himself to read at the age of fifteen) had, by a long struggle, become Professor of Comparative Philology at Oxford. One of his achievements was the six large volumes of his *English Dialect Dictionary*. As well as his studies with Wright, Tolkien also took up studying Welsh — the language that had enraptured him as a boy — and discovered Finnish. He began about this time to invent Elven languages, one of which he called

Quenya, based on Finnish, related to another one he named Sindarin, based on Welsh. Forty years later Tolkien reflected that it is common for children to start to create imaginary languages, and some develop them further — he had done this since he learned to write. In the summer of 1913 Tolkien gained a Second Class grade for his honour moderations and switched course to the English School after getting an "alpha" in comparative philology. At this time he read the great eighth-century alliterative poem *Christ*, by Cynewulf and others. Many years later from the poem he cited *Eala Earendel engla beorhtost* ("Behold Earendel brightest of angels") from *Christ* as "raptuous words from which ultimately sprang the whole of my mythology." As he studied in Oxford his thoughts returned again and again to Edith Bratt, as his twenty-first birthday neared.

Father Morgan's decree had meant a long separation, but Tolkien was loyal to his benefactor, the only father he had really known. He faced another obstacle besides the separation to daunt him: persuading Edith to renounce George Field in favor of an aspiring scholar with seemingly dubious prospects. When Tolkien wrote of their eventual engagement, Father Morgan accepted it without further fuss. The two were formally engaged when Tolkien was twenty-two, after Edith was received into the Roman Catholic Church in Warwick. She had moved there from Cheltenham the previous year with Jennie Grove, her mother's cousin, and her dog, Sam.

On August 4, 1914, Britain declared war on Germany, and demanded manpower for battle. That October, when Tolkien resumed his studies after the summer, it was in a rapidly emptying university. Clearly nothing would be the same again. After gaining a First Class (magna cum laude) in English language and literature the next summer, he was commissioned in the Lancashire Fusiliers, following his friend G. B. Smith of the T.C.B.S. On March 22, 1916, Tolkien married Edith at the Catholic Church of St. Mary Immaculate in Warwick.

☙❧

In the *Lewis Papers* there are some intriguing fragments relating to Lewis's youth. Warren Lewis, the compiler of the Papers, speaks about "the aloof and solitary nature of Clive's life during his adolescence," and inserts an incomplete piece of fiction of his brother's about a boy fourteen or fifteen years old and living in a house unmistakably like "Little Lea." The young C. S. Lewis wrote in this story that a boy had hoarded a special treasure over in a dark corner of his room. If he knelt in that corner, especially on a very "lonely" day, he could hear the winds swirling around the innards of the house. His "treasure" was an uneven stack of papers — songs, plays, and stories. These were everything he had tried to write over his youthful years. Under the papers, now faded with age, were many pictures that he had composed before he knew how to write. As well as his writings and drawings there were other things — paintboxes, plates extracted from boys' annuals, a small number of forbidden books, and, when funds allowed, cigarettes. This detritus made up the boy's treasure, "my religion: for it was my past, and the past was all I had yet made my own."

The young Lewis in fact increasingly made his own "religion" out of his memories, experiences, and literary discoveries, out of his deepest subjectivity. In September 1913 he had received a classical scholarship and entered Malvern College. Around this time he worked on "Loki Bound," a poetic tragedy about the Norse gods. Then, in April 1914, he came to know someone who would become a soul mate, Arthur Greeves (1895– 1966), who lived in a large house just up from "Little Lea." Lewis said of him, in 1933, that, after his brother, Warren, Arthur was his oldest and closest friend. A second life-changing event occurred soon after. On September 19, 1914, Lewis commenced private study with W. T. Kirkpatrick, "The Great Knock," in Great Bookham, Surrey, with whom he was to remain until April 1917. William T. Kirkpatrick (1848–1921) had been headmaster of Lurgan College, County Armagh, in the north of Ireland, from 1874 to 1899. Albert Lewis had attended Lurgan from 1877 to 1879 and later became Kirkpatrick's solicitor. After Kilpatrick retired from Lurgan in 1899, he began taking private students and had already successfully prepared Warnie for admission to the Royal Military College at Sandhurst. Kirkpatrick rigorously prepared Lewis for entrance to Oxford University. Lewis affectionately recalled the astringent Ulsterman in the character of Andrew MacPhee in *That Hideous Strength,* and there is a gentler version (with a different worldview) in the figure of Professor Digory Kirke in the Narnian Chronicles. Lewis commented in *Surprised by Joy:* "If ever a man came near to being a purely logical entity, that man was Kirk. Born a little later, he would have been a Logical Positivist. The idea that human beings should exercise their vocal organs for any purpose except that of communicating or discovering truth was to him preposterous. The most casual remark was taken as a summons to disputation." Lewis believed that "Kirk" had taught him how to think.

His private tutorage under the Irishman was one of the happiest periods of his life. Not only did he rapidly mature and grow under the stringent rationality of this teacher, but he discovered the beauty of the English countryside and fantasy writers such as William Morris. Discovering George MacDonald's *Phantastes* early in March 1916, Lewis wrote about its power to Arthur Greeves: "Of course it is hopeless for me to try to describe it, but when you have followed the hero Anodos along the little stream of the faery wood, have heard about the terrible ash tree . . . and heard the episode of Cosmo, I know you will agree with me." In *Surprised by Joy*, Lewis describes the effect as "baptising his imagination" and impressing him with a deep sense of the holy.

On June 6, 1916, Tolkien arrived in Calais on the flat coast of northern France. He served from July to October in the Battle of the Somme. It was one of the deadliest battles of World War I. Rob Gilson of the T.C.B.S. died on the very first day. When it was over in mid-November the total Allied gain was about eight miles, at a cost of 615,000 Allied and about 500,000 German casualties. Tolkien didn't write while he was in the trenches, as some have thought. "That's all spoof," he rejoined in an interview. "You might scribble something on the back of an envelope and shove it in your back pocket but that's all. You couldn't write. This [pointing to his converted garage] would be an enormous dugout. You'd be crouching down among flies and filth." He could soon write again however. In November 1916 Tolkien was returned to England suffering from "trench fever." The memories of modern war would haunt his later writing, as in "The Passage of the Marshes" in *The Lord of the Rings*: Here we read of Sam tripping as he hurried forward. His hand sank into the bog. Springing back, he had cried out in horror that there were dead faces in the water. Gollum had laughed at his reaction, and explained the name, "the Dead Marshes." There had been a great battle long ago, in which men and elves had fallen in great numbers. For Tolkien, those long-dead faces staring up from under the water could include his fallen friends, Smith as well as Gilson.

Soon after Tolkien arrived back in England, on December 3, 1916, G. B. Smith of the T.C.B.S. was injured by shellfire and died a few days later from gangrene. He wrote to Tolkien shortly before his wounding, saying how the T.C.B.S. — the "immortal four" — would live on, even if he died that night. Smith concluded: "May God bless you, my dear John Ronald, and may you say the things I have tried to say long after I am not there to say them, if such be my lot." The loss of two of his three closest friends was a strong motivation for Tolkien to write down his mythology, to make some sense of their aspirations. He later observed, "A real taste for fairy-stories was wakened by philology on the threshold of manhood, and quickened to full life by war."

Early in 1917 Tolkien, recovering in Great Haywood, a Staffordshire village (where he, Edith, and Jennie Grove had moved to from Warwick), began seriously shaping and writing the tales that would become *The Silmarillion*, putting "the Fall of Gondolin" on paper. Tolkien explained, "Long before I wrote *The Hobbit* and long before I wrote this [*The Lord of the Rings*] I had constructed this world mythology." After a temporary posting to Yorkshire (near Hornsea) the return of ill health put him into a sanatorium in Harrogate. He created another story for an early version of "The Silmarillion,"* *The Book of Lost Tales* — the tale of Túrin Turambar, influenced by the Finnish story of Kullervo from the *Kalevala*. Most of the *Book of Lost Tales* and his "Gnomish Lexicon" were written during his convalescence, during 1916–17. Tolkien commented, "My stories seem to germinate like a snowflake around a piece of dust."

---

*Throughout the book I have distinguished "The Silmarillion" and *The Silmarillion* (italics). "The Silmarillion" refers to the vast body of unfinished material — including stories in prose and verse, annals, and notes on Elven languages — covering the three Ages of Middle-earth. These were published after Tolkien's death in *Unfinished Tales,* and the twelve volumes of *The History of Middle Earth*. *The Silmarillion* (italics) refers to the book published in 1977, edited by Christopher Tolkien, which gives a concise, reconstructed, and coherent text as close as possible to the content envisaged by Tolkien.

On November 16, 1917, Tolkien's first son, John Francis Reuel Tolkien (died 2003), was born, named after his father, and his father's guardian, Father Francis Morgan. "Reuel" was a name favored in family tradition. Mother and child moved to Roos, north of the Humber estuary, to be near Tolkien's current military camp. Edith helped to inspire the great tale of Lúthien and Beren, his first story of "there and back again," which he created early on in the development of "The Silmarillion." It tells of the love between the elven Lúthien and the human Beren, and her renunciation of her immortality in order to marry him. In his turn Beren has to cut a silmaril, a magical gem, from the Iron Crown of Morgoth to win Lúthien. The story had such a personal meaning for Tolkien that Lúthien and her lover Beren became pet names for Edith and himself. The conception of the story was tied up with an incident where the two of them had wandered in a small wood in Roos. There, among hemlock, she danced and sang to him. Beren, in the story, first encounters Lúthien dancing among hemlock in the woods of Neldoreth. When Edith died in 1971 he included "Lúthien" on her gravestone. Later his own pet name, "Beren," was added.

Around the time Tolkien returned from the Battle of the Somme Lewis, now eighteen, sat for a classical scholarship and was elected to University College, Oxford, and was a student there from April 26 until September 1917. There was no conscription for people born in Ireland, so at the same time he voluntarily enlisted in the army and was billeted in Keble College, Oxford, for officer's training. His roommate at Keble College was fellow Irishman Edward Courtnay Francis "Paddy" Moore (1898–1918). Paddy was the son of Janie King Moore (1872–1951), who had left an unhappy marriage and Ireland in 1907 to live in Bristol with Paddy and his sister Maureen Daisy Helen (1906–97). With Paddy's commission, Mrs. Moore and Maureen moved to Oxford to be near him. She and Lewis first met in June 1917. Lewis himself was commissioned an officer in the 3rd Battalion, Somerset Light Infantry, on September 25, 1917, and reached the front line in the Somme Valley in November, about the time of his nineteenth birthday. Maureen, who was eleven at the time, remembered: "Before my brother went out to the trenches in France he asked C. S. Lewis...'If I don't come back, would you look after my mother and my little sister?'" Maureen's first impression of Lewis is also on record: "Rather slim, but nice looking, talkative." We do not know Lewis's impressions of Maureen then, but we do know that he was immensely attracted to Mrs. Moore, a feeling intensified by Albert Lewis's apparent inattention to his son at that time. By January 1918 Lewis had survived his first few weeks in the trenches, and was hospitalized at Le Tréport, France, with "trench fever." He returned to the front at the end of February and had, he says, a pretty quiet time of it until the great German Spring offensive, one of the worst bloodlettings of the war. During the Battle of Arras Lewis was in or near the front line. He remembered "the frights, the cold, the smell of H.[eavy] E.[xplosive], the horribly smashed men still moving like half crushed beetles, the sitting or standing corpses, the landscape of sheer earth without a blade of grass, the boots worn day and night until they seemed to grow to your feet." Soon after Lewis rejoined his battalion, he took sixty German prisoners who had surrendered. On April 15 Lewis was wounded by "friendly fire" on Mount Bernenchon (near Lillers, France) during the Battle. Pieces of shrapnel remained in his chest for much of his life. He recuperated in England and was able to return to military duty in October, being assigned to a camp at Ludgerhall, Andover. He was discharged in December 1918, just after the end of the war. He learned that his former roommate and friend, Paddy Moore, had been killed in battle and buried just south of Peronne, France. There was a promise to fulfill.

Various recurring illnesses prevented Tolkien's return to the front, and likely death. He wrote early versions of much of "The Silmarillion" while convalescing. In fact most of the legendary cycle of "The Silmarillion" was already constructed before 1930 — before the writing and publication of *The Hobbit,* the forerunner of *The Lord of the Rings.* In the latter books there are numerous references to matters covered by "The Silmarillion": ruins of once-great places, sites of battles long ago, strange and beautiful names from the deep past, and elven swords made in Gondolin, before its fall, for the Goblin Wars.

Just as science-fiction writers generally make use of plausible technological inventions and possibilities, Tolkien used his deep and expert knowledge of language in his fiction. The invention in his youth of two forms of the Elven tongue, inspired by his discovery of Welsh and Finnish, started a process that led to the creation of a history and a geography to surround these languages, and peoples to speak them (and other tongues). He explained that he had to suppose an underlying phonetic structure of primitive Elven, and then modify this by a sequence of changes such as really occur in actual languages. The resulting Elven languages therefore had a consistent character and structure, but were distinct.

Equally important to language in Tolkien's complicated makeup was a passion for myth and for fairy story, particularly, he says in a letter, for "heroic legend on the brink of fairy-tale and history." Both in his linguistic and his imaginative interests he was constantly seeking "material, things of a certain tone and air." Myths, fairy stories, and ancient words constantly inspired and sustained the unfolding creations of his mind and imagination — his Elven languages and the early seeds of "The Silmarillion." He identified the tone and quality that he sought with northern and western Europe, particularly England. He attempted to embody this quality in his fiction and invented languages.

The stories he created in the war years — such as "The Fall of Gondolin" — came to him as something given, rather than as conscious creation. This sense of givenness and discovery remained with him throughout his life. "The Silmarillion" essentially belongs to this period even though a full and developed version was not published until 1977, after Tolkien's death. In fact, developments of the mythology, history, and tales of Middle-earth conceived in World War I are found in unfinished drafts spanning over half a century, with considerable developments and changes in narrative structure.

But with his health restored, the war over, and with a young family, Tolkien had to find employment. He was soon able to take up work with the new *Oxford English Dictionary*, on the "W" section, and move the family in November 1918 to 50 St. John's Street, Oxford. He quickly realized he had to augment his slight income with teaching. Students would come to his home. It became necessary for the family to move again, now to 1 Alfred St. (later renamed Pusey Street). By 1920 Tolkien had enough students to end his work on the dictionary. In October 1920 the family celebrated the birth of Michael Hilary Reuel Tolkien (died 1984). Christmas that year saw the beginning of Tolkien's Father Christmas letters, annual letters he wrote and illustrated for his children.

Barely had normality settled in when, in 1921, Tolkien took up a senior post at the University of Leeds as Reader in English literature. For a few months after their arrival the family rented Hollybank, a house owned by Miss Moseley, a niece of Cardinal Newman's. Then they moved to 11 St. Marks Terrace, near the university.

Tolkien recalled the early days as a student and young academic in his Oxford valedictory address in 1959: "I cannot help recalling some of the salient moments in my academic past. The vastness of Joe Wright's dining-room table (when I sat alone at one end learning the elements of Greek philology from glinting glasses in the further gloom). The kindness of William Craigie [one of the editors of the *Oxford English Dictionary*] to a jobless soldier in 1918. . . . My first glimpse of the unique and dominant figure of Charles Talbut Onions, darkly surveying me, a fledgling prentice in the Dictionary Room (fiddling with the slips for WAG and WALRUS and WAMPUM). Serving under the generous captaincy of George Gordon [Professor of English] in Leeds. Seeing Henry Cecil Wyld [the Merton Professor of English Language and Literature before Tolkien] wreck a table in the Cadena Café with the vigour of his representation of Finnish minstrels chanting the *Kalevala*."

In Leeds Tolkien soon collaborated with Canadian Eric Valentine Gordon, who joined the university in 1922, on an edition of *Sir Gawain and the Green Knight*. This presentation of the text of the finest of all the English medieval romances helped to stimulate study of this work, much loved by Tolkien. The edition also contains a major glossary. Nancy Martsch speculates, "Perhaps, had he remained at Leeds, with Gordon, Tolkien would have written more philology; as it was, he became friends with Lewis and wrote the Mythology instead." Gordon and Tolkien formed the

Viking Club — which included translating nursery rhymes into Anglo-Saxon. During this period Tolkien made a beautiful verse translation of the great Early English poem *Beowulf*. It displays his remarkable mastery of the alliterative meter, which he also used in his unfinished poetic version of a tale from "The Silmarillion," that of Túrin Turambar.

In October 1924 Tolkien was appointed to the Chair of English Language at Leeds University, aged thirty-two. The next month Tolkien's third son, Christopher Reuel, was born. Through this period Tolkien told stories to young John when he was unable to sleep, a habit which ultimately lead to the creation of *The Hobbit*.

Tolkien's area of teaching at Leeds, and later at Oxford, was essentially philology. According to Tom Shippey, in *The Road to Middle-earth* (1982), Tolkien's fiction resulted from the interaction between his imagination and his professional work as a philologist. Owen Barfield said of his friend Lewis that he was in love with the imagination. It could be said of Tolkien that he was in love with language.

It was in October 1925 that Tolkien was appointed Rawlinson and Bosworth Professor of Anglo-Saxon at Oxford. As was the custom, he was at the same time assigned a fellowship with one of the Oxford colleges, in his case Pembroke. At this time of the Oxford English School's infancy the only three Chairs in the school were Tolkien's Chair for Anglo-Saxon, which he held from 1925 to 1945, and two Merton Chairs, one for literature (then held by George Gordon, who had also been at Leeds before) and one for language. Tolkien was to hold the language Chair from 1945 until his retirement in 1959. His academic work continued to be intimately related to his construction of the languages, peoples, and history of the three Ages of Middle-earth. He commented, late in his life, that he sought to create a mythology for England, but arguably he also tried to create a mythology for the English language.

As professorships were university-wide, not college appointments, the responsibilities were quite varied: Tolkien was required to give a quota of open lectures to undergraduates (around thirty-five a year, though Tolkien did many more than this); to teach the relatively few graduate students; and, primarily, to advance his subject area, particularly by publication. Tolkien in fact published modestly in his subject, choosing to invest his knowledge in generations of students and graduates, whom he always treated courteously and conscientiously.

✧❀❀✧

The February 1919 issue of *Reveille* contained "Death in Battle," Lewis's first publication other than in school magazines. The issue also included poems by Robert Bridges, Siegfried Sassoon, Robert Graves, and Hilaire Belloc. The next month Lewis's *Spirits in Bondage* was published under the name Clive Hamilton (his mother's maiden name) by Heinemann. From January 1919 until June 1924, he resumed his studies at University College, Oxford, where he received a First Class degree in classical honour moderations (Greek and Latin Literature) in 1920, a First in Greats (philosophy and ancient history) in 1922, and a First in English in 1923. The same year he won the Chancellor's Prize for an English essay. His tutors during this time included Edgar Frederick Carritt for philosophy, Frank Percy Wilson and George Gordon in the English School, and Edith Elizabeth Wardale for Early English. While an undergraduate Lewis helped Paddy Moore's mother and sister move permanently to Oxford, renting a house in Headington Quarry. Lewis lived with the Moores from June 1921 onward, quasi-adopting Mrs. Moore as his mother while having deeper feelings for her. Whether the relationship went further into sexual intimacy no one really knows. Around this time Mrs. Moore became known by her nickname, "Minto," perhaps because of her fondness for a popular mint confectionary, Nuttall's Mintos. Maureen remembered Lewis's remarkable powers of concentration. She had to practice music around five hours a day, sometimes in the same room he was working in — but he could concentrate, forgetting everything. According to Maureen her mother hardly went out after Paddy was killed. She no longer had the heart for the things she used to do, becoming "more and more obsessed with household things and the hands and the gardens."

From October 1924 until May 1925, Lewis served as philosophy tutor at University College during E. F. Carritt's absence on study leave in America. Then, on May 20, 1925, Lewis was elected to a fellowship in Magdalen College, Oxford, as tutor in English language and literature. His father's reaction to Lewis's appointment is recorded in *The Lewis Papers* (from his diary entry for that day). There we are told that Albert was waiting to be called for dinner. Mary Cullen, the housekeeper, came into his study to let him know that the Post Office was on the phone. Albert went to take the call and was informed that there was a telegram for him. "Read it," he asked. The message was stark: "Elected Fellow Magdalen. Jack." Albert thanked the anonymous voice and then climbed the stairs to his son's room. There he burst into tears. With joy filling his heart he knelt down by the bed and thanked God. "My prayers have been heard and answered," his entry concludes.

Lewis joined the Oxford English School (with his appointment to Magdalen College) the same year that Tolkien took up his post as Rawlinson and Bosworth Professor of Anglo-Saxon there.

2

Meeting of Minds and Imaginations

"Tolkien and I were talking of dragons...."
(1926–1929)

On Tuesday, May 11, 1926, Britain is full of its first general strike in history, which started less than a week before. The nationwide strike was precipitated by the breakdown of negotiations between coal miners and their employers over a large pay cut and longer working hours. The strike is the topic of conversation in every household. Oxford undergraduates, stockbrokers, solicitors, and white-collar workers throughout the country rally to beat the strike by manning the abandoned trains and buses. Many citizens sign up as special constables, anticipating a breakdown in civil order. There is a palpable danger of a class war splitting the nation. The previous day the Trade Union Congress had begun talks to end the strike. Chancellor of the Exchequer, Winston Churchill, acting as editor-in-emergency of *The British Gazette*, set up to print officially approved news, had heightened tensions by refusing to print an influential peace appeal from the Archbishop of Canterbury, Randall Davidson, and emotively labelled the strikers "the enemy."

Lewis finds himself no exception to the national mood. Mrs. Moore expresses strong opinions about the situation over the lunch table in "Hillsboro," in Oxford's Holyoake Road, where she, Maureen, and Lewis have lived for three years. Lewis keeps his own counsel, but this does not mean the issues of the strike have not preoccupied him since it began.

He finds the sort of atmosphere created by Minto's reaction to national or world events can be very trying. But he knows that if he abstains from too much contradiction, the clouds do not last too long.

The shadows have lengthened considerably by the time Lewis leaves the house and walks up the street the short distance to London Road, where buses come down from Headington on their way to town. Lewis normally catches the Number 2 bus, a double-decker, alighting opposite Magdalen College, where he has been a Fellow for a year now. But not this afternoon. With the strike affecting public transport he walks briskly down Headington Hill towards the town. Lewis had not managed to get home early from college for lunch as he had hoped. He had been thwarted that morning by the arrival, against the odds, of first one then a second pupil (as students were then called). The conversation quickly turned to the strike, with one of the pupils strongly in favor of the archbishop's appeal.

Lewis is down to go to a meeting that is likely also to discuss momentous issues. This is the four o'clock "English Tea" at Merton College. The Oxford English School is a relatively new institution, where approaches to the subject — particularly the views of its Professors — can strongly influence its future direction. In 1926 the school has only three Chairs, one of which had been occupied the year before by Professor Tolkien. Lewis thinks that he will use the occasion to talk to him afterwards.

As four o'clock approaches Lewis crosses Magdalen Bridge and hurries past the Botanic Gardens, turning left into Merton Street. When Lewis enters the meeting room in Merton College he takes in the various people already assembled — the Revd. Ronald Fletcher, a don (as the college tutors are called); George Gordon (Professor of English Literature); Margaret Lee, another don; and Professor Tolkien. The latter is a slight man, rather dapper in dress, shorter than Lewis and not much older. He speaks quickly, and one has to listen carefully to catch all his words. He is, in Lewis's impression, "a smooth, pale, fluent little chap."

The meeting seems cocooned from the outside world — there is hardly any talk of the strike. Tolkien finally manages to get the talk around to the English School syllabus, but isn't able to say very much. Lewis is interested to hear his approach. He *seems* to wish to bring language and literature studies in the school together more.

Talking to Tolkien afterwards, Lewis quizzes him obliquely. What does he think of Spenser (one of Lewis's favorite authors)? Tolkien reveals that he can't read Spenser "because of the forms." What are his views on language and literature in the English School (a loaded issue)? Oh, he thinks "language is the real thing in the school." Not only that, Tolkien makes matters worse by expressing his opinion that "all literature is written for the amusement of *men* between thirty and forty." Lewis records in his diary that night that, according to Tolkien, "we (in the English School) ought to vote ourselves out of existence if we are honest — still the sound-changes and the gobbets are great fun for the dons." Lewis concludes: "No harm in him: only needs a smack or two."

The Oxford English School was then in its infancy as a separate faculty. There were marked differences with its rival and also fledgling Cambridge English School, differences that were to deepen in the next few years, and which would increasingly preoccupy Lewis in particular. In wishing to bring the teaching of English language and literature together, Tolkien was drawing upon an older view of learning that had its roots in the earlier ages that he and Lewis loved. He hoped to install or at least consolidate an attitude in Oxford that would make it natural to be an imaginative writer as well as a don or Professor. He attempted in fact to rehabilitate what he later saw as a lost unitary consciousness. By the end of 1929, a little over three years after their first meeting, Lewis would be supporting Tolkien's proposed changes to the Oxford English School, changes that would integrate language and literature, and stop the syllabus with the Romantics at around 1830, the point after which the modern reader was familiar with the predominant worldview of literary authors and thus, in the view of Lewis and Tolkien, did not need the kind of help teachers in the English School were best suited to give. This was help in obscure texts, shifts in the meaning of words, and in tasting the imaginative worlds of previous ages, especially the imaginative splendor of the Middle Ages. A comment made by Lewis near the end of his life sums up the Tolkien-Lewis attitude: "If you take your stand on the 'prevalent' view, how long do you suppose it will prevail? ... All you can really say about my taste is that it is old-fashioned; yours will soon be the same."

                        ⁞⁞

In the early years of the twentieth century in England, idealism predominated in philosophy, particularly in Oxford when Lewis began his academic career as a philosophy tutor. The philosopher John Mabbott, a colleague of Lewis's during that period, pointed out the intellectual isolation of Oxford during this period in his *Oxford Memories*. He wrote:

> Oxford philosophy, as we found it, was completely inbred. It had practically no contacts with Cambridge, or the Continent, or America. The traditional doctrine was Hegelian idealism, filtered through the great Scottish prophets, [Edward] Caird, [Andrew Seth] Pringle-Pattison, ... [David George] Ritchie and [William] Wallace, and our own T. H. Green, [Bernard] Bosanquet and [F. H.] Bradley. The basic issue was between the idealists and their view that reality is spiritual and therefore that the world around us is akin to or determined by mind, and our realists, [John] Cook Wilson, [Sir W. David] Ross, [Harold Arthur] Prichard, holding that the objects of knowledge and perception are independent of mind.

Idealism was linked in many minds with Christianity, or with spiritual views which opposed a rapidly spreading naturalism that Lewis would later attack in his book *Miracles*. The idealists typically held that physical objects can have no existence apart from a mind which is conscious of them. For them the divine mind and the human mind had fundamental similarities. As a young Oxford atheist Lewis was at first staunchly opposed to idealism. He defined his naturalism of that time as the view that "every finite thing or event must be (in principle) explicable in terms of the Total System." Nature, in other words of his, is "the whole show." Naturalism is reflected in his early poetry, *Spirits in Bondage* and to a lesser extent in *Dymer*. Thus, when Lewis first met Tolkien, the two men had radically opposing worldviews. Tolkien was an old-fashioned supernaturalist, who had believed the orthodox doctrines of Christianity since childhood.

It was not only in philosophy that Oxford in the 1920s had an affinity with the nineteenth century. It was also, in the study of language and literature, still gripped by the model of philology — the historical and comparative study of language. The philologist at his humane best was embodied in Tolkien. Lewis gradually took on many of Tolkien's concerns, such as the serious writing of fantasy and fairy story, and shared his passionate love of language, especially after his conversion to Christianity. One day the two would even plan to collaborate on a book on language, a project that never materialized.

For Tolkien "Philology is the foundation of humane letters." In his essay, "The Oxford English School" (1930), Tolkien made clear that he regarded both literary and linguistic approaches as too narrow to gain a full response to works of art. He felt that this was particularly true of early literary works, very distant from contemporary culture. Philology was a necessary dimension of both approaches. It could give a proper depth of response. Tom Shippey points out that Tolkien saw works of literary art philologically, and his own fiction came out of a philological vision. In this he was like the nineteenth-century German philologists Jacob and Wilhelm Grimm, who produced collections of fairy tales as well as learned scholarship, just as Tolkien's imaginative work sprang out of his philological study.

Perhaps the most radical current crossing the 1920s was what Lewis and his friends dubbed "the new psychology," stemming particularly from the insights of Sigmund Freud (satirized as Sigismund Enlightenment in Lewis's *The Pilgrim's Regress*). Lewis's narrative poem, *Dymer,* was published in 1926. In his preface to the 1950 edition, explaining the context of its writing, he commented: "In those days the new psychology was just beginning to make itself felt in the circles I most frequented at Oxford. This joined forces with the fact that we felt ourselves (as young men always do) to be escaping from the illusions of adolescence, and as a result we were much exercised about the problem of fantasy or wishful thinking." Fantasy was increasingly seen as unreal and escapist. A new literary criticism, stemming from the influential Ivor Armstrong Richards (1893–1979) at Cambridge University, was underpinned by this new psychological approach. He radically reformulated the criteria and techniques for evaluating literature, particularly in *Principles of Literary Criticism* (1924) and *Practical Criticism, A Study of Literary Judgment* (1929). Like Freud, Richards was ultimately a naturalist. He adapted the methods of positivism in philosophy to literary criticism. He reduced values (such as beauty) to what was measurably available to the reader. Values in literature, he believed, are merely a capacity to satisfy the feelings and desires of readers. The language of literature is subjective and emotive, rather than describing an objective state of affairs in the real world. I. A. Richards stimulated a more precise debate about how a work of literature creates meaning than had been common under the sway of idealism.

In 1922 a "Great War" had begun between Lewis and his closest friend in this period, Owen Barfield (1898–1997), a fellow undergraduate studying at Oxford's Wadham College. The "war" was, for Barfield, "an intense interchange of philosophical opinions" and, for Lewis, "an almost incessant disputation, sometimes by letter and sometimes face to face, which lasted for years." The dialogue ensued soon after Barfield's acceptance of anthroposophism, a "spiritual science" based on a synthesis of Eastern and Christian thought and developed by Rudolf Steiner (1861–1925). It trailed off by the time of Lewis's conversion to Christian faith in 1931. The dispute centered on the nature of the imagination and the status of poetic insights. It cured Lewis of his "chronological snobbery," making him hostile to the modern period, and provided a rich background of sharpened thought for Barfield's important study, *Poetic Diction* (1928).

Lewis believed that one of the strongest myths of his time was that of progress. Change was considered to have a value in itself. Until meeting Barfield he had been seduced by this myth, intellectually at least. He came to see that we are increasingly cut off from our past (and hence a proper perspective on the strengths and weaknesses of our own age). He explained in *Surprised by Joy*.

> Barfield...made short work of what I have called my "chronological snobbery," the uncritical acceptance of the intellectual climate common to our age and the assumption that whatever has gone out of date is on that account discredited. You must find out why it went out of date; was it ever refuted (and if so by whom, where and how

conclusively) or did it merely die away as fashions do? If the latter, this tells us nothing about its truth or falsehood. From seeing this one passes to the realization that our age is also "a period," and certainly has, like all periods, its own characteristic illusions. They are likeliest to lurk in those wide-spread assumptions which are so ingrained in the age that no one dares to attack or feels it necessary to defend them.

The "war" with Barfield not only refuted his chronological snobbery; it also convinced him that his materialism, if true, in fact made knowledge impossible! It was self-refuting — a view strengthened by his reading of Arthur Balfour's *Theism and Humanism* in 1924, though he resisted Balfour's Christian conclusions at the time. Barfield jokingly said to his friend after their "war" was over that while Lewis had taught him *how* to think, he had taught Lewis *what* to think. Lewis undoubtedly forced him to think systematically and accurately, passing on hard-won skills he had acquired from his tutelage under W. T. Kirkpatrick. Barfield in his turn helped Lewis to think more imaginatively, to combine his imagination with his formidable intellect. This was a "slow business," remembered Barfield.

After graduating in English with a B.A. in 1921 Barfield began a B.Litt., the thesis of which became his book *Poetic Diction*. In 1925 he published a children's book, *The Silver Trumpet*, which later was a success in the Tolkien household. In 1926 his study, *History in English Words*, appeared. *Poetic Diction* deeply influenced Lewis and Tolkien.

Barfield believed that there has been an evolution of human consciousness, in which the imagination has played an integral role. This development of consciousness is reflected precisely in changes in language and perception. There was originally a unity of consciousness, now fragmented; Barfield believed, however, that in the future humans would achieve a greater and richer consciousness, in which spirit and nature will be reconciled. Barfield's concept inspired Lewis, especially as it was translated into highly original insights into the nature of poetic language. These insights were embodied in *Poetic Diction*, which concerns the nature of poetic language and a theory of how words originally embodied an ancient, unified perception. *Poetic Diction* offers a view of how human knowledge is attained, in which poetry plays a central role. Barfield's be-lief was that "the individual imagination is the medium of all knowledge from perception upward." The poetic impulse is linked to individual free-dom: "[T]he act of the imagination is the individual mind exercising its sovereign unity." The alternative, argued Barfield, is to see knowledge as power, to "mistake efficiency for meaning," leading to a relish for control. He contrasted this misuse of knowledge as power with knowledge by par-ticipation (a key word in Barfield). One kind of knowledge "consists of seeing what happens and getting used to it" and the other involves "con-sciously participating in what is." The proper activity of the imagination is "concrete thinking" — this is "the perception of resemblance, the demand for unity" (the influence of Samuel Taylor Coleridge is apparent). There is therefore a poetic element in all meaningful language. With this state-ment, Barfield was refuting the increasingly popular view that scientific discourse was the only means of true knowledge.

In 1925, when Tolkien took up the Chair of Anglo-Saxon at Oxford, the distinguished poet W. H. Auden arrived as an undergraduate and developed a particular liking for Early English literature. Like Tolkien, Auden had a deep interest in Northern mythology and was influenced by Tolkien's enthusiasm for his subject. In later years Tolkien was greatly encouraged by Auden's excitement over *The Lord of the Rings*. Auden wrote influential reviews of *The Lord of the Rings*, corresponded about and discussed with Tolkien the meaning of his work, and counteracted some of the negative criticism of the trilogy. In Humphrey Carpenter's biography of Auden (1981) there is a photograph from the 1940s of Auden absorbed in reading *The Hobbit*.

Tolkien had a theatrical side. He had enjoyed acting as Mrs. Malaprop in the all-male King Edward's School production of Sheridan's *The Rivals* in 1911. In later years he was surprised at the dramatic power of his readings from his poetry and *The Lord of the Rings*, captured on a friend's early-model tape recorder. As a lecturer he quickly discovered the effectiveness of opening a lecture with reading *Beowulf* aloud. This Early English poem, as was the style of the period, began with *Hwaet*, listen! To novice undergraduates it sounded remarkably like "Quiet!" Auden referred to the effect that Tolkien had on him:

> I remember [a lecture] I attended, delivered by Professor Tolkien. I do not remember a single word he said but at a certain point he recited, and magnificently, a long passage of Beowulf. I was spellbound. This poetry, I knew was going to be my dish. I became willing, therefore, to work at Anglo-Saxon because, unless I did, I should never be able to read this poetry. I learned enough to read it, however sloppily, and Anglo-Saxon and Middle English poetry have been one of my strongest, most lasting influences.

A Canadian postgraduate also heard Tolkien lecture in these early days:

> He came in lightly and gracefully, I always remember that, his gown flowing, his fair hair shining, and he read *Beowulf* aloud.... The terrors and the dangers that he recounted — how I do not know — made our hair stand on end. He read like no one else I have ever heard. The lecture room was crowded — it was in the Examination Halls, and he was a young man then, for his position, long before *The Hobbit* or the Trilogy were to make him famous. I took a seminar from him also, on Gothic. He was a great teacher, and delightful, courteous, ever so kindly.

John Innis Mackintosh Stewart, a lecturer and famous crime writer (under the pseudonym of Michael Innis), was also a student of Tolkien's, and remarked, "He could turn a lecture room into a mead hall in which he was the bard and we were the feasting listening guests."

ᄃᄉᄋ

Lewis was elected as a fellow and tutor in English language and literature at Magdalen College, in May 1925, initially for five years, but ended up staying until near the end of 1954. He tutored in the college but lectured university-wide, to students of literature from across the colleges. On January 23, 1926, Lewis gave his first lecture in the Oxford English School on "Some Eighteenth-Century Precursors of the Romantic Movement," after frantic preparations. He had planned to lecture on selected poetry, but discovered in time that a distinguished colleague intended to cover the poets. He therefore had to turn to the relevant prose writings of the period, less familiar to him. In the fall (or Michaelmas) term of 1926 Lewis presented a twice-weekly course of lectures on the subject, "Some English Thinkers of the Renaissance (Elyot, Ascham, Hooker, Bacon)." He began another characteristic series a year later on "The Romance of the Rose and Its Successors," material that would eventually appear in his *The Allegory of Love* (1936). He explained to his father, with whom he was by now on much better relations, his approach to giving lectures (he was referring to a lecture series on philosophy, but his approach was the same for literary topics). He was, he said, plodding on with his preparation for fourteen lectures. He was not writing them out in full, only in note form. Though the introduction of this extempory element was dangerous for a beginner, lectures that were read simply sent his pupils to sleep. He had decided to make the plunge from the very beginning of his lecturing career. He would force himself to talk rather than recite.

Lewis's ability as a philosopher is easily overlooked because of his subsequent fame as a literary figure. Lewis had taught philosophy for the previous year. In fact his "Great War" with Owen Barfield was often carried on at a highly sophisticated philosophical level, and his philosophical interests were well known to others. Indeed, he continued teaching some philosophy after taking up his lecturing in English. On May 12, 1926, for example (the day after meeting Tolkien for the first time), he recorded conducting a philosophy class at Lady Margaret Hall with several female pupils. He noted with approval their continued interest in the thought of Bishop Berkeley (1685–1753), who saw all existence as dependent on God's perception (*"esse est percipi"*), and explained a distinction made by the contemporary philosopher, Samuel Alexander, between contemplation and enjoyment, a difference between looking *at* and looking *with* one's perceptions and sensations. It was a matter of where you placed your awareness: whether you were self-conscious (focused on your own moods, awareness, or experiences) or attending to something or someone other than your self. This distinction was becoming more and more important to Lewis, one that was already undermining his materialism. Lewis was particularly pleased that one pupil, Joan Colbourne, understood the difference. She responded to another pupil's comment that she wished to "know" the self: "It is as if, not content with seeing with your eyes, you wanted to take them out and look at them — and then they wouldn't be eyes."

John Mabbott describes the formation of a philosophical discussion club in the mid-twenties for young lecturers in which Lewis actively participated. This was the "Wee Teas" (named after the Free Church of Scotland, which broke away from the state Church, and was dubbed the "Wee Free"). It was the kind of discussion club in which Lewis (like Tolkien) thrived and which he always required.

> Our seniors had an institution called "The Philosophers' Teas." They met on Thursdays at 4 o'clock. Anyone present could raise a point for discussion. We juniors were invited to join and we found the occasions friendly and unstuffy (again the genuine democracy of the faculty could be clearly felt). But, as a forum for discussion, they were not a success.... Tea-time is not a philosophic hour: and, by the time the crumpets had gone round, it would be 4.15 or 4.30. We juniors were under such tutorial pressure that we had to teach daily from 5 to 7 o'clock, so we had to leave at 4.50 to get back to our Colleges.... We juniors established a group built on our experience of the "Teas." We agreed that evening is the time for thought.... Membership should be limited to the number ideal for a discussion, which we agreed to be six. To avoid competitive luxury, dinners were to be three-course, and with beer not wine. (This rigour was not pedantically maintained.) Our original membership was: Gilbert Ryle, Henry Price, Frank Hardie, C. S. Lewis, T. D. Weldon and myself. C. S. Lewis soon seceded from philosophy to English Literature, popular theology and science fiction; but not before he had assisted in a happy contribution to our proceedings....
>
> It was understood that opening remarks need not be finished papers but rather flying kites (even in note form if desired). We knew

each other so well that our basic methods and interests could be taken for granted, and our growing points exposed straightaway to lively, frank and friendly scrutiny.... I am sure that everything any of us published would have been considerably less well-argued but for running this gauntlet....

According to the eminent literary critic, William Empson, Lewis was "the best read man of his generation, one who read everything and remembered everything he read." His thoroughly book-centered nature well suited him to his task of lecturing and tutoring in the English School. What emerged from this background is a richness of thought, imagination, and writing that impregnated his later literary criticism, science fiction, children's literature, literary approaches to the Bible, and Christian apologetics. Lewis was always quick to acknowledge his enormous debt to his wide reading.

From childhood onwards, Lewis read voraciously and eclectically. Later in his career he typically defended the value of "low brow" reading such as Rider Haggard and John Buchan in the face of literary elitism. This book-centeredness and eclecticism was an important characteristic of Lewis throughout his life, and is reflected in his diaries and letters. The "house full of books" Lewis was indebted to is, he writes in *Surprised by Joy,* "almost a major character in my story."

Lewis's capacity for endless reading made him a natural library dweller from his undergraduate studies onwards. Oxford's Bodleian Library held a central place in Lewis's life, work — and affection, as he explained in a letter to his father. He spoke of spending his mornings in the Bodleian Library and remarked that, had he been able to smoke and relax in an upholstered chair, this would be one of the world's most delightful places.

The literary critic Helen Gardner noticed his reading habits in the Bodleian Library in later years with admiration:

One sometimes feels that the word "unreadable" had no meaning for him. To sit opposite him in Duke Humphrey [Library] when he was moving steadily through some huge double-columned folio in his reading for his Oxford history was to have an object lesson in what concentration meant. He seemed to create a wall of stillness around him.

Lewis's interest from the beginning, and increasingly so, was in the texts of an older period, pre-1830 like his ideal Oxford syllabus. For Lewis, all books before the period of modernism, spanning millennia at least since the ancient Greeks, shared important values, and thus interrelated in a constantly stimulating way. It was reading, even more so than intellectual debate and friendship (though he hungered for the latter), that fed his mind and imagination and kept him mentally alive. He saw the world with the help of texts, as part of a symbolic perception of reality. Thus, while experiencing the horrors of wartime trench warfare, he reflected: "This is War. This is what Homer wrote about."

Early in 1926, after taking up his Oxford Chair the previous year, Tolkien moved his family from Leeds to 22 Northmoor Road, in the leafy suburbs not far north of Oxford's city center. He found it easy to commute to Pembroke College, a little past Carfax, the busy crossroads named after the tower of the fourteenth-century church of St. Martin. According to his children, John and Priscilla, "He became a familiar figure cycling at deliberate speed down the Banbury Road on his exceptionally high-seated bicycle, often wearing his academic cap and gown!"

After World War I Edith had settled into the life of an academic's wife and a mother of young children, pursuing her more homely interests. Much of Tolkien's life was separate from Edith's world, in his study at home, and in the then male-dominated world of the university, and soon would include frequent meetings with Lewis. Beginning in 1933, there would be the Inklings, the informal literary club centered around Lewis and himself. This routine was broken each year by the family vacation. In 1927 and 1928 the Tolkiens traveled to Lyme Regis, Dorset. Another favorite location was Sidmouth in Devon. A family photo shows Tolkien kneeling in the sand with his children, happily building sand castles.

Tolkien's younger brother, Hilary, had bought a small orchard and market garden near Evesham, west of Oxford, the ancestral home of his mother's family, the Suffields. After leaving school, he had helped run a farm with his Aunt Jane Neave before enlisting in the British Army in 1914 and seeing action with the Royal Warwickshire regiment. The farm lay in a lane that led only to the house, which local people sometimes called the "Bag End." The brothers were able to keep in contact without too much difficulty.

Ronald and Edith's fourth child, Priscilla Mary Reuel Tolkien, was born in 1929. The following year the Tolkien family moved next door to 20 Northmoor Road. Tolkien set up his study, "the most exciting room," his children recalled. "The walls were lined with books from floor to ceiling, and it contained a great black lead stove, the source of considerable drama every day: first thing in the morning Ronald would light and draw it, then become distracted by other business, from which he would be aroused by shouts from the neighbours or the postman that the chimney was on fire, black smoke pouring out of it." Some of Tolkien's graduate students would come to the house for tutorials.

☜☞

Lewis began a diary in 1922, reflecting his introspection at that time. Selections have been published in *All My Road Before Me: The Diary of C. S. Lewis 1922–1927* (1991). Edited and abridged by Walter Hooper, these handwritten diaries record some of the days in Lewis's life between 1922 and 1927. The title is a quotation from *Dymer,* a poem that Lewis was writing at this time. The choice of events and contents is connected to Mrs. Moore, to whom he read most of the entries as he wrote them. Therefore, as Owen Barfield discovered upon reading them, there was no record of the "Great War" of ideas between himself and Lewis. The diaries vividly render the daily domestic life that Lewis led, as well as walks, weather, books, writing, and uncertainties over employment. The events center on "Hillsboro," the house on Holyoake Road, and its occupants, Lewis, Maureen, Mrs. Moore, and the occasional lodger. There is a charwoman dubbed "Phippy" after her name, Mrs. Phipps, and accounts of Lewis's friends and colleagues at Magdalen College. A dog called Pat (and later, another called Mr. Papworth) accompanies Lewis on many walks.

Lewis's diaries were most likely written for the benefit of Mrs. Moore, whom he refers to as "D" rather than her usual nickname, Minto. There is some speculation that "D." in the typescript made by Warren Lewis (in the *Lewis Family Papers*) may be transcribed from the Greek letter, Delta, and may stand for Diotima, a priestess in Plato's *Symposium* who introduces Socrates (in a platonic way, of course) to the meaning of love. Mrs. Moore, as Diotima, may have introduced love to the young Lewis in a less platonic way. Owen Barfield was acquainted with Mrs. Moore in the 1920s: "People have argued that Jack had a relationship with her. It's certainly possible, but unlikely to have been long-enduring; she was quite a lot older than him, and not, I should have thought, physically attractive."

The Christmas vacations of 1926 were the last time that Lewis, his father, and his brother spent all together. Relations between Albert Lewis and his two sons had often been strained in the past, but were improving. For the sons he was always the "P.B." or "the Pudaita-bird," based on his occasional lapse in pronouncing "potato." (Albert's Irish brogue was a constant source of amusement to his sons.) In *Surprised by Joy* Lewis portrayed his father as having little talent for happiness, and withdrawing into the safe monotony of routine. Biographer A. N. Wilson, however, believes the picture Lewis painted of his father as a "comic character" to be one-sided. Albert was a complex person scarred by the loss of his wife. The richest heritage he gave to Lewis was, literally, a houseful of old books which the gifted boy explored unimpeded. Lewis acknowledges this debt of books in *Surprised by Joy* and in his preface to *The Allegory of Love*. Albert Lewis shared his son's interest in writing and a power of rhetoric, including recounting "wheezes" (pithy observations often of humorous events).

Nearly eighteen months later, on May 2, 1928, Albert retired with an annual pension from his position as Belfast Corporation County solicitor. Just over a year into his retirement, on July 25, 1929, he had his first X rays to investigate a recurring complaint. The illness was serious enough to force Lewis, on August 13, to hasten to Belfast. On September 25 his father died, succumbing just after Lewis had returned to Oxford to care for some urgent matters. Two days later Warren received a telegram in Shanghai — "Sorry report father died painless twenty fifth September.

Jack." With his older brother away, it was left to Lewis to arrange the funeral and settle the estate.

Warnie Lewis had begun his military career when he entered the Royal Military College at Sandhurst shortly before the outbreak of World War I. After the war he served in Sierra Leone and Shanghai, before retiring as a major from the army in 1932 with a pension. His army life is vividly portrayed in his diaries. After his discharge he joined the unusual household run by his brother and Mrs. Moore. When he moved in with Lewis's ménage (at first on leave from the army, then permanently), he began the enormous task of arranging the Lewis family papers (letters, diaries, photographs, and various documents), typing and arranging the material in what ended up being eleven volumes. They are entitled *Memoirs of the Lewis Family: 1850–1930.* The volumes were completed in 1935 and, after his brother's death, bequeathed by Warren Lewis to The Wade Center in Wheaton, Illinois.

In October 1930, Mrs. Moore, Lewis, and Warren purchased jointly a property, "The Kilns," just outside the city boundaries near Headington, with the title being taken solely in the name of Mrs. Moore. The Lewis brothers held rights of life tenancy. Warren noted his first impressions in his diary.

> Jack and I went out and saw the place . . . the eight-acre garden is such stuff as dreams are made on. . . . The house . . . stands at the entrance to its own grounds at the northern foot of Shotover [hill] at the end of a narrow lane. . . . To the left of the house are the two brick kilns from which it takes its name — in front, a lawn and hard tennis court — then a large bathing pool, beautifully wooded, and with a delightful circular brick seat overlooking it. After that a steep wilderness broken with ravines and nooks of all kinds runs up to a little cliff topped by a thistly meadow, and then the property ends in a thick belt of fir trees, almost a wood. The view from the cliff over the dim blue distance is simply glorious.

A perfect touch was that the pond on the grounds had, according to Warren, associations with a favorite poet of Lewis's. It was known locally as "Shelley's Pool." Tradition has it that the poet "used to meditate there."

When Warren moved into The Kilns he soon felt at home, despite misgivings about Mrs. Moore. He increasingly perceived her as unsuited for his brother, due to the narrow range of her interests. According to Maureen her mother made The Kilns "a very Irish household," centered around herself. Eventually, there were as many hands about the place, as well as two or three dogs, and two or three cats. It was very much a "country place," which is why her mother liked The Kilns. A later visitor, Leonard Blake, who was to marry Maureen, recalled how Lewis and Warren would carry on conversation "at fortissimo strength." There are frequent references to Mrs. Moore's "marmalading" in Lewis's diaries, an event that would dominate the household. Lewis was often drawn into domestic chores. Lewis told David Wesley Soper that "he had to write by snatches, between walking the dog and peeling the potatoes."

Maureen remembered being drawn into the pattern of Lewis's day after a car was acquired. He would have tutorials in college from 9 A.M. until 1 P.M., and then from 5 to 7 P.M. throughout each Oxford eight-week term. Maureen would drive down to pick up Lewis at 1:10 P.M. to return to The Kilns for lunch. Then he would take the dog out for a walk. Maureen would later return him to Magdalen about 4:30 P.M. His social life, she recalled, was at the college. In fact, she socialized more with Warren than with Lewis, once they all lived together at The Kilns.

❧

Tolkien's lifelong study and teaching of languages was intimately related to his imaginative creations. In a letter to W. H. Auden, written many years later, he confessed that he always had had a "sensibility to linguistic pattern which affects me emotionally like colour or music." As basic as language in his complicated makeup from a very early age was a passion for myth and for fairy story, particularly for heroic legend which straddled fairy tale and history (as in the tales of King Arthur, or the story of Beowulf the dragon slayer). As an undergraduate it began to dawn on Tolkien that story and language were "integrally related." In his essay "On Fairy Stories" (1947) he would write, "The incarnate mind, the tongue, and the tale are in our world coeval." His imaginative and scientific interests were not on opposite poles. Myth and fairy story, he believed, must contain moral and religious truth, but allusively, not explicitly.

Yet he was still at this time working to integrate his thought and his imagination. The main audience for his stories were his children. He had no adult readership. In the 1920s there was no general adult readership for fantasy, or literature in which the story element was predominant — at least story in the sacramental way in which Tolkien saw it, as prefiguring the greatest story of all, in which a God and king comes to earth hidden in humble clothes to sacrifice himself in a seemingly foolish act that would lead to unimaginable joy — to the turning of the cosmic table. There was some truth in his throwaway comment to Lewis that literature was meant for men between thirty and forty. Tolkien sought to rehabilitate fairy stories as reading for adults, rather than being relegated to the safety of the nursery. Tales he loved, such as *Beowulf,* had once upon a time been standard fare for adults; indeed they did not embarrass tough warriors. According to Austin Olney, Tolkien's American editor at Houghton Mifflin for many years: "During the 1920s and 1930s Tolkien's imagination was running along two distinct courses that did not meet. On one side were the stories composed for the amusement of his children. On the other were the grander themes, sometimes Arthurian or Celtic, but usually associated with his own legends. . . . Something was lacking, something that would bring the two sides of the imagination together and produce a story that was at once heroic and mythical and at the same time tuned to the popular imagination." The notion that he would help to create a global adult readership for fantasy and fairy story, for myth on a heroic scale, would have been beyond even Tolkien's imagination. Yet he had a vision, perhaps born in his association with the T.C.B.S. in his Birmingham school years, which carried him slowly forward. He was soon to recognize a remarkably similar vision in Lewis.

In the summer of 1925, just before he started his new Chair at Oxford, Tolkien began writing a poetic version of the tale of Beren and Lúthien. This became one of the chief stories of "The Silmarillion," briefly retold in song by Aragorn in *The Lord of the Rings.* Like *The Lord of the Rings* it is a heroic romance, though on a smaller scale. Tolkien worked on both poetic and prose versions, though none of the poetic versions was ever completed. In A. N. Wilson's view, "though at times the verse is technically imperfect, it is full of passages of quite stunning beauty; and the overall conception must make it, though unfinished, one of the most remarkable poems written in English in the twentieth century."

The tale of Beren and Lúthien is set in Beleriand, during the First Age of Middle-earth. Lúthien was the daughter of the elven King Thingol, ruler of Doriath, and Queen Melian, and thus immortal. Beren was a mortal man. Many of Tolkien's characteristic themes emerge in this story, including healing and sacrifice, evil, death and immortality, and romantic love. Through the eventual marriage of Beren and Lúthien, an elven quality was preserved in future generations — even into the Fourth Age when humankind became ascendant, and the elves declined. This theme is repeated in *The Lord of the* Rings with the marriage of Arwen and Aragorn. Throughout the ages of Middle-earth the story of Beren and Lúthien brought hope and consolation both to elves and to those humans who were faithful against the powers of darkness. This hope is often expressed in *The Lord of the Rings*, by Aragorn and others.

While the "Great War" was raging with Owen Barfield, Lewis, then still a materialist, was working on a long narrative poem, *Dymer*, which he published on September 18, 1926, under the pseudonym Clive Hamilton (using his mother's maiden name, as he had done with *Spirits in Bondage*). The story had come to his mind, complete, when he was about seventeen; he had started writing it down in 1917, then returned to it in 1922. It is an antitotalitarian poem that has some similarities with *Spirits in Bondage*. Its hero, Dymer, escapes from a perfect but inhuman city into the soothing countryside. Various adventures overtake him. In contrast to Dymer's idealism, a revolutionary group rebel against the Perfect City in anarchy, claiming Dymer's name. Fresh in Lewis's mind when he began the poem were the bloody events of the Russian Revolution and of his native Ulster. He regarded popular political causes as "daemonic." In *Dymer* the young Lewis attacks Christianity bitterly, regarding it as a tempting illusion that must be overcome and destroyed in one's life. Christianity is lumped together with all forms of supernaturalism, including spiritism. By the time

Lewis finished writing *Dymer*, however, he had largely rejected atheism and naturalism in favor of a patched-up idealism.

Lewis was searching for an alternative to the views he had held for so long. This deepened his intellectual preoccupation with myth, and with the relationship between myth and reality. His imaginative life up to this time had been separated from his intellectual development. On April 26, 1926, he glimpsed a bridge to another country in an unlikely and surprising discussion with Thomas Dewar Weldon, a hard-bitten philosophy don at Magdalen College. They discussed the historicity of the New Testament Gospels. Lewis probably recorded this encounter in *Surprised by Joy:* "Early in 1926 the hardest boiled of all the atheists I ever knew sat in my room on the other side of the fire and remarked that the evidence for the historicity of the Gospels was really surprisingly good. 'Rum thing,' he went on. 'All that stuff of Frazer's about the Dying God. Rum thing. It almost looks as if it had really happened once.'" In his diary that night Lewis wrote, "We somehow got on the historical truth of the Gospels, and agreed there was a lot that could not be explained away." The diary concludes: "a wasted, tho' interesting evening."

Lewis had been intrigued by Tolkien's alluding to his linguistic and writing hobbies. Soon he was attracted by Tolkien's invitation to come along to The Coalbiters, an informal reading club Tolkien had initiated at Oxford in the spring of 1926. Its purpose was to explore Icelandic literature such as the Poetic Edda. The name referred to those who crowd so close to the fire in winter that they seem to "bite the coal." Lewis was soon attending meetings, as was his old friend Nevill Coghill (1899–1980), a research fellow in English at Exeter College. Lewis noted to Arthur Greeves that he was realizing a number of his very old dreams, which included reading *Sir Gawain and the Green Knight* in the original Middle English and learning Old Icelandic. He reported that The Coalbiters had already read the Younger Edda and the Volsung Saga. Next term they were going to read the Laxdale Saga. As a result of the Coalbiter gatherings Tolkien and Lewis were soon meeting regularly and talking far into the night. (Edith was used to her husband's late returns and his writing into the early hours of the morning — they had separate bedrooms in order not to disturb her sleep.) In another letter to Greeves in December 1929, Lewis recorded that after one meeting Tolkien came back with him to his college rooms and "sat discoursing of the gods and giants of Asgard for three hours." These conversations were to prove crucial both for the two men's writings, and for Lewis's eventual conversion to the Christian faith. As the Ulsterman Lewis remarked in *Surprised by Joy:* "Friendship with...J. R. R. Tolkien...marked the breakdown of two old prejudices. At my first coming into the world I had been (implicitly) warned never to trust a Papist, and at my first coming into the English Faculty (explicitly) never to trust a philologist. Tolkien was both."

Tolkien and Lewis's evolving friendship was of great significance to both men. Tolkien found in Lewis an appreciative listener for his burgeoning stories and poems of Middle-earth, a good deal of which were not published until after his death. He acknowledged that without Lewis's encouragement over many years, *The Lord of the Rings* would have never appeared in print. Lewis equally had cause to appreciate Tolkien, whose views on myth, story, and imagination helped him eventually to believe in God's existence. Seeing mind to mind on both imagination and the truth of Christianity became the foundation of their remarkable friendship. The Inklings, the group of literary friends around Lewis, was to grow out of this rapport between Lewis and Tolkien. From the beginning, Lewis clearly recognized Tolkien's remarkable literary gifts. On Tolkien's side, too, there was much gratefulness. He wrote in 1929, "Friendship with Lewis compensates for much."

3

A Story-Shaped World

"Mythopoeia" (1929–1931)

Imagine an early summer's day in the Trinity term of 1929, around lunchtime. The location is the upper deck of the Headington bus, starting its journey up the hill eastwards from the Oxford city center. A man sits there, about thirty, wearing a tweed jacket and baggy flannels, and a shabby hat on his head, with the brim turned down all around. He could be a young farmer, with his red complexion and thick-set form.

He looks out of the bus window, putting his cigarette to his lips and drawing its smoke into his lungs, apparently gazing over Headington Hill Park. The man is C. S. Lewis, and he is starting to grapple with a momentous decision, evoking the whole question of human freedom. Unprovoked by any particular event on the bus journey, Lewis suddenly feels presented with a fact about himself, a confrontation without words and perhaps even without images. He senses that he has been shutting something out, holding something at bay. He would describe it later as if wearing uncomfortable clothing — like a cumbersome suit of armor, or like the high-collared uniform he was exiled to school in. It is as if suddenly a door appears before him that he can push open, or leave shut. He chooses in an instant to go through the door, to shed his skin of harsh clothes. Yet at the same moment, he feels compelled to do so. As he acts, he is freer than ever before, yet the choice is demanded by his deepest nature.

The bus pulls to a halt with a jerk at the stop by Bury Knowle Park, and Lewis hastily disappears down the stairs.

⧽⧼

Shortly after this experience in an Oxford bus Lewis knelt and prayed to his unknown God, who appeared barely personal. He described himself as the "most reluctant convert in all of England." It is as if Lewis had been on a celestial omnibus, like the one he later described in the dream sequence *The Great Divorce* (1945), which transported him from the dark, dank streets of hell to the bright but distant fringes of the heavenly country.

Because of the epiphany on the Oxford bus, and many other conversations and books that he had encountered, Lewis eventually became a theist; he acknowledged some kind of personal God behind the show of reality: "In the Trinity Term of 1929 I gave in, and admitted that God was God, and knelt and prayed...." The movement of Lewis's thinking at this time would be vividly captured in his book *Miracles* (1947). He later confessed: "I never had the experience of looking for God. It was the other way round; He was the hunter (or so it seemed to me) and I was the deer. He stalked me like a redskin, took unerring aim, and fired. And I am very thankful that that is how the first (conscious) meeting occurred. It forearms one against subsequent fears that the whole thing was only wish fulfillment. Something one didn't wish for can hardly be that."

Lewis describes his conversion to believing in a personal God in terms approaching the mystical: "In the region of awe ... in the deepest solitude there is a road right out of the self, a commerce with something which, by refusing to identify itself with any object of the senses, or anything whereof we might have biological or social need, or anything imagined, or any state of our own minds, proclaims itself sheerly objective ... the naked Other, imageless (though our imagination salutes it with a hundred images)."

⧽⧼

Lewis was enjoying The Coalbiters, one of several groups he attended. Tolkien was the most fluent of the members; he could faultlessly translate straight from the page the Icelandic sagas they studied. Lewis and most of the others made much slower progress, maybe managing just half a page at a time. The readings took him back to his youthful discoveries of Northern myths, where the sudden stab of "northernness" struck him as a physical sensation. Tolkien, he knew, shared this love of a vast, northern world, with wide, pale skies, dragons, courage against the darkness, and vulnerable gods, one of whom in particular, Balder, blazed bright in his beauty.

It eventually became a regular habit for Tolkien to drop by Lewis's college around mid-morning on Mondays (a day when Lewis had no students). The two friends usually crossed the high street and went to the Eastgate Hotel or to a nearby public house for a drink. Sometimes they remained in his college rooms. Other times they met at Tolkien's home in Northmoor Road, or after meetings of The Coalbiters. Lewis wrote to his brother about now-regular weekly meetings with Tolkien. Meeting his friend, he said, was one of the most pleasant spots in the week. Sometimes they talked university English School politics. Other times they commented on each other's poems. They might drift into theology or "the state of the nation." On rare occasions they simply played with bawdy and pun. Among other things, they plotted in establishing a coherent undergraduate syllabus for the English School at Oxford. "Perhaps one of the most significant of [Lewis's] contributions to the study of English literature at Oxford," wrote Dame Helen Gardner, after his death, "was the part he played with his friend Professor J. R. R. Tolkien in establishing a syllabus for the Final Honour School which embodied his belief in the value of medieval (especially Old English) literature, his conviction that a proper study of modern literature required the linguistic training that the study of earlier literature gave, and his sense of the continuity of English literature and the syllabus, which remained in force for over twenty years, was in many ways an admirable one." Tolkien's reformed syllabus was accepted, in fact, by 1931, bringing together "Lang." and "Lit."

At this time it was their practice (common then) to call each other by surname or nickname (Tolkien was "Tollers" and Lewis was simply "Lewis"). Lewis didn't even know Tolkien's first names other than "Ronald" as late as 1957. Many years later he described Tolkien's conversational style: "He is the most unmanageable man (in conversation) I've ever met. He will talk to you alright, but the subject of his remarks will be whatever happens to be interesting him at the moment, which might be anything from M.[iddle] E.[nglish] words to Oxford [English School] politics." Tolkien too, long after, recalled conversation with Lewis at this period: "C. S. Lewis was one of the only three persons who have so far read all or a considerable part of my 'mythology' of the First and Second Ages, which had already been in the main lines constructed before we met. He had the peculiarity that he liked to be read to. All that he knew of my 'matter' was what his capacious but not infallible memory retained from my reading to him as sole audience." He also remembered: "In the early days of our association Jack used to come to my house and I read aloud to him The Silmarillion so far as it had then gone, including a very long poem: Beren and Luthien."

It was near the end of 1929 that Tolkien decided to give the "Lay of Leithien" — the poetic version of the tale of Beren and Lúthien — to Lewis to read. His friend read it during the evening of December 6. His response was enthusiastic — he wrote to Tolkien the very next day: "I can quite honestly say that it is ages since I have had an evening of such delight: and the personal interest of reading a friend's work had very little to do with it. . . . The two things that came out clearly are the sense of reality in the background and the mythical value: the essence of a myth being that it should have no taint of allegory to the maker and yet should suggest incipient allegories to the reader." Early the next year Lewis offered ingenious comment on the unfinished poem in the form of a mock academic commentary, which ran to fourteen pages. He presented the commentary in the form of several spoof literary critics, representing various critical positions including German source criticism (influential in theology) — Schick, Schuffer, Pumpernickel, Bentley, and Peabody. He had already discovered that Tolkien's response to criticism of his work was either to ignore it, or to go back to the beginning and start a total rewriting. He felt that the work had considerable merit, but would benefit from some changes — certainly not a radical rewrite.

Sharing his mythology with Lewis was an important step for Tolkien in finding an adult readership (then nearly nonexistent) for "fairy tales." Fairies for Tolkien were the noble elves of Middle-earth, such as the beautiful Lúthien, and her parents King Thingol and Queen Melian. He took another tentative step by presenting a paper called "A Secret Vice" to an Oxford society in 1931. This paper is of particular interest because of a number of references to his life. Tolkien speaks of the pleasure of inventing languages, and believes that this technical linguistic "hobby" is natural in childhood. It can survive to adulthood: he gives examples of his own invention, including Elvish languages.

One of the many issues that Tolkien and Lewis discussed was that of the nature of language, its changes over time, and the way language carried and was shaped by myth. Tolkien read Owen Barfield's *Poetic Diction;* he may have been lent a copy by Lewis. In an undated letter to Barfield, possibly written in 1929, Lewis observed: "You might like to know that when Tolkien dined with me the other night he said à-propos of something quite different that your conception of the ancient semantic unity had modified his whole outlook and that he was almost just going to say something in a lecture when your conception stopped him in time. 'It is one of those things,' he said, 'that when you've once seen it there are all sorts of things you can never say again.'"

They also shared a fervent interest in Early and Middle English literature. Though the range of Lewis's literary interests was far wider than Tolkien's he was nevertheless well read in this period. Undoubtedly poems such as *Pearl, Sir Orfeo,* and *Beowulf* frequently came up in their conversations. Tolkien is likely to have shown or read Lewis his verse translation of *Beowulf,* made while he was in Leeds. He certainly showed his friend the first of two prose translations of *Beowulf* he made in the late 1920s or early 1930s, as the typescript contains amendments in what is more than probably Lewis's handwriting. This indicates that Lewis read and commented on the translation. Tolkien incorporated the emendations into his final version.

At the end of the 1920s Lewis was filling out, whereas Tolkien remained slight of build. In his teens Lewis was thin and lanky but now he had become markedly solid. His physical size, booming voice, and appearance were easily remembered, as by Professor A. G. Dickens:

Perhaps the first thing you noticed about him, he had an extraordinary red complexion, rather as if he might have a stroke at any time.... He had rather solid well-marked features, fine expressive eyes, a very solid physical build, a clear, emphatic voice. He talked very good prose. One could have recorded it and put a little punctuation in it and made something like an essay. He dressed very informally. He always wore a tweed jacket and flannel trousers, which was at the time the uniform of the undergraduate population.

Professor Dickens added that many of the senior members of the university also wore this attire, but more tidily perhaps than Lewis.

Lewis wore "manly" wear in deliberate contrast with the foppish trend of the aesthete who could be seen — and liked to be seen — around Oxford in those days. Tolkien dressed more stylishly, but still in the uniform of the bookish academic: tweed jacket and flannel trousers. (Perhaps Tolkien wished to compensate for his less privileged upbringing by being smarter in appearance.) Tolkien confided in a much later letter his impressions of his friend: "C.S.L. of course had some oddities and could sometimes be irritating. He was after all and remained an Irishman of Ulster. But he did nothing for effect; he was not a professional clown, but a natural one, when a clown at all. He was generous-minded, on guard against all prejudices, though a few were too deep-rooted in his native background to be observed by him." In a letter years later to an American scholar Lewis in turn shed light on Tolkien, "He is a very great man. His published works (both imaginative & scholarly) ought to fill a shelf by now: but he's one of those people who is never satisfied with a [manuscript]." Lewis also called him in another letter "that great but dilatory and unmethodical man."

☙

Shortly after his conversion to theism in 1929, Lewis began writing a spiritual autobiography, a kind of forerunner to *Surprised by Joy*. Its purpose was to explain the importance of his experience of joy, associated with an inconsolable longing, in the process. This early manuscript was seventy-two pages long. It began with a statement of purpose, explaining that it was not an intellectual defense of theism as such, but the story of a persistent experience that led him to belief in God:

In this book I propose to describe the process by which I came back, like so many of my generation, from materialism to a belief in God. . . . I arrived where I am, not by reflection alone, but by reflection on a particular recurrent experience. I am an empirical Theist. I have arrived at God by induction.

This unfinished autobiography is an indication of a self-examination after Lewis's acceptance of theism. The great war between his intellectual and his imaginative life began to show signs of an armistice. Lewis found himself responding to John Bunyan's account of his inner distress and subsequent conversion, recorded in his confession, *Grace Abounding to the Chief of Sinners* (1666). He wrote about Bunyan's confession in one of his frequent letters to his Ulster friend Arthur Greeves:

I should like to know . . . in general what you think of all the darker side of religion as we find it in old books. Formerly I regarded it as mere devil-worship based on horrible superstitions. Now that I have found, and am still finding more and more the element of truth in the old beliefs, I *feel* I cannot dismiss even their dreadful side so cavalierly. There must be something in it: only what?

Around the time of the move into The Kilns on October 11, 1930, Lewis began reading John's Gospel in Greek — it soon became his practice to read some passage of the Bible more or less daily. He also started attending Magdalen College chapel on weekdays and his parish church on Sundays. Reading John began to change his picture of the life and person of Christ. Significantly, he also had been reading George MacDonald's *Diary of an Old Soul* (1880) early in 1930. Oxford's spring (or Hilary) term had then started, ruling out private reading except for MacDonald's calendar of verses, written after the death of two of his children. In a letter to Greeves, Lewis expressed satisfaction that when he had completed it, there were many other books of its general type. He saw this as "another of the beauties of coming, I won't say, to religion but to an attempt at religion — one finds oneself on the main road with all humanity, and can compare notes with an endless succession of previous travellers. It is emphatically coming home...." Similar thoughts were in his mind when he wrote to another friend, Alfred Kenneth Hamilton Jenkin, on March 21, 1930. He told Jenkin how his outlook was changing. He did not feel that he was moving exactly to Christianity, though, Lewis confessed, it may turn out that way in the end. The best way of explaining the change, he said, was this: Once he would have said "Shall I adopt Christianity"; now he was waiting to see whether it would adopt him. Another party was involved — it was as if he were playing poker, not patience, as he once supposed. Lewis around this time wrote in mock alarm to Barfield that terrifying things were happening to him. He said, in the language of his philosophical concerns, that the "Spirit" or "Real I" was tending to become much more personal and, to his alarm, was taking the offensive. In fact, it was behaving just like God. He concluded, "You'd better come on Monday at the latest or I may have entered a monastery."

❧

A little over two years have passed since Lewis's totally unexpected epiphany on a local bus journey in the summer of 1929. Then he had chosen reluctantly to bow the knee to a God somewhat without shape, but incorrigibly personal, and distinctly theistic; that is, a God who is creator of all that is not him — stars and galaxies, matter and space, rocks and water, vegetation, animal life, and human beings.

On Monday, September 28, 1931, on a very different form of transport, Lewis takes another sudden step in his spiritual journey. He lodges himself in the sidecar of Warren's Daudel motorcycle. His brother mounts the bike and pulls down his goggles. Soon they are racing along the country roads of a sunny Oxfordshire, their glimpses of passing woods, hedgerows, and streams sometimes obscured by the lingering wisps of morning fog. They are heading east towards Whipsnade Zoo.

It might seem an incongruous event: A brilliant Oxford don and a seasoned army major taking a day out to go to the zoo to visit Mr. Bultitude the bear and Wallaby Wood — with its carpet of bluebells, and the Wallabies springing about here, there, and everywhere, a veritable vision for the brothers of Eden regained. Admittedly, the two are joined by Mrs. Moore, Maureen, and an Irish friend, not forgetting the canine Mr. Papworth, who are lagging behind in the much slower car. The visit, however, is the brothers' freely chosen pleasure. Lewis often feels that all his labors in writing and teaching are for just such a time as this, for a happy, leisurely outing with his friend and brother, Warnie, where they can talk the old, old talk. Lewis is not an aesthete (this is obvious from how he dresses) even though he honestly follows the tracks left by beauty wherever he finds them. He, like his brother, wallows in the physicality of the world.

As the motorbike speeds towards Whipsnade Lewis's whole world suddenly turns around. A choice has been presented to him and he pushes open another door, transforming into the Christian writer and thinker who, his celebrity unsought, will eventually be known to many millions of people around the globe. Before this moment, he is an obscure poet halfway through his life, with aspirations of greatness, and a teacher known only to a few, who not many years previously had been an atheist. Lewis feels himself pulled forward in his seat as the motorbike slows at a crossroads. A road sign shows that they are almost at Whipsnade.

◦∿◦

The process of Lewis's conversion to Christianity had all started with his acceptance of theism a little over two years before, following the momentous bus journey up Headington Hill. The pilgrimage had come to a head just a few days before the trip to Whipsnade. The night of September 19–20, as they made their way down Addison's Walk, on the grounds of Magdalen College, Lewis had had a long conversation with Tolkien, now a fast friend, and a mutual friend, Henry "Hugo" Victor Dyson Dyson (1896–1975), which had shaken him to the roots. Like Tolkien, Dyson was a devout Christian. Tolkien's faith went back to his childhood, to his mother's conversion to Roman Catholicism, and to his first communion as a boy in Birmingham. Tolkien recorded the long night conversation on Addison's Walk, and many previous exchanges with Lewis, in his poem, *Mythopoeia* (the "making of myth"). He also noted in his diary: "Friendship with Lewis compensates for much, and besides giving constant pleasure and comfort has done me much good from the contact with a man at once honest, brave, intellectual — a scholar, a poet, and a philosopher — and a lover, at least after a long pilgrimage, of Our Lord."

Dyson had reinforced Tolkien's argument. Lewis had come to know him the year before, on one of his visits from Reading University, where he taught. Describing that meeting, on July 28, 1930, Lewis wrote: "He is a man who really loves truth: a philosopher and a religious man: who makes his critical & literary activities depend on the former — none of your damned dilettante." Lewis liked him very much, including his vivacity, quickness of speech, and merry laughter. Undoubtedly Dyson gave emotional weight to Tolkien's more measured argument that momentous night. Tolkien had argued for the Christian Gospels on the basis of the universal love of story which, for him, was sacramental. His poem *Mythopoeia* gives us a good idea of the flow of the conversation. Tolkien wrote of the human heart not being composed of falsehood, but having nourishment of knowledge from the Wise One, and still remembering him. Though the estrangement is ancient, human beings are neither completely abandoned by God nor totally corrupted. Though we are disgraced we still retain vestiges of our mandate to rule. We continue to create according to the "law in which we're made."

Lewis later wrote a powerful essay on the harmony of story and fact in the Gospels, remembering that life-changing conversation with Tolkien and Dyson: "This is the marriage of heaven and earth, perfect Myth and Perfect Fact: claiming not only our love and Obedience, but also our wonder and delight, addressed to the savage, the child, and the poet in each one of us no less than to the moralist, the scholar, and the philosopher." He realized that the claims and stories of Christ demand an imaginative as much as an intellectual response from us. He treated the theme more fully in his book *Miracles* (1947).

Tolkien in turn expounded his view more fully in his essay "On Fairy Stories." He argued that the very historical events of the Gospel narratives are shaped by God, the master story maker, having a structure of the sudden turn from catastrophe to the most satisfying of all happy endings — a structure shared with the best human stories. The Gospels, in their divine source, thus penetrate the seamless "web" of human storytelling, clarifying and perfecting the insights that God in his grace has allowed to the human imagination. In the Gospels, Tolkien concluded, "art has been verified." Among this art that pointed to the master story of the Gospels were the

Northern myths that Tolkien had loved from his boyhood, a love and fascination he shared with Lewis.

⟡

A voice carries through the misty air above like the mournful cry of passing cranes. It laments:

> Balder the Beautiful
> Is dead, is dead!

The pallid corpse of the dead sun is borne through the northern sky. Blasts from Niffelheim lift the sheeted mists around him as he passes. Balder is dead — Balder the Beautiful, god of the summer sun, fairest of all the gods! Light from his forehead beams, runes are upon his tongue, as on the warrior's sword. All things in earth and air are bound by magic spell never to do him harm; even the plants and stones — all except the mistletoe! Hoeder, the blind and silent old god, innocently had pierced through Balder's gentle breast with his sharp spear, made by trickery from the accursed mistletoe!

So runs, in paraphrase, Isaias Tegner's nineteenth-century Swedish poem, *Drapa,* which was read in the verse translation of the scholar Henry Longfellow by a youthful Lewis. It was one of many instances of Northern myth that enraptured him and was an important signpost in Lewis's imaginative journey, as he sought the source of his inconsolable longing, marked by joy.

Lewis's life up to his conversion at the age of thirty-two is recorded in *Surprised by Joy* (1955), and somewhat in his long allegory, *The Pilgrim's Regress* (1933). These tell us that his lengthy, varied, and reluctant pilgrimage was greatly influenced by a certain distinct tone of feeling that he discovered in early childhood, and which stayed with him on and off throughout his adolescence and early adulthood.

This longing for beauty or joy he learned, he tells us, from gazing at distant hills from his nursery windows, and from seeing his brother's miniature garden in the biscuit tin lid. Later reading of Northern myths and sagas intensified this dissatisfaction. Significantly, in 1922, Lewis wrote a poem on this theme, "Joy." Towards the end of his life Lewis personified the imaginative longing in a character of the Princess Psyche in *Till We Have Faces* (1956), based upon classical myth. Myths and otherworldly tales, Lewis found, often defined this longing for beauty.

In *Surprised by Joy* Lewis reported his sensations of joy, some of which were responses to natural beauty, while others were evoked by literature and art. He hoped that other people would recognize similar experiences of their own as they read his account. His early tastes of beauty taught him longing, and made him for good or ill a votary of the "Blue Flower" — the symbol of *sehnsucht* or inconsolable longing in German Romantic literature and Scandinavian ballads — before he was six years old.

The relationship between zest for life and the desire for beauty constantly fascinated Lewis. The stories of George MacDonald, which shaped Lewis's imagination, are dominated by a joyful quality of holiness or goodness in life — but it was no platonic spirituality. MacDonald's stories (including his novels) concern the homely and ordinary, transformed by a new light. Lewis captured this exactly when he wrote: "The quality which had enchanted me in his imaginative works turned out to be the quality of the real universe, the divine, magical, terrifying and ecstatic reality in which we all live."

Lewis's own imaginative creations such as *The Chronicles of Narnia* were to spring from this desire for beauty, cast into a Christian framework. The last chapter of *The Problem of Pain* (1940) speaks of it; a sermon, "The Weight of Glory" (1941), tries to define the desire; *The Voyage of the Dawn Treader* (1952) is about the Narnian mouse Reepicheep's quest for Aslan's Country at the World's End; *Surprised by Joy* traces the twin threads of Lewis's thinking and his longing for beauty up to his conversion; and in *Till We Have Faces* the princess Psyche has a love of this beauty that is stronger than death. Lewis wrote: "We do not want merely to see beauty....We want something else which can hardly be put into words — to be united with the beauty we see, to pass into it, to receive it into ourselves, to bathe in it, to become part of it. That is why we have peopled air and earth and water with gods and goddesses and nymphs and elves."

Lewis saw this unquenchable longing as a sure sign that no part of the created world, and thus no aspect of our experience, is capable of fulfilling humankind. We are dominated by a homelessness, and yet by a keen sense of what "home" means.

Samuel Alexander (1859–1938) created a philosophical distinction between enjoyment and contemplation that became pivotal to Lewis's thinking at this time, especially his preoccupation with the "dialectic of desire." In *Surprised by Joy* he was to confess: "All my waiting and watching for Joy, all my vain hopes to find some mental content on which I could, so to speak, lay my finger and say, 'This is it,' had been a futile attempt to contemplate the enjoyed." It was a momentous discovery. The secret of joy lay not within himself but outside of himself, somewhere in the world. Yet even the world, with its complexity and vastness, was not adequate. Like his mental and imaginative resources, features of the world could only provide a lens to see with. The same was true of the world's stories — tales of dying gods and quests for undying lands pointed to a fulfillment elsewhere. The source and object of joy lay "beyond the walls of the world."

With his conversion Lewis rejected the grand impersonality of systems spawned by materialism, and even by idealism. He grew to prefer the individuality of places and people, seasons and times, moods and tones of feeling. God himself, he concluded, was the most concrete and articulate of existences. Christ's incarnation had a splendid logic to it. The Gospel accounts were (as he learned through Tolkien) the epitome of human storytelling and myth making, with an astounding dimension of historical veracity. Everything was true in the actual, primary world without losing the quality of myth that engendered joy. The Gospel narratives thus demanded both an imaginative and a reasoned response. For the first time, both sides of Lewis — the philosophical Lewis and the imaginative Lewis — became engaged.

A God who is fully personal, Lewis discovered, is also more interesting. The deity is involved in the contingency of the world, including the stuff of history; he is not an unchanging, abstract entity (even though his character is unchanging), as Lewis was to argue powerfully in his book *Miracles* (1947). The fact that the Gospels are stories tells us a lot about ourselves, about who we are. The Gospel narrative is essentially interesting as story; a good story implies human interest and a human response. The narrative, the *evangelion,* displays God's knowledge of us and of our interests. In Lewis's logic, inspired by the arguments of Tolkien and Dyson, God is the storyteller who enters his own story, putting later novelists in the shade. But not only do the Gospel narratives provide the key to ourselves, they tell us a lot about God as their main subject. He is intrinsically interesting, demanding both our intellectual and our imaginative attention. Everything to do with him can be put in the form of a story. Everything about him is the stuff of richest myth and deepest philosophical and scientific reasoning.

Lewis succinctly explained his understanding of myth becoming fact, an understanding that would underpin his writing henceforward:

> The heart of Christianity is a myth which is also a fact. The old myth of the Dying God, *without ceasing to be myth,* comes down from the heaven of legend and imagination to the earth of history. It *happens* — at a particular date, in a particular place, followed by definable historical consequences. We pass from a Balder or an Osiris, dying nobody knows when or where, to a historical Person crucified (it is all in order) *under Pontius Pilate.* By becoming fact it does not cease to be myth: that is the miracle. To be truly Christian we must both assent to the historical fact and also receive the myth (fact though it has become) with the same imaginative embrace which we accord to all myths.

Lewis, in taking on this view, faced, like Tolkien, ancient tensions. The tension between realism and fantasy is just one such tension, expressed in the common charge that fantasy is escapism. Employing myth and fantasy, however, did not traditionally denote lack of confidence; this was a modern phenomenon. Its use in Lewis, and in Tolkien, retains a sense of confidence. When Lewis applied the categories of myth and story to the Gospels he was not displaying uncertainty about their historicity. Though the two were aware of tensions between myth and realism, the tension for them was basically reconciled, despite the fact that the tension is embedded in modern usage of the term "myth." Myth can be defined in terms of the embodiment of a worldview of a people or culture, thus having an important believed element. Myth can also be defined as untrue, fictional, and merely imaginative. The existence of myth writes large the dilemma that the "lies" of the poet, the fiction writer, and the maker of scientific models capture profound realities, realities impossible to capture in any other way. Fiction, poetry, and metaphor, though they are "lies," by necessity have an element that represents the world. In his poem *Mythopoeia*, reflecting his argument with Lewis, Tolkien fully takes on the charge that stories are "lies breathed through silver."

Other forms of the inherent tension of myth are evident. The tensions between myth and reason, myth and history, and myth and knowledge go back to ancient times. However, it is only in the modern period has this tension represented a crisis in knowledge. In ancient times, up to what Lewis would eventually describe as the Great Divide between the Old West and Post-Christian West, the tension between myth and fact was creative, resulting in great literature. The two friends had a tangible confidence that the separation of story and fact has been reconciled, which led them to continue in a tradition of symbolic fiction, telling stories of dragons and kings in disguise, talking animals and heroic quests, set in imagined worlds. For them, heaven at a particular, definable moment in space and time came down to earth, and our humanity subsequently was taken up to and remains in God. Our familiar world and a larger world, fractured by the ancient fall of humanity, have met and fused forever because of the heroism of Christ. Their confidence in this reconciliation of myth and fact directly led Tolkien and Lewis to create Middle-earth, Narnia, Glome, and Perelandra, which aim to present a true picture of reality that combines heaven and earth, spirit and nature.

4

The Thirties

The Context of Imaginative Orthodoxy

Some time during the long wars of the First Age of Middle-earth a dragon lies on the edge of a narrow, deep gorge through which a river races, known as the "Rainy Stair." It is sundown as the warrior Túrin arrives with two companions. He has fought for many years against Morgoth, the dark would-be ruler of Middle-earth, and seeks revenge against the dragon, Glaurung, for the evil it has done. Seeing his opportunity, Túrin plans that he will climb up the gorge underneath where Glaurung lies and surprise him. It will mean a perilous crossing of the river. On seeing the gorge in the dark of night, the heart of one of his companions fails, and only Túrin and Hunthor cross over. The roaring of the river drowns all sound they make. They start the ascent. Around midnight the dragon stirs and starts to pull his vast bulk across the narrow ravine, leaving his soft underbelly exposed. A dislodged rock strikes Hunthor and kills him, but Túrin climbs hastily and thrusts his black sword into the dragon's belly up to its hilt. Glaurung gives a great scream as he feels the deathblow, and pulls himself right across the chasm. At last his fire goes out and he lies still.

Wishing to recover his precious sword, Túrin re-crosses the rushing river and climbs to where the dragon sprawls. As he retrieves the great sword with a shout of victory, Glaurung opens his eyes one last time and looks with malice at his enemy. Túrin passes out like one dead.

༺ঞ৯༻

The tragic tale of Túrin Turambar, who among other things marries his long-lost sister in ignorance, is one of the central stories of Tolkien's *The Silmarillion*. It characteristically wrestles with the reality of evil. Tolkien commented that, in the tale of Túrin "are revealed most evil works of Morgoth," and that it was "the worst of the works of Morgoth in the ancient world." Tolkien was shaping his accounts of the early ages of Middle-earth through much of the 1930s, until he abandoned them for many years in favor of a sequel to *The Hobbit*. Tolkien in fact composed a version of "The Silmarillion" in 1930. This was the only account of the mythology of the First Age that Tolkien ever completed.

"The Silmarillion," as it existed in the 1930s, chronicled the ancient days of Middle-earth. It began with the creation of the Two Lamps that lit the world and concluded with the great battle in which Morgoth, the malevolent power, is overthrown. The unifying thread of the annals and tales of "The Silmarillion" is, as its title suggests, the fate of the Silmarils, the precious gems illumined with the original light of the world.

The Silmarillion, as it was published in 1977, is divided into several sections. The first is the Ainulindalë — the account of the creation of the world. This is one of Tolkien's finest pieces of writing, perfectly blending philosophical and theological matter into artistic form. The second section is the Valaquenta — the history of the Valar, the angelic powers behind creation. Then follows the main and largest section, the Quenta Silmarillion — the "history of the Silmarils." The next section is the Akallabêth, the account of the downfall of Númenor, the island kingdom west of Middle-earth, its Atlantis. The final section concerns the history of the Rings of Power and the Third Age, creating a background to the events of *The Lord of the Rings*.

The mythology, history, and tales of Middle-earth exist in unfinished papers drafted over most of Tolkien's life, with often surprising developments and narrative changes. Not least, some of the great tales exist in both poetic and prose versions.

"The Silmarillion" comprised a number of stories, a variety of beings, a consistent geography and history, and several invented languages which generate the names of people and places, creating a stylistic unity. The scope of these creations is formidable. Furthermore, they are not merely elements. Tolkien breathed life into them so that they constantly interrelate. He increasingly felt that the stories, languages, and peoples had taken on a life of their own, which he struggled to capture adequately. In writing first *The Hobbit* and then *The Lord of the Rings* Tolkien, however, was able to accomplish an artistic unity accessible for a popular readership. In the process he nearly single-handedly had to create the conditions under which such fantasy and mythopoeic fiction could gain an adult readership. Lewis wholeheartedly supported this task by writing his science-fiction trilogy, *Out of the Silent Planet, Perelandra,* and *That Hideous Strength* (1938–45); *The Great Divorce* (1945); and later *Till We Have Faces* (1956).

In 1932 Tolkien bought his first car, a Morris Cowley known as "Old Jo," after its number plate. (He later abandoned car ownership on principle, because of the environmental effect of massive car ownership and production.) Owning the car led to an eventful family trip to visit Hilary Tolkien in Evesham, in which two of the tires lost air and the erratically driven vehicle partially demolished a dry-stone wall near Chipping Norton. The consequences of having a car inspired another children's story, *Mr. Bliss* (illustrated in color throughout by Tolkien himself), and not in fact published until 1982. It is the story of Mr. Bliss, a man noted for his tall hats, who lives in a tall house, and his adventures after buying a bright yellow car for five shillings.

The strange figure of Tom Bombadil, "master of wood, water and hill," also sees life during this period. He is a nature spirit, mastered by none and refusing possession himself. Like the biblical Adam, he is a name giver.

Tom Bombadil started out as a Dutch doll belonging to Michael Tolkien as a young child, with a splendid feather in its hat. He became, in Tolkien's invention, the hero of "The Adventures of Tom Bombadil," published in a poetry collection in 1934. Tom Bombadil eventually reemerged in *The Lord of the Rings.* He gave to the ponies of the hobbits names that they "answered to for the rest of their lives." Like the wizards, his appearance was that of a man, though, unlike them, he had been in Middle-earth from earliest days. Tolkien's talent for songs, ballads, and witty riddles, voiced in Tom Bombadil, fit well into a hobbitish setting. In a letter to his publisher in 1937 Tolkien spoke of Tom Bombadil as the spirit of the vanishing countryside of Berkshire and Oxfordshire. He is a very timely figure, refusing domination of nature, who could well serve as the patron saint of the good scientist.

Early in 1938 Tolkien read a new story, *Farmer Giles of Ham*, to an undergraduate society at Worcester College, instead of the announced academic paper on fairy stories, which was not yet ready. Though suitable for children, it feels its way towards being an adult story, which is why perhaps Tolkien saw it as an adequate substitute for the academic paper. Not published until 1950, this lighthearted short story is subtitled, "The Rise and Wonderful Adventures of Farmer Giles, Lord of Tame, Count of Worminghall and King of the Little Kingdom." It begins with a mock-scholarly foreword about its supposed authorship, translation from Latin, and the extent of the "Little Kingdom" in "a dark period of the history of Britain," before the days of King Arthur, in the valley of the Thames.

This humorous story, though on the surface very different from the tales of Middle-earth, is characteristic of Tolkien in its themes. The story's inspiration is linguistic: it provides a spoof explanation for the name of an actual village east of Oxford, a favorite of Tolkien's, called Worminghall, near Thame. The Little Kingdom has similarities with The Shire, particularly Farmer Giles's sheltered and homely life. He is like a complacent hobbit, with unexpected qualities. The humor — with its mock scholarship — is similar to that in the book of hobbit verses, *The Adventures of Tom Bombadil*, not published until 1962.

Lewis read far more widely and eclectically than his friend, who was increasingly focusing his attention upon the English West Midlands of the Middle Ages, both in his fiction and in his linguistic work at Oxford. The fruit of this close reading was many literary essays over the years, most collected posthumously, and major studies like *The Allegory of Love: A Study in Medieval Tradition* (1936), on the growth of allegory and the developments of romantic love, and *English Literature in the Sixteenth Century* (1954), Lewis's contribution to the *Oxford History of English Literature.* Lewis began writing the latter, after the completion of *The Allegory of Love,* in 1935 at the suggestion of Professor F. P. Wilson, one of the series editors. Frank Wilson had been Lewis's tutor as an undergraduate. Like many of his contemporaries he had been wounded, badly, in World War I — like Tolkien he had fought in the Battle of the Somme. He would one day be involved in the election of Lewis for a Chair at Cambridge University. Lewis continued to work on a sixteenth-century author he loved, Edmund Spenser, the results of which were scattered through many books and academic papers. David L. Russell perceptively comments that "most literary criticism is dated within its generation, but Lewis's remains highly readable, provocative, and, perhaps more significantly, in print more than three decades after his death — a forceful testimonial to his powers as a scholar."

The Allegory of Love is considered by many to be among the outstanding works of literary criticism of the twentieth century. "To mediaeval studies in this country Lewis's logical and philosophical cast of mind gave a wholly new dimension," commented Professor Jack Arthur Walter Bennett (1911–81), Lewis's successor at Cambridge. This interest in fundamental ideas is shown in his concern with the philosophical and semantic development of the term "nature." Lewis traced this concept from the beginnings of literary allegory through Chaucer and Spenser, turning to it again near the end of his life in his book *Studies in Words* (1960).

Lewis began work on *The Allegory of Love* in 1928, finishing it in 1935, and so it spanned the period of his conversion to theism and then Christianity. In a letter written in 1934, as *The Allegory of Love* neared completion, he suggested that the secret to understanding the Middle Ages, including its concern with allegory and courtly love, was to get to know thoroughly Dante's *The Divine Comedy, The Romance of the Rose,* the Classics, the Bible, and the Apocryphal New Testament.

The Middle Ages provide the key and the background both to Lewis's thought and his fiction, just as they do to Tolkien's. Much of Lewis's scholarly work centered on the period, and he regarded writers of the sixteenth century, and the entire Renaissance, as part of the same intellectual and imaginative world. His science-fiction stories celebrate a medieval picture of the cosmos, as do his Narnian tales. He sought to rehabilitate imaginative and intellectual insights of this vast period for the contemporary reader.

While in search of a publisher for *The Allegory of Love* he submitted the book to Oxford University Press, which accepted it for publication. He explained that the book had two overall themes. The first concerned the birth of allegory and its growth from what is found in the poetry of Prudentius to what it becomes in Spenser. The second theme was the birth of the romantic idea of love and the long struggle between its earlier form, what Lewis called the romance of adultery, and its later form, what he calls the romance of marriage.

Something of the intellectual excitement of the book can be conveyed by a small selection of statements from it:

> We shall understand our present, and perhaps even our future, the better if we can succeed, by an effort of the historical imagination, in reconstructing that long-lost state of mind for which the allegorical love poem was a natural mode of expression.... "Love," in our sense of the word, is as absent from the literature of the Dark Ages as from that of classical antiquity.... We have to inquire how something always latent in human speech [allegory] becomes, in addition, explicit in the structure of whole poems; and how poems of that kind come to enjoy an unusual popularity in the Middle Ages.

Lewis illuminates the nature of allegory: "The allegorist leaves the given — his own passions — to talk of that which is confessedly less real, which is a fiction.... Allegory is a mode of expression.... [in which] men's gaze was turned inward.... The development of allegory [was] to supply the subjective element in literature, to paint the inner world."

The Allegory of Love demonstrates Lewis's concern to help the reader enter as fully as possible into an author's intentions. He concentrated on textual criticism, which he valued above other types of critical activity, as a later comment makes clear: "Find out what the author actually wrote and what the hard words meant and what the allusions were to, and you have done far more for me than a hundred new interpretations or assessments could ever do." Lewis was committed to the *autho*rity of the author. Harry Blamires points out that Lewis "revived the genre of historical criticism by his work on Mediaeval and Renaissance literature in *The Allegory of Love* (1936) and *English Literature in the Sixteenth Century* (1954)." His revival of this genre, in Blamires's view, is perhaps even more significant than these works themselves. Notably, while Lewis's conclusions in the books are by no means always accepted, the books as historical scholarship are almost universally admired.

In the preface to *The Allegory of Love* references are made to three significant friends, Tolkien, Hugo Dyson, and Owen Barfield — to whom the book is dedicated, and to whom Lewis acknowledges the greatest debt, after his father:

> There seems to be hardly any one among my acquaintance from whom I have not learned. The greatest of these debts — that which I owe to my father for the inestimable benefit of a childhood passed mostly alone in a house full of books — is now beyond repayment; and among the rest I can only select.... Above all, the friend to whom I have dedicated the book, has taught me not to patronise the past, and has trained me to see the present as itself a "period." I desire for myself no higher function than to be one of the instruments whereby his theory and practice in such matters may become more widely effective.

∽

Lewis increasingly found himself confronting a new approach to criticism, much of it coming out of the Cambridge University English School and identified with I. A. Richards, particularly at that time. Tolkien was more indirectly responding, by his reform and implementation of the Oxford Honours English School syllabus, which was accepted in 1931. This countered the Cambridge emphasis upon the modern movement in literature and its increasing preoccupation with literary theory. The Cambridge School was markedly different from Oxford's, especially after syllabus reform in 1928. Anglo-Saxon was optional, "practical criticism" was introduced, literature before Shakespeare was downplayed, and writers of the modern period were taught. The new approach tended to reevaluate the traditional literary canon, and some of Lewis's favorites, such as Milton and Shelley, were casualties. Lewis had already attacked T. S. Eliot's downgrading of Shelley in an essay reproduced in his *Rehabilitations* (1938), but he was also troubled by a wider tendency to see poetry as the expression of the poet's personality. He called this tendency "the personal heresy," a tendency he had addressed as early as 1930 in a paper to an Oxford undergraduate society, the Martlets, on "The Personal Heresy in Poetics." This stance led him into a courteous dispute with Cambridge don Eustace Mandeville Wetenhall Tillyard (1889–1962), who had helped to set up the English School there. He began with an essay citing Tillyard's book, *Milton* (1930), as an example of this treatment of poetry as a personal expression. Tillyard responded, leading to a reply from Lewis and eventually a jointly authored book. Lewis argued against the view that poetry expresses biographical information about the poet and that it is necessary to know about the poet in order to understand the poem. His focus was on the inherent character of a work of literature — on the poem as something crafted, which is the original meaning of *poiema*, from which the term "poetry" comes. Lewis did not deny the importance of the poet and his or her cultural and social context and intention in writing. But in reading a poem, Lewis argued, we look with the poet, rather than at his or her psychological makeup. We see with his or her eyes. The poet's consciousness is a condition of our knowledge, not the knowledge itself. Lewis's analysis was remarkable in anticipating new schools of literary criticism that would focus upon the inherent character of literature, expressed for instance in John Crowe Ransom's *The New Criticism* (1942).

What Lewis saw as misreadings of Milton, or, more seriously, downgradings of him (as found particularly in the criticism of the Cambridge critic Frank Raymond Leavis [1895–1978]), were for him symptomatic of a modern trend that he found more and more alarming. Lewis perceived the new approach to criticism to have a rather elitist emphasis. From his wide experience of reading he instinctively rejected a distinction between highbrow and lowbrow literature, serious and popular, and even between so-called good and bad books. A far more important and fundamental distinction for him was that between good and bad readers. Literature, he increasingly felt, exists for the enjoyment of readers, and books therefore should be judged by the kind of reading that they evoke. Instead of judging whether a book is good or bad, it is better to reverse the process and consider good and bad readers. "The good reader," argued Lewis in his *An Experiment in Criticism* (1961), "reads every work seriously in the sense that he reads it whole-heartedly, makes himself as receptive as he can." This is why Lewis wrote in appreciation of Rider Haggard, Tolkien, Sir Walter Scott, and science fiction, as well as of Spenser, Shakespeare, Bunyan, Chaucer, and Milton. His emphasis was on the reception of literature, rather than on its analysis.

Cambridge University was not, however, as monolithic in its espousal of modernism as Lewis and Tolkien supposed. In fact, ironically, Cambridge in 1954 eventually gave Lewis the honor Oxford had declined to offer him for so long — an English Chair. In the spring term of 1938 Lewis found himself lecturing once a week to the Cambridge English School on "Prolegomena to Renaissance Literature." He had been invited to lecture on the sixteenth-century period by Henry Stanley Bennett (1889–1972), an important figure in the Cambridge School. Bennett was growing uneasy about the increasing prominence of F. R. Leavis, who had been deeply influenced by the theories of I. A. Richards and who was to become one of the most important literary critics in English of his time. In preparing and giving his Cambridge lectures Lewis made a surprising discovery, which he explained to his friend A. K. Hamilton Jenkin in a letter: "I go to Cambridge to lecture once a week this term. Did I tell you I have discovered the Renaissance never occurred? That is what I'm lecturing on. Do you think it reasonable to call the lectures 'The Renaissance' under the circumstances?" His belief that the rise of modernism was a far more important historical change than any changes occurring in the Renaissance was to provide the subject for his Inaugural Lecture at Cambridge in 1954. Continuity rather than radical change was the theme of the long introduction to his *English Literature in the Sixteenth Century*, "New Learning and New Ignorance," which was based on the 1938 Cambridge lectures, and a later series given in Cambridge in 1944 — the Clark Lectures. He argued there for a deep continuity between the medieval period and the Renaissance.

⌒⌯

Unlike Lewis's, Tolkien's academic writings were sparing and rare. He gave great attention to his lecturing and tutoring. On November 25, 1936, however, he gave a lecture to the British Academy in London. Because of the importance of the occasion Edith accompanied him. Tolkien's title was "Beowulf: The Monsters and the Critics." According to Donald K. Fry, this lecture (published the next year) "completely altered the course of Beowulf studies." It was a defense of the artistic unity of that Early English tale. (The oldest surviving manuscript is dated around A.D. 1000.) Like his 1939 lecture, "On Fairy Stories," the *Beowulf* lecture provides an important key to his work both as a scholar and a writer of fiction.

The following passage from Beowulf, in a nineteenth-century translation, speaks of a dragon guarding its hoard, rather like Smaug in *The Hobbit,* and then being enraged by the theft of one of its treasures:

> In the grave on the hill   a hoard it guarded,
> in the stone-barrow steep.   A strait path reached it,
> unknown to mortals.   Some man, however,
> came by chance   that cave within
> to the heathen hoard.   In hand he took
> a golden goblet,   nor gave he it back,
> stole with it away,   while the watcher slept,
> by thievish wiles: for the warden's wrath
> prince and people   must pay betimes!

In his lecture, Tolkien expresses dissatisfaction with existing Beowulf criticism. In fact, it had not been criticism proper, he complained, as it had not been directed to an understanding of the poem as a poem, as a unified work of art. Rather, it had been seen as a quarry for historical data about its period. In particular, the two monsters that dominate it — Grendel and the dragon — had not been sufficiently considered as the center and focus of the poem. Tolkien argued that what he called the "structure and conduct" of the poem arose from this central theme of monsters.

It was clear to Tolkien that the *Beowulf* poet created, by art, an illusion of historical truth and perspective. The poet had an instinctive historical sense that he used for artistic, poetic ends. Tolkien told his audience that fall night: "So far from being a poem so poor that only its accidental historical interest can still recommend it, *Beowulf* is in fact so interesting as poetry, in places poetry so powerful, that this quite overshadows the historical content, and is largely independent even of the most important facts...that research has discovered." A literary study of *Beowulf*, Tolkien argued, must deal with a native English poem that is using in a fresh way ancient and mostly traditional material, and thus the focus should not be on the poet's sources, but what he did with them.

In considering the monsters, which are so pivotal to *Beowulf*, Tolkien explained that this choice of theme actually accounts for the greatness of the poem. The power comes from "the mythical mode of imagination." Tolkien's approach to *Beowulf* is strikingly true of his own stories: "The significance of myth is not easily to be pinned on paper by analytical reasoning. It is at its best when it is presented by a poet who feels rather than makes explicit what his theme portends; who presents it incarnate in the world of history and geography, as our [*Beowulf*] poet has done." Tolkien pointed out the danger and difficulty of accounting for the mythical mode of imagination in a work like *Beowulf*.

Its defender is thus at a disadvantage: unless he is careful, and speaks in parables, he will kill what he is studying by vivisection, and he will be left with a formal or mechanical allegory, and, what is more, probably one that will not work. For myth is alive at once and in all its parts, and dies before it can be dissected. It is possible, I think, to be moved by the power of myth and yet to misunderstand the sensation, to ascribe it wholly to something else that is also present: to metrical art, style, or verbal skill.

Beowulf was a dragon slayer. Tolkien saw the dragon as a potent symbol. "Something more significant than the standard hero, a man faced with a foe more evil than any human enemy of house or realm, is before us, and yet incarnate in time, walking in heroic history, and treading the named

70

lands of the North." According to Tolkien, the creator of *Beowulf* not only used the old legends in a fresh and original fashion, but provided "a measure and interpretation of them all." In this poem we see "man at war with the hostile world, and his inevitable overthrow in time." The question of the power of evil is central. Beowulf "moves in a northern heroic age imagined by a Christian, and therefore has a noble and gentle quality, though conceived to be a pagan."

In *Beowulf* there is a fusion of the Christian and the ancient North, the old and the new. Yet the imagination of the *Beowulf* author had not developed into an allegorical one. Allegory was a later development. His dragon, as a symbol of evil, retains the ancient force of the pagan Northern imagination; it is not an allegory of evil in reference to the individual soul's redemption or damnation. He is concerned with "man on earth" rather than the journey to the Celestial City. "Each man and all men, and all their works shall die.... The shadow of its despair, if only as a mood, as an intense emotion of regret, is still there. The worth of defeated valour in this world is deeply felt." The poet feels this theme imaginatively or poetically rather than literally, yet with a sense of the ultimate defeat of darkness.

The author of *Beowulf* explored insights that may be found in the pagan imagination, a theme that would be powerfully explored by Tolkien in *The Lord of the Rings*. Indeed most of Tolkien's fiction is set in a pagan, pre-Christian world. Tolkien concluded his lecture by pointing out that "In *Beowulf* we have, then, an historical poem about the pagan past, or an attempt at one.... It is a poem by a learned man writing of old times, who looking back on the heroism and sorrow feels in them something permanent and something symbolical. So far from being a confused semi-pagan — historically unlikely for a man of this sort in the period — he brought probably first to his task a knowledge of Christian poetry...."

There are a number of parallels between the author of *Beowulf,* as understood by Tolkien, and Tolkien himself. Tolkien was a Christian storyteller looking back to an imagined northern European past — his Middle-earth. The *Beowulf* poet was a Christian looking back at the imaginative resources of a pagan past. Both made use of dragons and other potent symbols, symbols that unified their work. Both were concerned more with symbolism than allegory. As with *Beowulf,* what is important is not so much the sources but what was made of them. Like the ancient author, also, Tolkien created an impression of real history and a sense of depths of the past.

In March 1939 Tolkien traveled by train up to St. Andrews University in Scotland to give the annual Andrew Lang lecture. His was entitled, "On Fairy Stories." It set out Tolkien's basic ideas concerning imagination, fantasy, and what he distinctively called "sub-creation."

This lecture is the key source for Tolkien's thinking and theology behind his creation of Middle-earth and its stories: Tolkien links God and mankind in two related ways. In the first, he, as a Christian, sees humankind as being made in the image of God. This point makes a qualitative difference between mankind and all other things that exist in the universe. Our ability to speak, love, and create fantasy originates in this imageness of God. The second way Tolkien links God and humankind is in the similarities that exist by necessity between the universe of God's making and human making. Human making derives, that is, from our being in God's image.

The actual course of Tolkien's lecture did not so starkly highlight these two related links between God and mankind, but they clearly underlie both this lecture and Tolkien's fiction. The goal of "On Fairy Stories" was to rehabilitate for adults the idea of the fairy story, which had been relegated to children's literature, and fantasy in general. Regarding fairy stories as trivial — suitable only for children — in his view failed to do justice to both fairy stories and children.

Tolkien, who had by then written much of the basic matter of *The Silmarillion,* and published *The Hobbit* (in 1937), attempted to set out a structure underlying good fairy tales and fantasies, a structure that would demonstrate that fairy tales were worthy of serious attention.

Fairy tales, he pointed out, were stories about faerie: "the realm or state where fairies have their being." Listeners who had read his essay, "Beowulf: The Monsters and the Critics," may have noticed a similarity here with Tolkien's portrayal of the Old English poem. Tolkien had spoken of the poet making his theme "incarnate in the world of history and geography." Fairy tales, he told his audience at St. Andrews, were fantasy, allowing their hearers or readers to move from the details of their limited experience to "survey the depths of space and time." The successful fairy story in fact was "sub-creation," the ultimate achievement of fantasy, the highest art, deriving its power from human language itself. The successful writer of fairy story "makes a Secondary World which your mind can enter. Inside it, what he relates is 'true': it accords with the laws of that world."

In addition to offering a secondary world, with an "inner consistency of reality," a good fairy tale in Tolkien's view has three other key structural features. First, it helps to bring about in the reader what Tolkien called recovery — that is, the restoration of a true view of the meaning of ordinary and humble things that make up human life and reality, things like love, thought, trees, hills, and food. Second, the good fairy story offers escape from one's narrow and distorted view of reality and meaning — the escape of the prisoner rather than the flight of the deserter. Third, the good story offers consolation, leading to joy (similar to the experience Lewis was to chart in *Surprised by Joy*). Such consolation, argued Tolkien, only had meaning because good stories pointed to the greatest story of all, the Gospel of Jesus. This first-century account had all the structural features of a fairy tale, myth, or great story, and, in addition, it was true in actual human history — the greatest storyteller of all had entered his own story. Tolkien believed in fact that God himself came to earth as a humble human being, a king like Aragorn, in disguise, a seeming fool, like Frodo, who risks his life in order to destroy the ruling Ring.

This opportunity to air in public his deepest thoughts about fantasy and fairy tale was an important encouragement to Tolkien; he faced many more years of labor on *The Lord of the Rings,* the "new Hobbit," a task of composition and incessant revision that had begun in December 1937.

⌒⌒⌒

The 1930s marked what literary historian Harry Blamires (a former student of Lewis's) has called a "minor renaissance" of Christian themes in English literature. It was not a self-conscious movement, as such, as many of the writers were part of smaller groups, such as the Inklings. This resurgence took place in the face of a strong theological liberalism — the latter an impact of a climate of modernism. Many writers, however, dissatisfied with materialism, turned back to orthodox Christian belief, as Lewis did in 1931. Others, like Tolkien and Charles Williams, had never lost their childhood faith. Lewis and Tolkien were very much part of this significant trend in writing.

An indication that something was happening occurred in 1928 when George Bell, then dean of Canterbury Cathedral, decided to bring theater back into the church, picking up a great tradition that had fallen into neglect. He instituted the Canterbury Festival, which soon attracted a following. In 1935 T. S. Eliot's verse drama *Murder in the Cathedral* was first performed there. The next year saw the staging of *Thomas Cranmer of Canterbury,* by Charles Williams.

Aside from T. S. Eliot, other Christian writers like Graham Greene, Evelyn Waugh, and Christopher Fry had an impact in the 1930s. Dorothy L. Sayers was writing her Lord Peter Wimsey crime novels, begun in the 1920s, and Charles Williams was bringing out literary criticism and supernatural thrillers like *The Place of the Lion,* which enraptured Lewis, Tolkien, and others in 1936. At Williams's suggestion, Dorothy L. Sayers was approached to write for the Canterbury Festival. Tolkien himself published *The Hobbit* in 1937, and, in 1940 a young poet named W. H. Auden began composing his "New Year Letter," under the influence of Charles Williams's inimitable history of the church, *Descent of the Dove,* published the year before.

Lewis and Tolkien were not as isolated and disconnected with contemporary culture as they thought. This point is summed up admirably by Harry Blamires:

> Lewis began writing just at the point when this minor Christian Renaissance in literature was taking off. His *Pilgrim's Regress* came out in 1933. And the 1930s were a remarkable decade in this respect. Eliot's *Ash Wednesday* came out in 1930, *The Rock* in 1934, *Murder in the Cathedral* in 1935 and *Burnt Norton* in 1936. Charles Williams's *War in Heaven* was published in 1930, *The Place of the Lion* in 1931, *The Greater Trumps* in 1932, and his play *Thomas Cranmer of Canterbury* in 1936. Helen Waddell's *Peter Abelard* came out in 1933. Meanwhile on the stage James Bridie had great popular successes with his biblical

plays *Tobias and the Angel* (1930) and *Jonah and the Whale* (1932). Then by 1937 Christopher Fry was launched with *The Boy with a Cart*. That same year saw Dorothy Sayers's *The Zeal of Thy House* performed, and David Jones's *In Parenthesis* and Tolkien's *The Hobbit* published. Lewis's *Out of the Silent Planet* followed in 1938 along with Williams's *Taliessin through Logres* and Greene's *Brighton Rock*, Eliot's *Family Reunion* followed in 1939, Greene's *The Power and The Glory* in 1940. During the same decade Evelyn Waugh was getting known and Rose Macauley was in spate. Edwin Muir, Andrew Young and Francis Berry appeared in print.

So when the literary historian looks back at the English literary scene in the 1930s and 1940s he is going to see C. S. Lewis and Charles Williams, not as freakish throwbacks, but as initial contributors to what I have called a Christian literary renaissance, if a minor one.

Looking back decades later, it is easier for us to see such a pattern emerging. Of more significance at the time for Tolkien and Lewis was the informal club they had started in 1933. The fall term of that year marked the beginning of Lewis's convening of a circle of friends dubbed "the Inklings." For the next sixteen years, on through 1949, they continued to meet, often in Lewis's rooms at Magdalen College on Thursday evenings and, before lunch on Mondays or Tuesdays, in a snug back room at The Eagle and Child, a public house on St. Giles known to locals as "The Bird and Baby." After 1949 meetings were more limited, and no longer saw the reading of manuscripts in progress. Members of the Inklings in the very earliest years included Tolkien, Lewis, his brother Warren, Hugo Dyson, Robert Emlyn "Humphrey" Havard (1901–85), Adam Fox (1883–1977), Charles Leslie Wrenn (1895–1969), and, very occasionally, Owen Barfield. Nevill Coghill dropped in from time to time and unpredictably.

The Tuesday meetings of the Inklings became such a local institution that they were memorialized in Edmund Crispin's 1947 crime novel, *Swan Song*. This is one of a number of stories featuring Gervase Fen, an Oxford Professor of English language and literature, and a private detective.

"Oh, for a beakerful of the cold north," said Fen, gulping at his Burton. "Impossible murders, for the present, must wait their turn."

They were sitting before a blazing and hospitable fire in the small front parlour of the "Bird and Baby." . . . Adam, Elizabeth, Sir Richard Freeman, and Fen were now toasting themselves to a comfortable glow. Outside, it was still attempting to snow, but with only partial success. . . .

"There goes C. S. Lewis," said Fen suddenly. "It must be Tuesday."

"It is Tuesday." Sir Richard struck a match and puffed doggedly at his pipe.

"You seem to smoke the most incombustible tobacco," Fen commented.

5

The Inklings Begin

Friendship Shared? (1933–1939)

Lewis pushes open the front door of the Eagle and Child public house to a welcome roar of conversation. It is a wintry morning late in 1937. A few snowflakes stick to his shabby overcoat. He is slightly breathless from rushing up St. Giles, slightly late. His second tutorial had run over time. It is already past eleven-thirty, though Lewis doesn't know that precisely — he never carries a watch. One has to remember to wind it.

As he fights his way through the customers in the cheerful front parlor on his way to the more private back room he catches a reference to murders and then the sound of his name in one of the many conversations going on. Startled, and glancing to his right, he glimpses a fleeting tableaux: four people warming themselves by the roaring fire — a pretty young woman and three men, one of whom wears the tweeds and flannel trousers of an Oxford academic, and another, with a military bearing, lighting his pipe. They could have come straight out of a crime novel, Lewis notes, puzzled by the reference to murders. He never reads the newspapers. Then, without giving the group further thought, for he is used to being a local character, at least in the pub, he pushes on.

The other Inklings are already assembled. Lewis can hear their loud voices and laughter before he reaches the snug, called The Rabbit Room. Tolkien is attempting a conversation about hobbits while fumbling with the pipe in his mouth; Dr. "Humphrey" Havard finishes asking Warnie

Lewis about his motorbike; Adam Fox pulls at his tight clerical collar to loosen it. No Dyson this week, or the volume would have been louder — he is tied up with his duties at Reading University. Nevill Coghill is busily examining a copy of *The Hobbit,* published recently, which Tolkien has brought along for the barmaid. (She overheard part of their conversation last week, and suddenly realized that that nice gentleman Mr. Tolkien had written a book for children.) Beer and cider glasses jostle with each other on the long table. Tolkien's pipe is now well alight. Coghill has a cigarette at his lips, his large head nodding at some comment as he turns over the pages. Looking up he quickly asks, "Can I buy you a pint, Lewis?" When the newcomer is settled, and greetings over, Tolkien resumes his conversation.

"Hobbits have what you might call universal morals — they are the common man."

"Do you mean they are common in Oxford?" asks Coghill in a drawl, his smile revealing somewhat battered teeth.

Tolkien refuses to be drawn. "I should say they are examples of natural philosophy and natural religion."

"I take it you mean they exemplify the best in paganism without the light of Christ," breaks in Lewis, interest in his face.

"I do," returns Tolkien. "I'm still trying to formulate some ideas for a lecture. As Lewis knows, it's to be on the nature of fairy stories. That they are not meant in the first place for children — that's what I've got wrong with *The Hobbit.* That the best of stories anticipate the greatest of stories, the *Evangelium.*"

"The marriage of myth and fact," adds Lewis.

Fox, the theologian among them, has been silent. "I think there's a lot in the idea of looking at the Gospels like that. The modernists haven't really understood that the Gospels are narrative. They don't understand imagination, for that matter — they don't know their Plato."

The conversation is interrupted by Havard's offer to buy another round of drinks.

Tolkien described the Inklings as an "undetermined and unelected circle of friends who gathered around C.S.L[ewis]., and met in his rooms in Magdalen. . . . Our habit was to read aloud compositions of various kinds (and lengths!). . . . " The Inklings embodied the ideals of life and pleasure of Tolkien and Lewis, especially Lewis. Both friends had a penchant for informal clubs. Tolkien remembered how much Lewis felt at home in this kind of company. "C.S.L. had a passion for hearing things read aloud, a power of memory for things received in that way, and also a facility in extempore criticism, none of which were shared (especially not the last) in anything like the same degree by his friends."

In a letter many years later to Donald Swann, Tolkien explained that the name, "the Inklings," originally belonged to an undergraduate group (of a type common in Oxford in those days). He spoke of reading an early version of his poem, *Errantry,* to them (later set to music by Swann). The student club, explained Tolkien, used to hear its members read unpublished poems or short tales. The better ones were minuted. The students came up with the name *Inklings,* and not he or Lewis, who were among its few members from the university staff. The name was a pun on the fact that its members aspired to write. Tolkien remembered that the club lasted the usual year or two of undergraduate societies. After it folded in the summer term of 1933, its name "became transferred to the circle of C. S. Lewis."

From its onset the Inklings played an important part in Tolkien's life. They were to be particularly significant during the writing of *The Lord of the Rings* (1937–49). The group had no formal constitution so there were no minutes taken. As Tolkien and Lewis met frequently they rarely corresponded with each other, so little was recorded in this way of their conversations. Tolkien, thinking of James Boswell's magnificent *The Life of Samuel Johnson* (1791), pointed out that "The Inklings had no recorder and C. S. Lewis no Boswell." Tolkien was undoubtedly a central figure in this literary group of friends, though it was held together by Lewis's zest and enthusiasm. Tolkien was a much more reserved person than Lewis, naturally having fewer intimate friends, even though he was personable and friendly to all types of people.

The two patterns of Inklings meetings emerged in the 1930s: Tuesday mornings in the pub and Thursday evenings, usually in Lewis's college rooms in Magdalen. The evenings had the more literary bent — here members would read to each other works in progress, receiving criticism and encouragement. The "new Hobbit," *The Lord of the Rings*, began to be read in this way after 1937.

A question niggles when we focus upon the relationship between Lewis and Tolkien. Did the Inklings friendships mean as much to Tolkien as they did to Lewis? The group undoubtedly expanded from the deep friendship between Tolkien and Lewis. Lewis, in his book *The Four Loves*, explains the process by which friendship expands. He uses illuminating examples from the Inklings — "Ronald" is of course Tolkien, and "Charles" is Williams (a later Inklings member):

> In each of my friends there is something that only some other friend can fully bring out. By myself I am not large enough to call the whole man into activity; I want other lights than my own to show all his facets. Now that Charles is dead, I shall never again see Ronald's reaction to a specifically Caroline joke. Far from having more of Ronald, having him "to myself" now that Charles is away, I have less of Ronald. Hence true Friendship is the least jealous of loves. Two friends delight to be joined by a third, and three by a fourth, if only the newcomer is qualified to become a real friend.... Of course the scarcity of kindred souls — not to mention practical considerations about the size of rooms and the audibility of voices — set limits to the enlargement of the circle; but within those limits we possess each friend not less but more as the number of those with whom we share him increases.

Though Lewis was wise in pointing out that friendship is the least jealous of our loves, people, and thus their friendships, are complex. Lewis meant a great deal to Tolkien as their friendship developed. Tolkien remembered with fondness the deep bonds — ideological and emotional — between the members of the T.C.B.S., but the war had destroyed that group. The two survivors, he and Christopher Wiseman, had grown apart. Tolkien was not at Leeds long enough to establish close friendships. Now, at Oxford, he was able to share his so-called secret vice — his philological creations and tales of Middle-earth — with Lewis. In fact, he increasingly relied upon Lewis's encouragement to further his creations, creations that sometimes moved Lewis to tears. While the Inklings was a small and intimate group in the thirties, everything was very much to Tolkien's liking. But as the group expanded, particularly by embracing Charles Williams, he began to feel somewhat left out from Lewis's attentions. The dynamics of a larger group worked for Lewis, but did not seem to work for Tolkien. Jealousy is too strong a word for Tolkien's feeling of loss; it was more perhaps a gradual and barely articulated hurt. He was a warm and generous man, however, and continued to participate in the Inklings, showing affection and interest to each member.

Speaking in America in 1969, several years after Lewis's death, Owen Barfield remembered the way Lewis affected all the groups he was part of, including the Inklings. One way was unconsciously and unobtrusively by the sheer force and weight of Lewis's personality, and, as Barfield put it, "a rather loud voice when he was in high spirits." He would set the tone and decide the topic of conversation. Barfield recalled that, on one occasion, when the topic was not of interest to Lewis (it could have been politics or economics) he merely turned aside from the conversation, picked up a book, and proceeded to read it instead of talking. Second, irrespective of the subject that was brought up, Lewis always turned it round to the point where it was a moral issue or problem. If anyone did not think that a moral issue was involved, Lewis reminded him that there *ought* to be.

❧

The formation of the Inklings in the fall of 1933 coincided with the natural ending of the Coalbiters, which had by now fulfilled its purpose. Three of the Coalbiters — Tolkien, Lewis, and Nevill Coghill — became Inklings. Charles Wrenn helped Tolkien with the teaching of Anglo-Saxon, having joined the university in 1930. Soon after the formation of the Inklings he was invited to come along. A later recruit was Canon Adam Fox, dean of Divinity at Lewis's college.

The group was informal, requiring no membership. The only "require-
ment" was that visitors were friends of Lewis, or had been invited. The
entire group recognized Lewis as the natural leader. Even though his personality was dominant, however, there was no coercion on his part over
what would happen at any given meeting. Being part of the Inklings was
a free choice of equals.

We can only speculate about the subjects of conversations in the "Bird
and Baby," or about what pieces were read aloud to the club, since there
is no documentation of the early days. Lewis had finished writing *The Pilgrim's Regress* before the Inklings began. Much of *The Hobbit* was complete
by late 1932; we know this because Tolkien had lent the manuscript then
to Lewis to read. Perhaps the final chapters of *The Hobbit* were read to
the group, but we do not know.

Not until Dr. Robert Havard — nicknamed "Humphrey" by Hugo
Dyson, when he couldn't remember his name on one occasion — was
invited to join do we begin to glimpse concrete details of the group. Recalling events many years later, Havard believed that he had become a
member in 1935. In the early part of the year Havard attended Lewis, as his
general practitioner, for influenza. They were discussing Aquinas within a
matter of minutes. Perhaps Lewis had remarked on the provenance of the
term — he was to point out, in his book *The Discarded Image* (1964), that
influenza refers to the influence of the starry heavens in medieval times.
Soon after, Havard recalled, he was invited to join the Inklings, because
of his evident interest in "religio-philosophical discussion." The Inklings
were described to Havard as a group that met on Thursday evenings, read
papers they had written, and discussed them. The group, he discovered,
was made up of friends of Lewis's. It was years later, Havard said, that he
woke up one morning to find that his Inklings friends had become famous.

Affectionately known as the "Useless Quack," Havard was the son of an
Anglican clergyman. He had studied medicine after graduating in chem-
istry at Oxford in 1922. In 1934 he took over a medical practice in Oxford
with surgeries in Headington as well as in St. Giles, near "The Bird and
Baby" pub. Havard had converted to Roman Catholicism in 1931, influenced by Ronald Knox, and soon found he had a lot in common with
Tolkien.

According to Havard, the group was composed of critical Christians. All of them, in one way or another, were dissatisfied with the Church as it existed there and then, but not with the Christian faith itself.

Havard recalled that they did not take Lewis all that seriously. They had no idea that he was going to develop into a celebrity. For them he was simply one among others. They either liked or didn't like what he read to them; usually they liked it, and would say so. It seemed to Havard that none in the group was aware of being anything special; they were simply a group of friends. There were no rules, and "no subscription except Lewis's hospitality." According to Havard the Inklings meetings had a free and easy atmosphere — as informal a gathering as he had ever attended. Members said what they thought "without let or hindrance."

Havard described the friendship between Lewis and Tolkien he had seen at first hand:

> They were very different men. Lewis was a big, full-blown man — overbearing, almost, both in his weight of personality and his physical weight. Tolkien was a slight figure — I'd say three quarters the weight of Lewis. [Tolkien's] remarks were always made by the way, and not [with a] knock you down, take them or leave them attitude. His whole manner was elusive rather than direct, whereas Lewis came straight out at you. These are superficialities, but there's a great difference in mental makeup. The word "flighty" crosses my mind in connection with Tolkien. It's misleading, because I don't mean it in the ordinary sense at all. But he would hop from subject to subject, in an elusive sort of way. You could see his mind was working more like a carpenter at a carpenter's bench. These are very imperfect descriptions of their differences, but they are very apparent in close contact. They were two very different people. And the surprising thing, really, is that they became such close friends, rather than that differences appeared and separated them.

Owen Barfield speculated, many years later, that what the Inklings "had in common...was more like a world outlook, a *Weltanschauung*, than a doctrine." A few centuries back, he remarked, its outlook might have been described as "The Matter of the Inklings." Barfield was interested in cultural changes and realities, not simply in the history of ideas, an interest he shared with Lewis.

Barfield is almost certainly right. This world outlook was not only part of the character of the Inklings, but some kindred writers outside of the club also shared it. It was defined and hammered out in the 1930s, setting the pattern for future writings, particularly those of Lewis and Tolkien. It would be fair to say that writers or friends who were discovered to share the outlook were sometimes invited into the circle. (There were obvious limitations of size.) One contemporary writer sharing this outlook (who could not be one of the Inklings because, as was the custom of such groups in those days in Oxford, they were all male) was Dorothy L. Sayers. As early as 1916, in a lecture in Hull entitled "The Way to the Other World," she speculated about the presence of the eternal in the temporal:

> One must remember that though in one sense the Other World was a definite place, yet in another the kingdom of gods was within one, Earth and fairy-land co-exist upon the same foot of ground. It was all a matter of the seeing eye. . . . The dweller in this world can become aware of an existence on a totally different plane. To go from earth to faery is like passing from this time to eternity; it is not a journey in space, but a change of mental outlook.

Her words could have been written by either Lewis or Tolkien. A similar world outlook can be discovered (as it was by Lewis) in the nineteenth-century poet, novelist, and fantasy writer George MacDonald, both in his fiction and in his essays "The Imagination: Its Functions and Its Culture" (1867) and "The Fantastic Imagination" (1882). Changes in outlook and consciousness, captured by and caused by glimpses of another world, were the very heartbeat of MacDonald, Sayers, and the key Inklings: Lewis, Tolkien, Williams, and Barfield. They were concerned with the presence of the eternal in the temporal, which was the world outlook to which Barfield was referring.

In 1936 Lewis discovered Charles Williams's novel *The Place of the Lion.* While visiting Nevill Coghill at Exeter College in February of that year

Lewis heard from him the basic plot in vivid terms. On the strength of Coghill's colorful description, Lewis had borrowed a copy of the "spiritual shocker." Reading it enraptured Lewis, and in a letter to Arthur Greeves he characterized it as a blend of Genesis and Plato, concerned with the days of creation. It was based, he told Greeves, on Plato's theory of the other world. Here the archetypes or originals of all earthly qualities exist. In Williams's novel these primeval archetypes are pulling our world back to them. The processes of creation reverse and the world is in danger. The novel opens north of London with two men awaiting a bus on the Hertfordshire Road; they encounter a search party for an escaped lioness. Caught up in the search they see the animal on the grounds of a large house. Anthony, one of the men, has a fiancée who is writing a dissertation on Platonic ideas, little realizing the potent powers they represent. They see another lion, which begins to transform dramatically:

> Anthony and Quentin saw before them the form of a man lying on the ground, and standing over him the shape of a full-grown and tremendous lion, its head flung back, its mouth open, its body quivering. It ceased to roar, and gathered itself back into itself. It was a lion such as the young men had never seen in any zoo or menagerie; it was gigantic and seemed to their dazed senses to be growing larger every moment.... Awful and solitary it stood.... Then, majestically, it moved ... and while they still stared it entered into the dark shadow of the trees and was hidden from sight.

By a strange turn of events, Charles Williams had been reading the proofs of Lewis's *The Allegory of Love*, not to correct them, but to give them a hasty read in order to prepare some copy to help in the marketing and selling of the book. Williams had been on the staff of the London office of Oxford University Press for many years, but rarely had he been so excited by one of its publications. He decided to take the unusual step of writing to its author, in appreciation. Before he put pen to paper, however, he received a remarkable letter, on March 11, 1936, from Lewis praising his own *The Place of the Lion*, and inviting Williams to attend an Inklings meeting in Oxford:

A book sometimes crosses one's path which is . . . like the sound of one's native language in a strange country. . . . It is to me one of the major literary events of my life — comparable to my first discovery of George MacDonald, G. K. Chesterton, or Wm. Morris. . . . Coghill of Exeter put me on to the book: I have put on Tolkien (the Professor of Anglo Saxon and a papist) and my brother. So there is three dons and one soldier all buzzing with excited admiration. We have a sort of informal club called the Inklings: the qualifications (as they have informally evolved) are a tendency to write, and Christianity. Can you come down some day next term (preferably *not* Sat. or Sunday), spend the night as my guest in College, eat with us at a chop house, and talk with us till the small hours?

Charles Williams replied by return of post:

If you had delayed writing another 24 hours our letters would have crossed. It has never before happened to me to be admiring an author of a book while he at the same time was admiring me. My admiration for the staff work of the Omnipotence rises every day. . . . I regard your book as practically the only one that I have ever come across, since Dante, that shows the slightest understanding of what this very peculiar identity of love and religion means. . . .

Williams did visit the Inklings soon after (the exact date is not recorded), and Lewis reciprocated by accepting an invitation to see Williams in London. Later, in a tribute to Williams, Lewis remembered the London meeting as "a certain immortal lunch" which was followed by an "almost Platonic discussion" in St. Paul's Cathedral churchyard which lasted for about two hours. On that occasion Williams presented his new friend with a copy of his *He Came Down from Heaven*, hot from the press and published by William Heinemann. On the book's flyleaf is written, "At Shirreffs, 2.10, 4th July 1938." Shirreffs was Williams's favorite restaurant, now long gone. It was close to his office in the City of London, and located at the bottom of Ludgate Hill, under the railway bridge.

Not far from the London office of Oxford University Press at Amen Corner, near St. Paul's Cathedral, was a cluster of other prestigious and privately owned publishing houses, most of them now absorbed into publishing giants like HarperCollins or Random House. Among these was George Allen & Unwin, Tolkien's publisher in Museum Street (named after The British Museum nearby). On February 18, 1938, Tolkien wrote to Stanley Unwin about a science-fiction story that his friend Lewis had written. It had been, he said, read aloud to the Inklings ("our local club"), which went in for "reading things short and long aloud." He recorded that it had proved to be exciting as a serial, and was highly approved by all of them.

Lewis's story, which was eventually published as *Out of the Silent Planet* (1938), was just one of many stories that benefited from the honest criticism all of the Inklings members received. Their meetings would continue to play a significant role in the lives of both Tolkien and Lewis for many years to come.

6

Two Journeys There and Back Again

The Pilgrim's Regress and The Hobbit (1930–1937)

On a summer's day around the end of the 1920s a slight man — indistinct in contrast to the brightness outside — sits by an open window at his desk, a pen in hand, a Toby Jug sprouting pipes and a wooden tobacco jar nearby. A slant of sun touches him. His hair is so fine that the light makes the crown of his head shine. The comparative gloom of the study is emphasized by an abundance of dark-bound books — books lining the walls of the room from floor to ceiling, books even creating the sides of a tunnel through which one enters the study, shelves protruding outwards on either side of the door. The man is silent, except for an occasional muttered "O lor," reluctantly concentrating upon the task in hand. For beside him are two piles of papers. The larger is made up of unmarked school certificate exam papers. The smaller pile is made up of the already marked ones. Abandoned sheets of elegant manuscript perch on the edge of the desk.

Tolkien, like Lewis, undertakes the seasonal task of grading papers to supplement his meager university income. Both have households to support. Tolkien would rather be working on his poetic version of "The Tales of Beren and Lúthien Elf-maiden," teasing out some detail of the chronology of the First Age of Middle-earth, or checking out the origin and formation in an Elven variant of the name of a particular character who has sprung, unbidden, into the story.

This particular summer's day seems likely to be uneventful, as many before it. There are the familiar sounds of his boys playing in the garden, and the undeniable mountain of scripts to be evaluated before his voluntary imprisonment is over. All changes, however, when Tolkien turns over a page and, instead of a hastily written answer, finds it blank. This is joy indeed. One of the candidates, mercifully it seems to him, has left one of the folios with no writing on it. Tolkien hesitates a moment, then inscribes boldly across the sheet: "In a hole in the ground there lived a hobbit." As always, names generate a story in his mind. Eventually he decides that he had better find out what these mysterious hobbits are like.

By late 1932 Tolkien was able to hand Lewis a sheaf of papers to read. It was the incomplete draft of what became *The Hobbit: or There and Back Again*. Lewis described his reaction to it in a letter to Arthur Greeves: "Reading his fairy tale has been uncanny — it is so exactly like what we would both have longed to write (or read) in 1916: so that one feels he is not making it up but merely describing the same world into which all three of us have the entry." Lewis had already written to Greeves in rosiest terms of his friendship with Tolkien, comparing it favorably with their own — like them, Lewis said, he had grown up on William Morris and George MacDonald. In a letter a few weeks later he mentions Tolkien sharing their love of "romance" literature, and in the same sense: "He agreed that for what *we* meant by romance there must be at least the hint of another world — one must hear the horns of elfland."

The Hobbit was eventually published on September 21, 1937, complete with Tolkien's own illustrations; the initial printing was fifteen hundred copies. W. H. Auden, when he reviewed *The Fellowship of the Ring* for the *New York Times* on October 31, 1954, wrote: "in my opinion, [*The Hobbit*] is one of the best children's stories of this century."

Though Tolkien probably began writing the book in 1930, his eldest sons, John and Michael, remembered the story being told to them before the 1930s. Perhaps various oral forms of the story merged into the more finished written draft. What is significant from these indistinct memories is that *The Hobbit* began as a tale told by a father to his children. It was consciously written as a children's story, and this fact shapes its style. It also seems that at first the story was independent of Tolkien's burgeoning mythological cycle, "The Silmarillion," and was only later incorporated into his invented world and history. The tale introduced hobbits into Middle-earth, dramatically affecting the course of events there. *The Hobbit* belongs to the Third Age of Middle-earth, and chronologically precedes *The Lord of the Rings.*

At the time of publication Lewis reviewed his friend's book for *The Times Literary Supplement:* "Prediction is dangerous: but *The Hobbit* may well prove a classic." Another critic, in the *New Statesman,* remarked of Tolkien: "It is a triumph that the genus *Hobbit,* which he himself has invented, rings just as real as the time-hallowed genera of Goblin, Troll, and Elf." Lewis believed that the hobbits "are perhaps a myth that only an Englishman (or, should we add, a Dutchman?) could have created." Instead of a creation of character as we find it in standard novels, much of the personality of Bilbo, Frodo, and Sam derives from their character as hobbits, just as we identify Gandalf in character as a wizard or Treebeard as an Ent. Tolkien sustains the collective qualities of these different mythological species with great skill.

The title of *The Hobbit* refers to its unlikely hero, Mr. Bilbo Baggins. He is a creature of paradox, summed up in his oxymoronic role as a bourgeois burglar in the story. Before Bilbo, hobbits aimed at having a good reputation with their peers — not only by being comfortably off, but by not having any adventures or doing anything unexpected. Bilbo's house was a typical dwelling place of a wealthy hobbit. It was not a worm-filled, dirty, damp hole, but a comfortable, many-roomed underground home. Its hall, which connected all the rooms, had "panelled walls, and floors tiled and carpeted, provided with polished chairs, and lots and lots of pegs for hats and coats — the hobbit was fond of visitors." Hobbits generally liked to be thought respectable, not having adventures or behaving in an unexpected way. They were lifted from Tolkien's childhood world of the rural West Midlands, the inspiration for The Shire.

Bilbo's reputation is tarnished forever when he is suddenly caught up in the quest for dragon's treasure. He reluctantly finds this more congenial than he ever thought. A whole new world is opened up to him, and in later years he even becomes somewhat of a scholar, translating and retelling tales from the older days. The quest also develops his character, though he always retains the quality of homeliness associated with hobbits and The Shire where they live.

In *The Hobbit* a party of dwarves, thirteen in number, are on a quest for their long-lost treasure, which is jealously guarded by the dragon, Smaug. Their leader is the great Thorin Oakenshield. They employ Bilbo Baggins as their master burglar to steal the treasure, at the recommendation of the wizard Gandalf the Grey. At first the reluctant Mr. Baggins would rather spend a quiet day with his pipe and pot of tea in his comfortable hobbit-hole than partake in any risky adventure.

But as their journey unfolds, the dwarves become increasingly thankful for the fact that they employed him, despite initial misgivings, as he gets them out of many scrapes. He seems to have extraordinary luck. At one point in the adventure Bilbo is knocked unconscious in a tunnel under the Misty Mountains, and left behind in the darkness by the rest of the party.

Reviving, Bilbo discovers a ring lying beside him in the tunnel. It is the ruling ring, the One Ring, that would eventually form the subject of *The Lord of the Rings*, but at this stage Bilbo is to discover only its magical property of invisibility. After putting the ring in his pocket, Bilbo stumbles along the dark tunnel. Eventually, he comes across a subterranean lake, where Gollum dwells, a living vestige of a hobbit, his life preserved over centuries by the ring he has now lost for the first time. After a battle of riddles, Bilbo escapes, seemingly by luck, by slipping on the ring. Following the vengeful Gollum, who cannot see him, he finds his way out of the mountains, on the other side.

After the encounter with Gollum, the plucky Bilbo eventually leads the party successfully to the dragon's treasure, and the scaly monster perishes while attacking nearby Lake-town. Bilbo and Gandalf in the end journey back to the peaceful Shire — they have gone "there and back again." Bilbo decides to refuse most of his share of the treasure, having seen the results of greed. The events have in fact changed him forever, but even more, the ring he secretly possesses will shape the events eventually to be recorded in *The Lord of the Rings*.

Thorin's remark concerning Bilbo is perhaps an apt summary of his many-sided character: "a hobbit full of courage and resource far exceeding his size, and if I may say so possessed of good luck far exceeding the usual allowance." The "good luck" noticed by Thorin is in fact the unusual presence of providence working out in events using him as a key agent.

Tolkien draws attention to unusual blood in Bilbo's makeup inherited from his mother. This unhobbitlike quality emerges and develops as Bilbo partakes in the adventure. Most important for him, however, is not the finding of the treasure (which leads to Smaug the dragon's death), but his finding of the One Ring.

Bilbo's discovery of the ring was eventually to provide Tolkien with the link between *The Hobbit* and its large sequel, *The Lord of the Rings*. However, Tolkien realized he had to partially rewrite chapter 5 of the former book to provide proper continuity between the two works over the great significance of the ruling ring. He drafted the revision ten years after the publication of *The Hobbit*, in the midst of finalizing *The Lord of the Rings*. The new edition, incorporating the revised chapter, first appeared in 1951.

What is striking about Tolkien's story is his skill in adjusting to the level of children the scale of his great mythology of the earlier ages of Middle-earth. Names for instance are simple, in complete contrast to the complexities of "The Silmarillion." Erebor is simply The Lonely Mountain. Esgaroth is usually called Lake-town. Elrond's home in Rivendell is described as the Last Homely House west of the Mountains. In his review in *The Times Literary Supplement* Lewis remarked on "the curious shift from the matter-of-fact beginnings of his story ('hobbits are small people, smaller than dwarfs — and they have no beards — but very much larger than the Lilliputians') to the saga-like tone of the later chapters ('It is in my mind to ask what share of their inheritance you would have paid had you found the hoard unguarded')." This shift in tone marked a dawning recognition on Tolkien's part that it would be possible to write a modern fairy tale for adults. Tolkien's own journey there and back again led to a sequel thirteen years in the writing that is no longer a children's story, even though of course countless children have enjoyed *The Lord of the Rings* since it was first published in 1954–55.

While Tolkien painstakingly was completing *The Hobbit,* Lewis drafted a symbolic story directly for adults during a two-week vacation. Though it was not a fairy tale, it had the elements of such stories; like *The Hobbit,* it was a tale of "there and back again" and was called *The Pilgrim's Regress* (1933) in echo of the Puritan John Bunyan's *The Pilgrim's Progress* (published in two parts in 1678 and 1684). Like *The Hobbit* it marked Lewis's first publication of the kind of symbolic fiction that the two friends admired and developed. Even though Tolkien did not share Lewis's taste for allegory, he reportedly liked the book. Lewis may have read some or all of the manuscript to him, and Tolkien quoted, approvingly, a poem from it about a dragon in early versions of his essay on "Beowulf: The Monsters and the Critics." *The Pilgrim's Regress* at once shows the differences and the affinities between Lewis, with his Protestant upbringing, and Tolkien, with his sacramental Roman Catholicism. Lewis's book delights in the imaginative dimension of ideas, Tolkien's in the rich world of the Northern imagination, concerned with capturing a tone or quality he saw as the essence of a disappearing English West Midlands. Lewis was also attempting to capture a quality, but it was a quality of joy and inconsolable longing that is just as likely to appear, however fleetingly, in a classical Greek or Roman story as in an Old Norse myth like that of the death of the beautiful god Balder. Whereas Tolkien took several years conceiving and gestating *The Hobbit,* gradually weaving it in to his history, languages, and geography of Middle-earth, Lewis composed his story essentially in a couple of weeks. *The Pilgrim's Regress* is remarkable both as a spiritual journey in the tradition of Bunyan and as a map of contemporary thought in the 1920s and early 1930s that still has much relevance today. Both friends, working on these books, were honing skills that would one day help them to become celebrated authors. They were clearly scholars and storytellers in the Oxford mold.

Lewis was researching the method of allegory in literature for his study, *The Allegory of Love,* when he wrote *The Pilgrim's Regress: An Allegorical Apology for Christianity, Reason and Romanticism.* In literature, allegory is a figurative narrative or description that conveys a hidden meaning, often moral. Leading examples in English literature are John Bunyan's *The Pilgrim's Progress* and Edmund Spenser's *Faerie Queene*, both firm favorites of Lewis. The biblical parables have allegorical elements; allegory is a type of instruction. Lewis gave his own definition in a letter: "a composition . . . in which immaterial realities are represented by feigned physical objects." Lewis's fondness for allegory was part of his eclecticism. He was at home in the vast range of the premodern imagination, from the ancient Greeks through the entire medieval and Renaissance periods.

In fictional and more general form, *The Pilgrim's Regress* covers the ground of his later account of his life up to his conversion to Christianity in 1931, *Surprised by Joy,* published over twenty years later in 1955. He wrote *The Pilgrim's Regress* during a vacation in Northern Ireland in the second half of August 1932. Now that "Little Lea" had been sold, Lewis stayed at "Bernagh," a hundred yards or so over the road from his old house, with the Greeves family. When corresponding later with Arthur, asking him if he minded the book being dedicated to him, Lewis added: "It is yours by every right — written in your house, read to you as it was written, and celebrating (at least in the most important parts) an experience which I have more in common with you than anyone else." Lewis was referring to his experience of longing, marked by joy.

The Pilgrim's Regress is in fact an intellectual, early-twentieth-century version of John Bunyan's *The Pilgrim's Progress* and *The Holy War.* Instead of Bunyan's allegorical figure of Christian, the central protagonist is John, a contemporary Everyman or pilgrim, based loosely upon Lewis himself. The name "John" possibly was an allusion to Lewis's model, John Bunyan. Another influence was Boethius. *The Consolation of Philosophy* (written around A.D. 525 while its author awaited execution) was one of Lewis's favorite books, intermingling poetry and prose as Lewis does in *The Pilgrim's Regress,* and with a female figure representing Boethius's companion, Philosophy. In *The Pilgrim's Regress,* Reason — one of the themes of the book — is conveyed by an armored woman in a cloak of blue who rescues John from the Giant, the Spirit of the Age:

> The rider threw back the cloak and a flash of steel smote light into
> John's eyes and on the giant's face. John saw that it was a woman

in the flower of her age: she was so tall that she seemed to him a Titaness, a sun-bright virgin clad in complete steel, with a sword naked in her hand.

As in *The Pilgrim's Progress*, John's quest can be mapped. Indeed, Lewis provides his readers with a *Mappa Mundi*, in which the human soul is divided into north and south, the north representing arid intellectualism and the south emotional excess. A straight road passes between them. Needless to say, John's route strays far off the straight and narrow. Like the young Lewis, he tends towards intellectual rather than sensual follies.

In this *Mappa Mundi*, very significantly, Lewis characterized the modern thought of his time in religious terms as representing a cosmic war. He and Tolkien increasingly saw themselves as against the modern spirit, against modernism both as a literary movement and, more deeply, as an intellectual stance. They shared a mission against the Zeitgeist. In a letter written on May 8, 1939, Lewis observed, "My memories of the last war haunted my dreams for years." Modern warfare for him, a preoccupation of a generation of writers who had survived World War I, was an image of a permanent cosmic war between good and evil. In a later essay, "Learning in Wartime," he commented, "War creates no absolutely new situation; it simply aggravates the permanent human situation so that we can no longer ignore it." Though in *The Pilgrim's Regress* the story powerfully illuminates the intellectual climate of the 1920s and early 1930s, its geography of thought applies much more widely. The *Mappa Mundi* shows military railways both to the north and south. In his preface to the third edition (1943), Lewis observed that "the two military railways were meant to symbolize the double attack from Hell on the two sides of our nature. It was hoped that the roads spreading out from each of the enemy railheads would look like claws or tentacles reaching out into the country of Man's Soul."

Lewis explained the overall map as a scheme of "the Holy War as I see it." It depicts "the double attack from Hell on the two sides of our nature" (the mind and the physical sensations). Theologian James I. Packer pointed out that the idea of the Holy War, drawn from Bunyan and others, as well as Lewis's own war experience, not only informs *The*

Pilgrim's Regress but "gives shape and perspective to Lewis's output as a whole." The attack on the soul from north and south represent, in Lewis's words, "equal and opposite evils, each continually strengthened and made plausible by its critique of the other." The Northern people are cold, with "rigid systems whether sceptical or dogmatic, Aristocrats, Stoics, Pharisees, Rigorists, signed and sealed members of highly organized 'Parties.'" The emotional Southerners are the opposite, "boneless souls whose doors stand open day and night to almost every visitant, but always with the readiest welcome for those . . . who offer some sort of intoxication. . . . Every feeling is justified by the mere fact that it is felt: for a Northerner, every feeling on the same ground is suspect."

Both tendencies, according to Lewis's schema, actually dehumanize us, a thesis he was to explore in 1943 in his Riddell Memorial Lectures at the University of Durham, subsequently published as *The Abolition of Man* later that year. To remain human, Lewis argued, we have no choice but the straight and narrow, the "Main Road" of common humanity: "With both the 'North' and the 'South' a man has, I take it, only one concern — to avoid them and hold the Main Road. . . . We were made to be neither cerebral men nor visceral men, but Men."

John's way is a regress rather than a progress because he in fact is going away from rather than towards the beautiful Island that he seeks. The Island is Lewis's equivalent to the Celestial City of Bunyan. Glimpsed in childhood, it is both the cause and object of his sweet desire, a longing that evokes joy. When he gains the knowledge of how to achieve his Island, through Mother Kirk (the embodiment of what he later would call "Mere Christianity"), John finds he has to retrace his steps eastwards.

John's quest for the Island is a fine embodiment of the theme of joy that is so central in Lewis's autobiography, *Surprised by Joy*. The quest helps John to avoid the various snares and dangers he encounters as he lives out the "dialectic of desire."

Born in Puritania, John early on was taught to fear the Landlord of the country. Puritania is on the western edge of the Eastern Mountains to which he eventually returns. Though not intended as a portrait of Lewis's native Ulster, there are echoes of his childhood in the speech patterns of John's mother and father, the cook, the Steward, and Uncle George, and no doubt such voices rang in his ears during the fortnight in Northern Ireland in which he composed the book. The following extract displays dialogue that exemplifies an Ulster influence, with expressions like "indeed we did not," "to be sure," "it seems cruelly hard," and "not at all":

"Poor Uncle George has had notice to quit," [John's mother] said.

"Why?" said John.

"His lease is up. The Landlord has sent him notice to quit."

"But didn't you know how long the lease was for?"

"Oh, no, indeed we did not. We thought it was for years and years more. I am sure the Landlord never gave us any idea he was going to turn him out at a moment's notice like this."

"Ah, but he doesn't need any notice," broke in the Steward. "You know he always retains the right to turn anyone out whenever he chooses. It is very good of him to let any of us stay here at all."

"To be sure, to be sure," said the mother.

"That goes without saying," said the father.

"I'm not complaining," said Uncle George. "But it seems cruelly hard."

"Not at all," said the Steward. "You've only got to go to the Castle and knock at the gate and see the Landlord himself. You know that he's only turning you out of here to make you much more comfortable somewhere else...."

When Sheed and Ward republished the book in 1935, Lewis disagreed with them over paralleling Puritania and Ulster on their cover blurb ("This story begins in Puritania [Mr. Lewis was brought up in Ulster]"). In fact, he always held his birth country in highest regard, despite the excesses of Orangeism he disliked. Its landscapes, particularly County Down, not only fleetingly yet vividly featured in the early chapters of *The Pilgrim's Regress*, but helped to inspire the world of Narnia in later years. He was also appreciative of the Ulster people, such as the nurse of his childhood, Lizzie Endicott, and his hard-edged tutor, W. T. Kirkpatrick, the inspiration for the skeptical gardener Andrew MacPhee in Lewis's *That Hideous Strength*.

In the new edition of *The Pilgrim's Regress* in 1943 he provided a detailed foreword and notes to the chapters to help his readers with the obscurer points of the allegory. It is in fact best to enjoy the book as a story and not be too concerned with the meaning of every allusion. Read as a quest for joy, and in parallel with *Surprised by Joy*, it yields its main meanings, especially in the context of its mapping of the human soul in its *Mappa Mundi*.

7

Space, Time, and the "New Hobbit"

(1936–1939)

Lewis looks thoughtfully out of the window of his big sitting room in Magdalen College on to the deer park it overlooks. It's the spring of 1936. The parkland scene before him is one he considers beautiful beyond compare. Past a stretch of carefully groomed grass lies a grove of freshly clothed trees. A few deer stray among the trees or on the turf. Half a dozen are chewing the cud directly under his window. On his right hand is the reassuring sight of his favorite path — Addison's Walk — where, five years before, Tolkien, Hugo Dyson, and he had had that momentous nighttime conversation that led to his conversion.

He turns to address his friend, who is perched on a threadbare armchair, the room's handsome white-paneled walls behind him. Tolkien reaches for an enamel beer jug on the table and refills his tankard.

"You know, Tollers, there's far too little of what we enjoy in stories. You liked Williams's *The Place of the Lion* just as much as I did. Really it struck me how rare such books are."

Tolkien exclaims through dispersing wisps of smoke, "Not enough echoes of the horns of Elfland."

He sucks on his pipe to encourage its dying embers. "Some of the Scientifiction around evokes wonder — sometimes offers fleeting glimpses of genuine other worlds. There's some deplorable stuff, too, but that's true of all the genres. Space and time stories can provide Recovery and

Escape." He says the last two nouns with sudden loudness, perhaps to emphasize that they should have capitals. "I hope to lecture soon on this as a quality of Fairy Story. I relish stories that survey the depths of space and time."

"To be sure, to be sure," agrees Lewis, drawing attention to the slight Ulster in his vowels. He is unusually quiet this morning. "Take H. G. Wells. Even Wellsian stories can touch on the real other world of the Spirit. His early ones I care for — it's a pity he sold his birthright for a pot of message. These kinds of stories that create regions of the spirit — they actually add to life, don't they? They're like some dreams that only come from time to time — they give us sensations we've never had before. You could say they enlarge our very idea of what's possible in human experience."

"Your *Pilgrim's Regress* had something of what we like — romance. It's a pity it didn't do well with the public," Tolkien puts in. "Was a bit obscure in places. It can be a deuce of a labor to get it right."

"You know, Tollers," Lewis says decisively, pipe in hand. "I'm afraid we'll have to write them ourselves. We need stories like your *Hobbit* book, but on the more heroic scale of your older tales of Gondolin and Goblin wars. One of us should write a tale of time travel and the other should do space travel."

Tolkien reminds his friend of a rather similar challenge well over a century ago — Lord Byron, at Lake Geneva in 1816, had challenged Percy Shelley and Mary Shelley to write a ghost story . . . and Mary, a mere girl at the time, went on to write *Frankenstein*. They needed, Tolkien continues, his eyes brightening, stories today that expose modern magic — the tyranny of the machine.

"Let's toss for it, Tollers. Heads, you write about time travel; tails, you try space travel. I'll do the other." Tolkien nods his agreement, grinning.

Lewis fishes in the pocket of his crumpled and baggy flannels and a coin spins in the air.

"Heads it is."

❧

Tolkien's response to the challenge to write an "excursionary thriller" into time soon took shape, unlike his planned lecture on the subject of fairy

stories. He had continued for many years to gnaw on the problem of a satisfying framework for his tales of ancient Middle-earth — "the Silmarillion."
Time travel might just provide a narrative bridge for modern readers and
allow an encounter with myth. A new dimension to "the Silmarillion" had
started to unfold, linked to a nightmare he had of giant waves overwhelm-
ing green inlands, a nightmare that had recurred from childhood. This was
his version of the Atlantis myth. He called this doomed island far over
the western seas Númenor; it was star-shaped, given to the Elf-friends of
mankind who had resisted Morgoth, the first Dark Lord, at the close of
the First Age of Middle-earth. Though barely distinguishable from elves
in their nobility, the Númenoreans were mortal, like all humans, but had
a far longer life span.

The story Tolkien had begun writing shortly after the challenge from
Lewis was entitled "The Lost Road," and it explored the idea of an unusual
father-and-son relationship that repeats itself at various times in history.
This particular kinship represented a continuity in language, culture, and
ancestry that allowed vestiges of an ancient history of northern Europe to
be discovered. The father and son of "The Lost Road" are contemporary
figures, living by the Atlantic, perhaps in Cornwall or West Wales. Oswin
Errol is a history teacher. His son, Alboin, is haunted by names that emerge
in deep dreams. Great dark clouds over the western sea evoke for him the
sight of the eagles of "the Lord of the West" looming over Númenor,
not knowing the significance of these names. Later, after Oswin's death,
Alboin's own son, Audoin, has similar insights or postmonitions, but more
visual than linguistic, concerning "things and descriptions." These mental
discoveries allow Alboin and Audoin to travel back in time to Númenor,
where there are a father and son similar and in some ways equivalent to
them called Elendil and Herendil (in fact, Alboin has sometimes thought
of his own son by this mysterious name). Elendil and Herendil live at the
time Númenor is destroyed, and when Sauron, the banished Morgoth's
lieutenant and the epicenter of evil in *The Lord of the Rings*, is taking over
the island by subtle means. At this time Sauron is still fair to look upon,
and can win people over by plausible reasoning rather than naked power.
Númenor's fate plays an important role in the history of Middle-earth,
because the noble race of humans fleeing its destruction go on to found

the great kingdoms of Arnor in the north and Gondor in the south of Middle-earth.

Tolkien abandoned the story after writing only four chapters and some notes on plot and development. The idea of the "lost road" or "straight road" remained integral, however, to his conception of Middle-earth. After the downfall of Númenor the world was turned into a sphere, and the seas bent. Some Elven ships were allowed to pass beyond the world to the undying lands. They used the straight road, the same road taken by the Ring Bearers Bilbo and Frodo after they left the Grey Havens for the Uttermost West in *The Lord of the Rings*. Tolkien employed the idea of a lost road in early formulations of his mythology, involving the voyage of the mariner Aelfwine to the Elven island of Tol Eressëa, where he hears the tales of "the Silmarillion."

"The Lost Road," as far as it went, was most likely read to the Inklings. If so they would have pointed out the difficulties it would present to a contemporary reader. Lewis certainly heard it read aloud, because Tolkien himself explained that this is why Lewis misspelled some of the names or echoed them in his science-fiction stories *Perelandra* and *That Hideous Strength*. Tolkien wrote of his own influence on Lewis's stories in a letter to Roger Lancelyn Green, explaining that "Numinor" was Lewis's version of a name he had only heard from Tolkien's reading — Númenor.

Another example of Tolkien's influence are the characters of Tor and Tinidril in Lewis's *Perelandra*. These were clearly Tuor and his elf-wife Idril, from "The Silmarillion," merged with Tinúviel, the second name of Lúthien. Lewis's angelic Eldils, in the science-fiction trilogy, owe something to the Eldar (the high elves) of Middle-earth.

Lewis himself explained his inspiration by Tolkien and the idea of Atlantis in a letter written several years before the publication of *The Lord of the Rings*. There he explained that his Numinor is a misspelling of Tolkien's Númenor. Númenor, he said, belonged to the then "private mythology" which grew out of the "private language" that Tolkien had invented. This was, he added, a real language having sound laws and roots such as only a "great philologist" had the ability to create. Tolkien found that it was impossible to fashion a language without at the same time inventing a mythology. His private mythology, said Lewis, was appropriated by our world at the moment when "the participle *atlan* (fallen or shattered)" was applied to the vanished land of Númenor. Sound laws had produced this participle with no clear anticipation on Tolkien's part of its result: a connection with the mythological land of Atlantis in our world.

Not only did this unfinished story (and later pieces concerning the island of Númenor) influence Lewis, but other elements in the story appealed to him as well. Indeed they may have contributed to the imaginative matrix that inspired other stories by Lewis.

The parallels between Alboin and his son Audoin in western England and Elendil and his son Herendil in Númenor may have helped to suggest the doubles of Scudamour and Camilla — though they had a different purpose — in Lewis's abandoned story, "The Dark Tower" (possibly written between 1938 and 1939). Lewis also makes use of the idea of doubles in his fragment of a story, "After Ten Years" (written near the end of his life), which features both a real and an idealized Helen of Troy.

A second element that would have appealed to Lewis, and perhaps influenced his writing, was Tolkien's use of time. During the period that Alboin and his son are time traveling to Númenor, no time at all passes in the present. The two find themselves back in the twentieth century at the very same point in time. Tolkien may well have discussed this point with Lewis. His friend used the same device whenever children visit Narnia, with the exception of *The Last Battle*, where the visitors have already died in this world from a railway accident.

A further influence upon Lewis may have been *The Ainulindalë*. Tolkien was reworking this beautiful cosmological myth during the 1930s (probably including the time during which he wrote "The Lost Road"), and is likely to have shared it at some stage with Lewis. In *The Silmarillion*, this is "The Music of the Ainur" (the Ainur — or Valar — are the angelic beings behind creation). It is also called "The Great Music" or "The Great Song." The music expressed the blueprint of creation, the providence and design of Ilúvatar, the name of God in Tolkien's mythology of Middle-earth. The music parallels the personification of Wisdom in one of the most beautiful passages of the Bible, Proverbs 8. There Wisdom represents the standard by which God works as he envisages the creation he is to make. The Great Music was synonymous with the conception and creation of the world out of nothing, as well as its subsequent development. The rebellion of Morgoth (a figure like the fallen angel, Lucifer) is incorporated into the music and works out throughout the invented history of Middle-earth, becoming a central theme in Tolkien's work, for instance, in the rise of Sauron, Morgoth's greatest servant. The Valar, or angelic powers, first take on the role of preparing the world for the arrival of elves and, later, humankind. They steward the world and provide its light, first the Two Lamps, then the Two Trees, and finally the sun and moon. In the Third Age, when the events of *The Lord of the Rings* take place, several lesser Valar, or Maiar — most famously Gandalf — take on human form in order to serve as guardians against the reviving power of Sauron. Lewis may have been partly inspired by *The Ainulindalë* as he described the creation of Narnia by the song of Aslan in his *The Magician's Nephew* (begun in 1949), and in the Great Dance at the climax of his science-fiction story *Perelandra* (begun in 1941).

"The Lost Road" is not only of great interest for its insight into Tolkien's growing power as a storyteller, grappling with momentous themes of cosmology, providence, and theology, but also for its rare glimpse of his personality. Apart from the occasional aside in his lectures on *Beowulf* and on fairy stories, the only other document that has such strong autobiographical references is his *Leaf by Niggle* (1945). "The Lost Road" features two generations of motherless boys, and an idealized father, which might point to Tolkien's loss of father and mother in his childhood. Alboin is particularly like Tolkien, born about the same time as him, and fictionally illuminating the creative process of discovery that led Tolkien to write "The Silmarillion" material, and eventually *The Lord of the Rings*. We are told that as a child, "Alboin liked the flavour of the older northern languages, quite as much as he liked some of the things written in them." This tone or quality was "related to the atmosphere of the legends and myths told in the languages." Unaccountable names and phrases slipped into Alboin's consciousness, which, by following their trail, led to further discoveries. Alboin's son in later years observed this process in his father. He "was used to odd words and names slipping out in a murmur from his father. Sometimes his father would spin a long tale round them."

Most remarkably, perhaps, the story highlights Tolkien's preoccupation with the ancient past of Europe, the foreground of which was the Worcestershire and Warwickshire of his childhood. This was entirely appropriate within the frame of a story of time travel into the deep past. It also illuminates Tolkien's artistic purpose in *The Lord of the Rings,* which he would begin to write soon after, at the same time turning aside from writing "The Silmarillion" — it was to remain essentially unaltered for about thirteen years. Alboin, as he gets older (and pretty much the age of Tolkien as he wrote "The Lost Road"), reflects on his life:

> Surveying the last thirty years, he felt he could say that his most permanent mood, though often overlaid or suppressed, had been since childhood the desire *to go back.* To walk in Time, perhaps, as men walk on long roads; or to survey it, as men may see the world from a mountain, or the earth as a living map beneath an airship. But in any case to see with eyes and to hear with ears: to see the lie of old and even forgotten lands, to behold ancient men walking, and hear their languages as they spoke them, in the days before the days, when tongues of forgotten lineage were heard in kingdoms long fallen by the shores of the Atlantic.

Tolkien's publisher, Stanley Unwin, had been pressing for more from his pen after the publication of *The Hobbit* in September 1937. In November of that year Tolkien sent Unwin the four chapters he had written of "The Lost Road." At the same time he offered his publisher much of "The Silmarillion" material, which he described as his "private and beloved nonsense." He agreed with Unwin that a "sequel or successor to The Hobbit is called for," but was at a loss about what more hobbits could do. He confessed this in a letter of December 16, but only three days later, on December 19, he told Unwin of a breakthrough: "I have written the first chapter of a new story about Hobbits." Published seventeen years later, this was to be the opening chapter of *The Lord of the Rings.*

While Tolkien was writing his abortive tale of time travel, "The Lost Road," Lewis was pressing ahead with his story of space travel, *Out of the Silent Planet*, reading it chapter by chapter to the Inklings as it was written. Remarkably, Lewis's story *also* casts light upon the complex character of Tolkien.

As we have seen, Tolkien's work teaching Early and Middle English was intimately related to his construction of the languages, peoples, and history of Middle-earth. From his creation of Elven languages he had gone on to invent a fantasy world as if it were a forgotten world he had unearthed from the ancient past of northern Europe. This was patterned on his professional construction, as a philologist, of dim and distant contexts and earlier forms from vestiges of actual old languages like Early English.

In *Out of the Silent Planet*, Lewis captured the instincts and austere passions of a linguist just like Tolkien in the figure of the Cambridge philologist Elwin Ransom. Elwin means "Elf-friend," like the name Aelfwine. Dr. Ransom had a war wound, and was a "sedentary scholar." One of his publications was *Dialect and Semantics*. He combined intellectual and heroic qualities, though he tended to put himself down. He was tall, slightly built, golden-haired, aged about thirty-five to forty in the late 1930s when the events of *Out of the Silent Planet* take place. He didn't have much dress sense, and, at first sight, might have been mistaken for a doctor or schoolteacher.

Ransom is kidnapped by his evil colleague Edward Weston and transported to Malacandra (Mars) in a spacecraft, where he escapes his captors. He fears meeting alien life forms called sorns in the wild until a startling event takes place, which dramatically overturns his perceptions; he encounters an alien creature that proves to be intelligent:

> The creature, which was still steaming and shaking itself on the bank and had obviously not seen him, opened its mouth and began to make noises. This in itself was not remarkable; but a lifetime of linguistic study assured Ransom almost at once that these were articulate noises. The creature was talking. It had language. If you are not yourself a philologist, I am afraid you must take on trust the prodigious emotional consequences of this realization in Ransom's

mind. A new world he had already seen — but a new, an extra-terrestrial, a non-human language was a different matter. Somehow he had not thought of this in connection with the sorns; now it flashed upon him like a revelation. The love of knowledge is a kind of madness. In the fraction of a second which it took Ransom to decide that the creature was really talking, and while he still knew that he might be facing instant death, his imagination had leaped over every fear and hope and probability of his situation to follow the dazzling project of making a Malacandrian grammar. *An Introduction to the Malacandrian language — The Lunar verb — A concise Martian-English Dictionary* . . . the titles flitted through his mind. And what might one not discover from the speech of a non-human race? The very form of language itself, the principle behind all possible languages, might fall into his hands. Unconsciously he raised himself on his elbow and stared at the black beast. . . . Minute after minute in utter silence the representatives of two so far-divided species stared each into the other's face.

Ransom's thought, "What might one not discover from the speech of a non-human race?" is the kind of notion that would naturally occur to Tolkien. Indeed, the creation of Elvish languages — non-human languages of a kind — were for him an explanation of the dazzling possibilities of language for illuminating our knowledge of reality, both natural and supernatural, seen and unseen.

Lewis based the character of Elwin Ransom at least partially on his friend. Tolkien was aware of this resemblance, writing several years later to his son Christopher, "As a philologist I may have some part in [Ransom], and recognize some of my opinions Lewisified in him."

At the core of the friendship of Tolkien and Lewis was their shared antipathy to the modern world. They were not opposed to dentists, buses, draft beer, and other features of the twentieth century, but what they viewed as the underlying mentality of modernism. They were not against science or scientists, but the cult of science, found in modernism, and its tendency to monopolize knowledge, denying alternative approaches to knowledge through the arts, religion, and ordinary human wisdom. Tolkien and Lewis felt that this mentality was a malaise that posed a serious threat to humanity. The fictional character of Elwin Ransom embodied what the friends viewed as the contrasting old, perennial values common to humanity — values later referred to by Lewis as the Tao.

These positive values are displayed in Ransom's perception, which is premodern and essentially draws on medieval insights about nature and humanity. Lewis, like Tolkien, loved the Renaissance and medieval cosmos, its imaginative model of reality, and this world picture is the one "smuggled" into the minds of modern readers as they enjoy Lewis's story. In deep space, en route to Malacandra in a spacecraft, Ransom finds himself unexpectedly feeling well, despite the ordeal of his kidnapping. He begins to regain what Lewis regarded as humanity's lost consciousness:

> He lay for hours in contemplation of the skylight. The Earth's disk was nowhere to be seen; the stars, thick as daisies on an uncut lawn, reigned perpetually, with no cloud, no moon, no sunrise to dispute their sway. There were planets of unbelievable majesty, and constellations undreamed of: there were celestial sapphires, rubies, emeralds and pinpricks of burning gold; far out on the left of the picture hung a comet, tiny and remote: and between all and behind all, far more emphatic and palpable than it showed on Earth, the un-dimensioned, enigmatic blackness. The lights trembled: they seemed to grow brighter as he looked. Stretched naked on his bed, a second Danaë, he found it night by night more difficult to disbelieve in old astrology: almost he felt, wholly he imagined, "sweet influence" pouring or even stabbing into his surrendered body.

Ransom's positive values are contrasted with the negative values of his kidnapper, Professor Edward Weston, an eminent physicist who represents all that Lewis disliked about the modernist world. Weston, along with his henchman Dick Devine, has abducted Ransom in the mistaken belief that a human sacrifice is required by the mysterious rulers of Mars, an act he considers completely justifiable. He has a disdain for all values of common humanity. His guiding value is biological survival, the replication of enlightened men at any cost.

After escaping his captors Ransom is at first terrified and disoriented by the red planet and its diversity of terrain and inhabitants — various forms of rational life related in a harmonious hierarchy. However, the inhabitants turn out to be civilized and amiable. Ransom, as a linguist, is soon able to pick up the rudiments of their language, Old Solar. Ransom also encounters the barely perceptible but audible rulers of the planet, the Oyarsa, who are incorporeal.

Lewis was annoyed at the tendency of science fiction at the time to portray extraterrestrial beings as evil, as the enemies of mankind. In his view the medieval image of the universe was exactly the reverse, and this appealed to him. His portrayal of peaceful, spiritual alien life forms had a profound impact on science fiction that has lasted to this day. Half humorously, Lewis noted in a letter in 1939 to a reader: "You will be both grieved and amused to hear that out of about 60 reviews only two showed any knowledge that my idea of the fall of the Bent One was anything but an invention of my own. . . . Any amount of theology can now be smuggled into people's minds under the cover of romance without their knowing it." This sort of response was one of the factors in Lewis's decision to continue writing theology and ethics on a broad front.

In her study *Voyages to the Moon* (1948), Marjorie Hope Nicolson paid this tribute:

> *Out of the Silent Planet* is to me the most beautiful of all cosmic voyages and in some ways the most moving. . . . As C. S. Lewis, the Christian apologist, has added something to the long tradition, so C. S. Lewis, the scholar-poet, has achieved an effect in *Out of the Silent Planet* different from anything in the past. Earlier writers have created new worlds from legend, from mythology, from fairy tale. Mr. Lewis has created myth itself, myth woven of desire and aspirations deep-seated in some, at least, of the human race. . . . As I journey with him into worlds at once familiar and strange, I experience, as did Ransom, "a sensation not of following an adventure but of enacting a myth."

When Lewis told Tolkien that he had been invited by Stanley Unwin to submit *Out of the Silent Planet*, Tolkien wrote to Unwin of it "being read aloud to our local club (which goes in for reading things short and long aloud). It proved an exciting serial, and was highly approved. But of course we are all rather like-minded." Within a couple of weeks Unwin sent a negative reader's report on Lewis's manuscript to Tolkien and asked for his opinion of the story. He replied almost immediately expressing his detailed unease at the report and confessing: "I read the story in the original MS. and was so enthralled that I could do nothing else until I had finished it." Various criticisms he had made to Lewis had been implemented to his satisfaction. There was praise indeed in his comment, "The linguistic inventions and the philology on the whole are more than good enough." Nevertheless Unwin decided that the book was not for his publishing house, and passed it on to John Lane, the Bodley Head. It was published the next year, in 1938. The book proved a success, especially after the publication of *The Screwtape Letters* in 1942 and Lewis's popular wartime broadcast series in 1941, 1942, and 1944. L. P. Hartley, in the *Daily Sketch*, spoke for many readers when he enthused, "I warmly recommend this original, interesting and well-written phantasy."

☙❧

The first chapter of the new hobbit story that Tolkien had mentioned to Stanley Unwin on December 19, 1937, began in its original draft like this:

> When Bilbo, son of Bungo of the family of Baggins, prepared to celebrate his seventieth birthday there was for a day or two some talk in the neighbourhood. He had once had a little fleeting fame among the people of Hobbiton and Bywater — he had disappeared after breakfast one April 30th and not reappeared until lunchtime on June 22nd in the following year. A very odd proceeding for which he had never given any good reason, and of which he wrote a nonsensical account....

On March 4, 1938, Tolkien informed Unwin that his sequel to *The Hobbit* had reached the end of a third chapter, and that Black Riders had made an unexpected appearance, radically affecting the plot. He observed the

tendency of stories to have a life of their own, and his had taken an unexpected turn with the Riders. Up to that point Tolkien may have still
been thinking of the sequel as another children's book. The Black Riders
indicated a darker terror that would forever change the scale and tone of
the book. Around this time he made a rough map of The Shire, filling in
details of his invented world. This map remained essentially unchanged
as the work developed, and showed an increasing emphasis on consistent
geography and history, comparable to the earlier tales of "The Silmarillion," which he had now abandoned in favor of the "new Hobbit" — *The
Lord of the Rings*.

This new work, not "The Lost Road," turned out to be Tolkien's enduring story of "time travel," his unrivaled exploration of the nature of
time. While there is no obvious device of time-traveling into the past, he
was able to create the illusion of Middle-earth as part of the history and
background of northern Europe. Though an imagined history, there is a
sense of familiarity, in which this ancient and seemingly discovered history
can be appropriated by the reader of today, as any history is appropriated.
We travel in time as we enjoy the story. On our own familiar terms we
walk in time, perhaps, as people "walk on long roads"; or survey it, as we
may "see the world from a mountain," or "the earth as a living map" be-
neath an aircraft. We view "the lie of old and even forgotten lands," and
stare at ancient peoples walking. We sometimes hear their languages as
they speak them, "in the days before the days, when tongues of forgotten
lineage were heard in kingdoms long fallen by the shores of the Atlantic."

8

World War II and After

Charles Williams Comes to Oxford (1939–1949)

Shouts and the laughter of children's voices come from the normally tranquil woods nearby.

"What's that?" Lewis wonders, as he slams shut the car door. His thoughts are elsewhere, and the sounds startle him. He has just been picked up from town, where he has passed a pleasant couple of hours with Tolkien at the Eagle and Child pub. The Michaelmas term is not due to start for another month. With war imminent, Tolkien has had to cancel his family vacation in Sidmouth and is at a loose end. He has been ill quite a bit this year, and also is struggling with the chapters he has written of the *The Lord of the Rings*. He told Lewis that he needs to make some important changes to the narrative. He is also changing the names of some of the characters — Bingo is to become Bilbo Baggins. When the Inklings reconvene in the fall he will have more chapters to read to them.

"The evacuee children have arrived. I collected them earlier from the station," explains Maureen, smiling at Lewis's surprised face. She is now in her early thirties and often takes care of tasks that require driving the car. Mrs. Moore — Minto — rarely leaves The Kilns.

War with Germany is inevitable. It is the beginning of September 1939. The evacuees, all giggly girls, have been assigned to The Kilns, to the care of Mrs. Moore. Like one and a half million children hurriedly dispersed around the country they bring little — a gas mask, in a large box attached to a shoulder strap, spare clothing, toothbrush, comb, a handkerchief, and a bag of food for the day they travel. Some evacuees bring head lice, too, but not the girls who arrive today at Lewis's home.

Frequently interrupting each other, the children explain to Lewis and Mrs. Moore at tea time how, when they arrived at Oxford station from Waterloo in London, first billeting officers met them, then Maureen.

Lewis, who hitherto had had little experience of children, instantly warms to them. He writes that night to Warren, recalled to active service as part of the war preparation, that the evacuees seem "very nice, unaffected creatures and all most flatteringly delighted with their new surroundings." He adds that they are fond of animals, a good thing both ways — for them, and for the Kilns household.

 ❧

Most evacuees, coming from deeply urban areas, had little or no experience of the countryside. The evacuees at The Kilns were no exception. In the few years since Lewis, Warren, Mrs. Moore, and Maureen moved into The Kilns it superficially had come to resemble a small farm, and this resemblance deepened as the war progressed. A succession of evacuees were presented with the sight of a low, rambling brick house in acres of land, a tennis court, an apple orchard, a pond in the distant trees, and many hens. Eggs were on the menu every day. There were coops for hens and cages for rabbits to be cleaned.

The expanse of garden was presided over by general factotum Fred Paxford, then in his forties, who would be the lugubrious model for Lewis's Puddleglum in the Narnian story, *The Silver Chair* (1953). He lived in a wooden bungalow on the grounds. His hymn singing could be heard from a great distance. Minto had taught him to cook, and the meals he served were often accompanied by a plate-rattling rendition of "Abide with me."

One evacuee — Patricia Boshell — remembered, long after, her first encounter with Lewis, that he was "a shabbily clad, rather portly gentleman, whom I took to be the gardener, and told him so. He roared — boomed! — with laughter."

The evacuees took to Minto, by then in her late sixties, and frail. She was kind to them and they were not put off by the cigarette constantly hanging on her lower lip scattering ash, sometimes on to their food (which they didn't care for). They all noticed that Minto made a huge fuss of Lewis — he was the center of attention. For her he was the axis around which life revolved. One evacuee, Jill "June" Flewett (pronounced "Juin" by Lewis) remarked: "The running of the house, the cooking, the meals — everything she did — was geared for Jack's happiness and comfort. The whole household revolved on the premise that Jack must be looked after, and Warnie was expected to tag along."

One young man assigned to The Kilns during this period by the Social Services had quite severe learning difficulties. Every night for about two months Lewis would give him lessons in reading. Lewis had quite a talent for illustration, and made drawings and letter cards as aids for his teaching. The lad, whose mental age was about eight, found difficulty in retaining even these simple lessons, but Lewis persevered nonetheless.

The evacuees made a deep impression on Lewis. Soon after the first children arrived he started to write a story, soon abandoned.

This book is about four children whose names were Ann, Martin, Rose and Peter. But it is most about Peter who was the youngest. They all had to go away from London suddenly because of Air Raids, and because Father, who was in the Army, had gone off to the War and Mother was doing some kind of war work. They were sent to stay with a kind of relation of Mother's who was a very old Professor who lived all by himself in the country.

Lewis would pick up the story again ten years later, in 1949, and it became the first story of Narnia, *The Lion, the Witch and the Wardrobe,* in which evacuee children enter another, magical world through an old wardrobe.

❧

In the Tolkien household the meager wartime rations were eventually augmented by turning the tennis court in the garden into a vegetable patch and keeping chickens. The family would gather around Edith's large Pye radio to listen intently to news bulletins from the BBC. They also heard with dismay the intrusive nasal voice of propagandist "Lord Haw-Haw,"

William Joyce the traitor, broadcasting from Germany. Priscilla Tolkien got used to the staccato thud from upstairs of her father's heavy and ancient Hammond typewriter, as he typed his way through successive drafts of his emerging *The Lord of the Rings*.

Oxford's University examination buildings were turned into a military hospital. Tolkien's college at that time, Pembroke, was partially requisitioned by the ministry of agriculture as well as the army. At lunch one day Tolkien, chuckling, told the family that a notice had appeared in the college lodge which announced, *Pests: First Floor.*

❧

Not all evacuees were children bearing their sandwiches and gas masks. Fifty employees of the London office of Oxford University Press were moved to Oxford, almost immediately after Britain's declaration of war on September 3, 1939, among them Charles Williams. It was two weeks before his fifty-third birthday. He was billeted at the home of Professor H. N. Spalding, at 9 South Parks Road, close by the city center. Williams settled into the domestic establishment, which included the Professor and his wife, their two daughters, and Gerry Hopkins, his OUP colleague — nephew of the poet Gerard Manley Hopkins. Williams cut bread for everyone at meals, even though his hands habitually shook; opened windows to air the rooms; and reliably dried dishes after the washing up. The friendship between Lewis and Williams had consolidated since their exchange of letters in 1936, with Williams visiting the Inklings perhaps a couple of times, and the two had sat together in gatherings of the Christendom Group. This think tank explored the social implications of the Christian faith, other members including Hugo Dyson, T. S. Eliot, and the distinguished theologians E. L. Mascall and Donald Mackinnon.

Soon Williams was regularly meeting with Lewis and Tolkien, and attending the Inklings. Williams spoke with a marked East London accent, which was unusual to the ears of mostly private school–educated university academics. E. L. Mascall remembered him like this: "Physically, Williams was not particularly impressive until one noticed the vivacity of his facial expression. He was rather below middle height and peered through rather thick glasses. It was in the excitability and volubility of his speech that his enormous interior energy and enthusiasm was manifested and became infectious. Though largely self-educated, he was a man of profound intellectual depth and, with this, of great spiritual integrity."

Poet Anne Ridler, a publishing friend of Williams, captured his essence when she wrote, "In Williams' universe there is a clear logic, a sense of terrible justice which is not our justice and yet is not divorced from love." This echoes George MacDonald's view of God's "inexorable love." For Anne Ridler "the whole man...was greater even than the sum of his works." T. S. Eliot also greatly admired Charles Williams. He said in a broadcast talk after the war: "It is the whole work, not any one or several masterpieces, that we have to take into account in estimating the importance of the man. I think he was a man of unusual genius, and I regard his work as important. But it has an importance of a kind not easy to explain."

Williams was born in Islington, London, on September 20, 1886. His father was a foreign correspondence clerk in French and German to a firm of importers in London until his failing eyesight forced the family to move away from the city, to St. Albans in Hertfordshire. There they set up a shop selling artists' material. The talented boy gained a county council scholarship to St. Albans Grammar school. Then he won a place at University College, London, beginning his studies at the age of fifteen. The family unfortunately was not able to keep up paying the fees, and Williams was forced to discontinue his studies. He managed to get at job in a Methodist bookshop in the capital.

His fortunes changed through meeting an editor from the London office of the Oxford University Press, who was looking for help with the proofs of the complete edition of Thackeray. Williams would remain with OUP until his death, creating a distinctive atmosphere affectionately remembered by those who worked with him, particularly women. He married, was considered medically unfit to serve in World War I, and, like Tolkien, lost two of his closest friends in the trenches.

Williams began what was to become a habitual event — giving adult evening classes in literature for the London County Council to supplement the modest family income. Later he wrote his series of seven supernatural thrillers for the same reason. The series included *The Place of the Lion*, which came to Lewis's attention and led to the friendship between the two men.

Like his friends Lewis and Tolkien, Williams's thought and writing centered on the three themes of reason, romanticism, and Christianity. Like Lewis, he was an Anglican, but whereas Lewis was relatively "Low Church" (preferring plain worship), Williams was an Anglo-Catholic (or "High Church"), which gave him more affinities with Roman Catholicism. His interest in romanticism is expressed, in a literary way, in his interest in and use of symbols (human love, for example, to him implied the love of God). He was interested in the experience of romantic and other forms of love, such as friendship and affection, and the theological implications of human love. As regards reason, he rejected the equation of rational abstraction with reality, and helped to introduce the writings of Søren Kierkegaard to English readers. Yet he felt passionately that the whole human personality must be ordered by reason to have integrity and spiritual health. Williams constantly sought the balance between the abstract and the "feeling" mind, between intellect and emotion, between reason and imagination. He tried to walk the straight main road of Lewis's *Mappa Mundi*.

Williams was in his early forties before his first novel, *War in Heaven*, was published in 1930; he was over five years older than Tolkien and nearly twelve years older than Lewis. Prior to *War in Heaven* he had brought out five minor books, four of them poetry, the other a play. His important work begins with the novels; after 1930 his noteworthy works appear, packed into the last fifteen years of his life. Between 1930 and his sudden death in 1945 twenty-eight books were published (an average of almost two a year) as well as numerous articles and reviews. The last of these years of maturity as a thinker and writer he spent in Oxford, from 1939 until 1945, a result of the war. They involved Williams's normal editorial duties with Oxford University Press; lecturing and tutorials for the university (set up by Lewis); constant meetings with Lewis, Tolkien, and the Inklings; and frequent weekends in his London home. His wife, Michal, had stayed behind to look after the flat when Williams was evacuated. He spent occasional weekends back in London, a city he loved.

Charles Williams's writings — encompassing fiction, poetry, drama, theology, church history, biography, and literary criticism — become more accessible in the light of those writings of Lewis that were influenced by Williams. There are many elements consciously drawn from him in Lewis's *That Hideous Strength*, *The Great Divorce*, *Till We Have Faces*, and *The Four Loves*. Lewis was particularly influenced by Williams's novel *The Place of the Lion*, and his Arthurian cycle of poetry (including *Taliesin Through Logres*).

Williams's move to Oxford, and his admittance into the Inklings, helped to exert this deep and lasting influence on Lewis. Tolkien was in later years to describe Lewis as being under Williams's "spell," and did not entirely approve of this, feeling that Lewis was too impressionable a man. Later also, he would refer to the Inklings as Lewis's "coven," alluding to Williams's fascination with the occult, a taste that disturbed Tolkien. At the time, however, Tolkien got a lot out of his friendship with Williams, and deeply appreciated Williams's attentive listening to episodes of *The Lord of the Rings* as they were written — in marked contrast to the cool attitude of another Inkling, Dyson. In a letter to his son Christopher, Tolkien wrote: "C. Williams who is reading it all says the great thing is that its *centre* is not in strife and war and heroism (though they are understood and depicted) but in freedom, peace, ordinary life and good living."

Tolkien, vice versa, would listen attentively to Williams reading, even though he confessed that, at times, he found Williams's work difficult to make out. Lewis described one such occasion when Williams read a piece of his that was more to Tolkien's liking, *The Figure of Arthur*, Williams's unfinished prose study of the Arthurian legend.

> Picture to yourself... an upstairs sitting-room with windows looking north into the "grove" of Magdalen College on a sunshiny Monday Morning in vacation at about ten o'clock. The Professor and I, both on the Chesterfield, lit our pipes and stretched out our legs. Williams in the arm-chair opposite to us threw his cigarette into the grate, took up a pile of the extremely small, loose sheets on which he habitually wrote — they came, I think, from a twopenny pad for memoranda, and began [reading]....

Dr. "Humphrey" Havard attended many of the Inklings' meetings during the war, despite being away for a long period on naval service. As usual he was an astute observer, recalling Williams with affection and praising his charm and humor: "He was always full of laughter, ready to join in any joke that was going. He would throw his arms back and his head to the ceiling, chuckling with joy. But when it came to reading his work, I couldn't understand a word of it." He felt that others in the group shared his view, except Lewis. But even Lewis, his greatest fan, protested at the obscurity, saying on one occasion, "Charles, you're impossible." Havard recalled too Tolkien's intense reservations about Williams "dabbling in the occult," a reference to plot features of his novels. In one novel, *The Greater Trumps*, for instance, the story centers around the Tarot pack. Havard observed that these reservations in fact strained the friendship between Lewis and Tolkien. "Lewis was fascinated by Williams, and rightly; he [had] a very extraordinary charm. You couldn't be in the same room with him without being attracted to him."

Both Tolkien and Lewis were too old now to be called up for service in the war, and, like many of their age, served in the Home Guard, or "Dad's Army" as it was nicknamed, fulfilling a variety of duties. Many a night they patrolled, observing the changes of the night sky, from cloudy to star-filled. One clear night in 1940, while on watch, Tolkien noticed a strong and strange light growing and spreading over the northern horizon. Next day he learned it was the burning of Coventry — Oxford escaped the blitz. Throughout 1942 Tolkien took particular interest in the phases of the moon and the sunsets — in his meticulous attention to detail he based the movements of the moon and sunsets during the journeys of the fellowship of the Ring on that particular year.

The war strongly affected Tolkien's family. First, his eldest son, John, set out in November 1939 for Rome, to train for the priesthood. Although Italy had not yet joined forces with Hitler it soon became clear that John would have to return to Britain. He got back just as traveling from France was becoming precarious, and then followed his college as it was moved first to the Lake District and then to Stoneyhurst in Lancashire. (On one occasion, when Tolkien visited Stoneyhurst College, he and Edith stayed in the small college lodge. In his skillful hand, Tolkien sketched a picture of the little house as Tom Bombadil's Cottage, complete with bean rows.) The next in the family to be affected was Michael, who enlisted in the Army early in the war and became an antiaircraft gunner. For his action defending airfields during the Battle of Britain he won the prestigious George Medal. In 1944 he was invalided out of service and resumed his studies at Oxford. Christopher's turn came when he joined the Royal Air Force in 1942, and was soon in South Africa training to be a fighter pilot. While there Tolkien sent him long letters reporting the progress of *The Lord of the Rings,* and providing glimpses of his meetings with Lewis, Williams, and the Inklings. Christopher, more than any of the Tolkien children, had been closely involved with the creation of the story since its beginning, and, in 1943, he made for his father a large and elaborate map of Middle-earth in pencil and colored chalks, closely based upon Tolkien's primitive but precise maps. These grew from the original sketching of The Shire in 1938. Christopher shared a special affinity with his father, which may be reflected in the father-son relationships in the unfinished story, "The Lost Road." This affinity gave Christopher a natural facility in untangling and making sense of the numerous drafts of "the Silmarillion" Tolkien left upon his death.

An important household event was the celebration of Tolkien and Edith's silver wedding anniversary in 1941, necessarily a modest occasion due to the limitations created by the war. Of the children only Priscilla, the youngest, who still lived at home, could attend, but guests included Dyson and Lewis. Edith ran the household through the severe rationing, supplemented by homegrown vegetables from the garden and eggs from the hens.

Despite the disruptions of war, including a shortage of students, the university carried on as normally as possible. Tolkien and Lewis continued to lecture, Tolkien oversaw his graduate students, and Lewis held his morning and early-evening tutorials for Magdalen undergraduates. Williams augmented the teaching of the English School with his wide knowledge of poetry, and his lectures were very popular with students.

After he spoke to a surprised audience of students on the theme of virginity in Milton's *Comus* Dyson quipped that Williams was in danger of becoming a thoroughgoing "chastitute." On one occasion in 1943 Tolkien and Williams found themselves lecturing at the very same time. Whereas Williams's lecture on *Hamlet* filled the auditorium, Tolkien's students all but deserted him to hear Williams. The only student who remained for the lecture on Anglo-Saxon was one who was there to take notes. So Tolkien was left to lecture to the single student. Tolkien magnanimously had a drink with the ebullient Williams afterwards.

Sometimes in the long, weary war years, progress halted on the writing of the *The Lord of the Rings*. During one such hiatus an intensely personal story was born. Uncharacteristically, Tolkien wrote it as an allegory. *Leaf by Niggle* was a purgatorial story, perhaps under the influence of Williams's fascination with Dante's *Purgatory*. Williams's novel *Descent into Hell* (1937) had a purgatorial theme, as had Lewis's *The Great Divorce* and Williams's *All Hallows Eve*, both written in the war years.

Leaf by Niggle was published in January 1945 in *The Dublin Review,* but written some time before. Niggle, a little man and artist, knew that he would one day have to make a Journey. Many matters got in the way of his painting, such as the demands of his neighbor, Mr. Parish, who had a lame leg. Niggle was softhearted and rather lazy.

Niggle was concerned to finish one painting in particular. This had started as an illustration of a leaf caught in the wind, then the work kept developing until it became a tree. Through gaps in the leaves and branches a forest and a whole world opened up. As the painting grew (with other, smaller paintings tacked on) Niggle had had to move it into a specially built shed on his potato plot.

Eventually Niggle fell ill after getting soaked in a storm while running an errand for Mr. Parish. Then the dreaded Inspector visited to tell him that the time had come for him to set out on the Journey.

Taking a train his first destination (where he seemed to be for a century) was at the Workhouse, as Niggle had not brought any belongings. He worked very hard there on various chores. At last, one day, when he had been ordered to rest, he overheard two Voices discussing his case. One of them spoke up for him. It was time for gentler treatment, the Voice said.

Niggle was allowed to resume his journey in a small train which led him to the familiar world depicted on his painting of long ago, and to his tree, now complete. "It's a gift!" he exclaimed. Niggle then walked towards the forest (which had tall mountains behind). He realized that there was unfinished gardening work that could be done here, and that Parish could help him — his old neighbor knew a lot about plants, earth, and trees. Just as he realized this he came across Parish, and the two of them worked busily together. At last, Niggle felt that it was time to move on into the mountains. Parish wished to remain behind to await his wife. It turned out that the region they had worked in together was called Niggle's Country, much to their surprise. A guide led Niggle into the mountains he longed to visit and no more was heard of him.

Long before, back in the town near where Niggle and Parish had lived before the Journey, a fragment of Niggle's painting had survived and been hung in the town museum, entitled simply, "Leaf by Niggle." It depicted a spray of leaves with a glimpse of a mountain peak. Niggle's Country became a popular place to send travelers to for a vacation, for refreshment and convalescence, and as a splendid introduction to the mountains.

Tolkien's little story suggests the link between art and reality. Even in heaven there will be room for the artist to add his or her own touch to the created world. The allegorical components could be interpreted as follows, much as suggested by Tom Shippey in his groundbreaking study, *The Road to Middle-earth:* Niggle's journey represents death. Niggle the painter stands for Tolkien the fastidious writer. The way he paints leaves rather than trees reflects Tolkien's perfectionism, and his ability to be easily distracted. Niggle's leaf may be the equivalent of Tolkien's *The Hobbit*. If this is so, it would follow that Niggle's tree resembles the large undertakings of *The Lord of the Rings* and "The Silmarillion." The country that opens up as Niggle works represents Middle-earth. Other pictures tacked on by Niggle may be interpreted as being Tolkien's poems, translations, and other works. Niggle's neglected garden may stand for Tolkien's professorial responsibilities. Parish's excellent potatoes might represent "proper" work. The Workhouse is likely to mean Purgatory. The figure of Niggle himself might symbolize the creative element in humans. By the same token, the figure of Parish may represent the practical element. The mountains that

Niggle longs to visit are likely to symbolize heaven. Potatoes in the story might, allowing for Tolkien's humor, represent scholarship. The meaning of trees is likely to be fantasy. Trees are a fundamental symbol in Tolkien's work.

This pattern of interpretation emphasizes the autobiographical aspect of the story. The tale has equal applicability to the artist in general, however. In particular, there is poignancy to the unfinished nature of Niggle's work. This inability turned out to be true of Tolkien's own work on "The Silmarillion." Yet there was a hope for him in recognizing that this is part of the human condition, brought about by an ancient fall. After completing *Leaf by Niggle*, Tolkien was able to resume his work on *The Lord of the Rings*, aided by Lewis's fervent encouragement.

$\sim\!\infty\!\sim$

For Lewis the years of war marked his establishment as a major popular communicator of Christian faith. *Time* magazine sent a reporter to research this Oxford phenomenon. The journalist painstakingly interviewed several of Lewis's friends and colleagues, including Williams, but failed to penetrate the mysteries of Lewis's domestic situation with Mrs. Moore. The article did not appear until September 1947, and by then Lewis was sufficiently celebrated to feature on the cover. This article, together with Chad Walsh's pioneering study, *C. S. Lewis: Apostle to the Skeptics* (1949), helped to establish Lewis's high profile in the United States, where, to this day, he continues to have greater recognition than in his homeland.

The popular theology Lewis published then — *The Problem of Pain* (1940), *The Weight of Glory* (1942), *Broadcast Talks* (1942), *The Screwtape Letters* (1943), *Christian Behaviour* (1943), and *Beyond Personality* (1944) — are still in great demand in various forms at the beginning of the twenty-first century. His popularity was immensely boosted by the four series of talks he gave on BBC radio in 1941, 1942, and 1944. The booklets based on the talks were eventually gathered into *Mere Christianity* (1952). The talks were straightforward and lucid, providing an outstanding example of early media evangelism. Their content is captured in the part titles of the book: "Right and Wrong As a Clue to the Meaning of the Universe," "What Christians Believe," "Christian Behaviour," and

"Beyond Personality: Or First Steps in the Doctrine of the Trinity." The BBC had invited Lewis to give these popular talks early in 1941, when war had made people generally more thoughtful about ultimate issues. Lewis had to weigh up two dislikes — the radio and traveling to London — but his sense of duty won. He, like Tolkien, increasingly regarded England as a post-Christian country. In Lewis's view, many people were convinced that they had left Christianity behind, when in fact they had never been true believers in the first place. His feelings about the first set of talks were recorded in a letter. The broadcasts, he revealed, were preevangelism rather than evangelism — their aim was to persuade modern people that there is a moral law, that we are guilty of disobeying it. The existence of a lawgiver followed very probably, at least, from the reality of the moral law. Unless the Christian doctrine of the atonement was added to this bleak analysis, he concluded, it imparted despair rather than consolation.

Tolkien strongly disapproved of Lewis as a popular theologian. Reflecting their differing church orientations Tolkien felt that this type of communication should be left to professional churchmen. In a letter to Kathleen Farrer in 1956, Tolkien wrote approvingly of her husband, the outstanding theologian Austin Farrer, but acidly of his friend: Austin Farrer was a gifted communicator. Tolkien commented that if real theologians like her husband had started writing theology for lay people ("oeuvres de vulgarisation") a few years earlier, "the world would have been spared" C. S. Lewis. Tolkien was committed to a much more allusive approach of the creative artist steeped in the Christian faith and had little sympathy for Lewis's direct approach. Particularly Tolkien explored the idea of the artist as "sub-creator," believing that people necessarily reflect the true nature of the world in artistic creation. Thus, while unhappy with Lewis's popular theology, he approved in principle of his imaginative writings at this time — *The Great Divorce* and *Perelandra* — and would have approved of *That Hideous Strength* (1945) if he didn't find it spoiled by the influence of Williams. There was much that Tolkien liked of *The Screwtape Letters*, though he was bemused as to why it was dedicated to him. His letters at the time often reflect concepts explored in *Screwtape*, just as he used the idea of Lewis's *hnau* (or embodied personal being) from his space stories in reflecting upon some developments in the narrative of *The Lord of the Rings*.

⟋⟍⟍⟋⟍⟍

Night falls on June 12, 1987, according to a new story Tolkien has started. A great storm rages over the midlands and southern England — the fiercest in living memory. Houses and hotels collapse, roads and railway lines are blocked by thousands of trees, and there is a swath of damage from Cornwall to East Anglia. The giant storm flattens acres of trees in woodland, parks, and forests as it strides across countryside and urban areas. In the stillness and heat before that storm a club of like-minded academics meets in the rooms of Michael Ramer, Professor of Finno-Ugric philology, in Jesus College, Oxford. They continue their exploration of dreams, words, and phrases that is beginning to build up a picture of an ancient disaster that had swallowed an island kingdom deep in the Atlantic. The group — called the Notion Club — bears some remarkable similarities to the Inklings that had met for so many years during Lewis's lifetime.

⟋⟍⟍⟋⟍⟍

Tolkien was reading this fictional account of a great storm and a literary club, set in the future world of 1987, to some of the Inklings in the summer of 1946. By remarkable coincidence, he was only about four months out in the timing of the great hurricane, for indeed the storm of the century struck England late on October 15, 1987.

The writing of *The Lord of the Rings* had temporarily dried up after reaching the end of what became *The Two Towers*, the second volume of the trilogy. He had returned to the challenge set long before by Lewis of writing a story of time travel, and he called it *The Notion Club Papers*. Warren recorded later the gist of one of the meetings at which Tolkien read from the story in his diary. He read on this occasion to a small gathering of the Inklings: to his son Christopher, and the Lewis brothers. Before Tolkien began, Lewis had read a poem on Paracelsus's view of gnomes, then "Tollers" read "a magnificent myth which is to knit up and concludes his Papers of the Notions Club" — on the downfall of Númenor. An early draft had a lighthearted title page:

Beyond Lewis
Or
Out of the Talkative Planet
Being a fragment of an apocryphal Inklings' saga,
made by some imitator at some time in the 1980s.

The Notion Club Papers was never completed. In a letter to his publisher, Stanley Unwin, in July 1946, Tolkien mentioned that it took up material employed in the aborted "The Lost Road," but in an entirely different time frame and setting. In the story, papers found early in the twenty-first century constitute the minutes of discussion of the Notion Club in Oxford from 1986 to 1987 — the years of the great storm. Linked with the story was a new version of his Atlantis legend of Númenor — "The Drowning of Anadûnê." While "The Lost Road" contained a soft-focus portrait of a father and son not unlike Tolkien and his son Christopher, *The Notion Club Papers* somewhat idealized the Inklings. Neither story, however, is direct biography or autobiography. Both mainly concern the discovery of clues to the lost world of Númenor through dreams and strange words discovered by people exceptionally sensitive to language, people who would fit in well to a club like the Inklings. The insights into the past they achieve in this way are in a curious manner as objective as the seemingly hard facts of traditional history. This facticity is demonstrated in the story by the intrusion of a great storm in late twentieth-century Oxford, a storm which issues from the calamity that befell Númenor far away and long ago. The world of Númenor — specifically its terrible destruction — intrudes into the future Western world in that summer of 1987. This is a direct consequence of the time link made by members of the Notion Club as they explore the ancient past through traces of forgotten languages and through persistent dreams. Some of the discussions of the Notion Club concern the importance of dreams, and time and space travel via a dream state. Behind it is an exciting exploration of the place imagination has in putting us in contact with reality.

Christopher Tolkien — who was a member of the Inklings at the time Tolkien created this fictional account of the group — assures us from his intimate knowledge that there is no direct connection between characters in the Notion Club and actual Inklings. However there are hints of actual characters — for instance, marked parallels between Havard and Dolbear, and between the restless and hyperactive Dyson and Arry Lowdham. One amusing fictional character is Wilfred Trewin Jeremy, an English Fellow at Corpus Christi College, who specializes in escapism and has written extensively on ghost stories, time travel, and imaginary lands. He is also an expert on C. S. Lewis, encouraging the members of the Notion Club to read his nearly forgotten writings! Tolkien himself is echoed in one draft of the story, in the elderly Rashbold (a translation of the Germanic "Tolkien"), professor of Anglo-Saxon at Pembroke College.

The large membership of the fictional Notion Club reflected the swelling of the Inklings by 1946. Only five years before Lewis had written to former pupil Bede Griffiths, the great propagator of Christian-Hindu dialogue, explaining his dedication of *The Problem of Pain* to the Inklings. Lewis listed them as Charles Williams, Hugo Dyson of Reading University, and his brother, Warren (all Anglicans), and Tolkien and Lewis's doctor, Havard (both Roman Catholics like Griffiths). Though not listed as Inklings by Lewis, Adam Fox, Charles Wrenn, and Nevill Coghill had attended meetings, and Owen Barfield put in an occasional appearance when he could get away from London. During the war and afterwards several new members joined, including Christopher Tolkien, John Wain (1925–94), the poet and novelist, and Roger Lancelyn Green (1918–87), the children's author.

The Inklings continued throughout the war years with their familiar pattern of two types of meetings, the literary gatherings usually in Lewis's rooms in Magdalen, and the more informal meetings in a public house such as The Eagle and Child. Lewis wrote: "My happiest hours are spent with three or four old friends in old clothes tramping together and putting up in small pubs — or else sitting up till the small hours in someone's college rooms talking nonsense, poetry, theology, metaphysics over beer, tea and pipes."

Lewis gives the flavor of a typical Thursday night literary meeting in a letter to an absent member — his brother — in November 1939. "On

Thursday we had a meeting of the Inklings . . . we dined at the Eastgate. I have never in my life seen Dyson so exuberant — 'A roaring cataract of nonsense.' The bill of fare afterwards consisted of a section of the new Hobbit book from Tolkien, a nativity play from Williams (unusually intelligible for him, and approved by all), and a chapter out of the book on the Problem of Pain from me." The piece read by Tolkien at this time may have been a reworked section of Book One of *The Fellowship of the Ring* — he was making momentous changes relating, among other things, to the nature of the ring and the identity of Aragorn. Whatever the piece it must have touched upon the nature of evil, as Lewis remarks later in his letter that the subject-matter of the readings that evening "formed almost a logical sequence." His own chapter likely enough touched on this theme, as Williams's play — *The House by the Stable* — concerns the battle to win the human soul to evil, effectively presenting the inverse perspective of hell. Two allegorical characters, Pride, in the form of a pretty woman, and Hell, her brother, seek to elicit the precious jewel of the soul from the breast of Man. The proceedings are interrupted by the figures of Joseph and Mary seeking shelter for the night.

This pattern of literary and informal meetings continued until, on one Thursday evening in October 1949, Warren and Lewis waited in vain for friends to arrive at his college rooms. The drinks were ready and the fire lit. Simply no one turned up. This effectively marked the end of the Inklings as a reading group, even though the friends continued to meet informally on Tuesdays (and sometimes Mondays) at The Eagle and Child, or other favorite pubs, until the year of Lewis's death.

According to John Wain, after Charles Williams's sudden death in 1945, which was a grievous blow to the Inklings, the two most active members became once more Tolkien and Lewis. Wain writes that "While C. S. Lewis attacked [the whole current of contemporary art and life] on a wide front, with broadcasts, popular-theological books, children's stories, romances, and controversial literary criticism, Tolkien concentrated on the writing of his colossal 'Lord of the Rings' trilogy. His readings of each successive installment were eagerly received, for 'romance' was a pillar of this whole structure." Writers admired by Tolken and Lewis ("the literary household gods" of the group, Wain calls them) included George

MacDonald, William Morris ("selectively"), and E. R. Eddison, who attended the Inklings on a couple of occasions. These fantasy writers all had in common the fact that they *invented.* According to Wain, "Lewis considered 'fine fabling' an essential part of literature, and never lost a chance to push any author, from Spenser to Rider Haggard, who would be called a romancer." Wain pointed out that, during the time he was involved with the Inklings (from around 1944 or 1945 to 1946), he was surprised by the "unexpected alliances" it was capable of forming. Yet he felt that the key to this unexpectedness lay in Lewis's character: "Lewis . . . is basically a humble man. While he will fight long and hard for his beliefs, he is entirely free of the pride which refuses reinforcement for the sake of keeping within its hands the sole glory of conquer or, if need be, of heroic defeat." The "unexpected alliances" included Dorothy L. Sayers, the children's author Roger Lancelyn Green, and the poet Roy Campbell. Wain concluded, "Lewis, during these years, had very much the mentality of a partisan leader: anyone who would skirmish against the enemy — the drab, unbelieving, sneering, blinkered modern world — should be his brother, be he ne'er so vile."

It is clear from Tolkien's *Letters* that the Inklings provided valuable and much-needed encouragement as he struggled to compose *The Lord of the Rings.* This sadly came to an end when, around the spring of 1947, Dyson started exercising a veto against the reading of further installments (though Tolkien continued to read when Dyson was absent). Legend has it that Dyson was tired of constantly hearing about elves. Clearly, he had not the interest in and was not in sympathy with Tolkien's unfolding epic, unlike Lewis, Williams, and the other Inklings (unless some kept a polite silence). Less than three years after Dyson began to veto Tolkien's reading, the literary meetings of the group foundered. Warren Lewis records one such silencing of Tolkien in his diary: "A well attended Inkling this evening — both the Tolkiens, J[ack] and I, Humphrey, Gervase, Hugo; the latter came in just as we were starting on the '[new] Hobbit,' and as he now exercises a veto in it — most unfairly I think — we had to stop." Without the chance to read his installments to the Inklings, Tolkien needed the encouragement of Lewis more than ever to complete the writing of *The Lord of the Rings.*

9

A Professor's Wardrobe and Magic Rings

(1949–1954)

It is a bright morning in 1949, fresh from a spring shower. The light brings out, in sharp relief, Oxford's towers, turrets, and spires to advantage. Merton College's deputy librarian, Roger Lancelyn Green, walks past the Porter's Lodge and out into Merton Street. He almost collides with Tolkien as he adjusts to the light.

"Hello, Professor," the young man greets.

He hears a fleeting and mumbled "hello," as Tolkien passes him by.

Roger Lancelyn Green is struck once more about how odd Tolkien could be — he could be miles away in a world of his own. They had met at several Inklings meetings. Roger is one of its youngest members and finds Tolkien invariably cordial. He remembers vividly meeting Tolkien together with Dyson and Jack Lewis for a drink while researching his B.Litt. and how the four talked intensively for a long time. In fact, Tolkien supervised him for a whole term on his thesis — "Andrew Lang and the Fairy Tale."

A few days later the two encounter each other again at the Merton College entrance.

"Er, hello, Professor," Roger greets, hesitating.

"Roger!" exclaims Tolkien. "So very good to see you." He flings his arm around Green's shoulders. "Come and have a drink." Roger is quickly propelled to a convenient pub.

As they sit at a small table, and Tolkien kindles his pipe comfortably, the Professor looks knowingly at Roger with a twinkle in his bright eyes.

"I hear you've been reading Lewis's children's story. It really won't do, you know! I mean to say — 'Nymphs and their Ways, The Love-Life of a Faun.' Doesn't he know what he's talking about?"

Though Tolkien is parodying slightly Roger nonetheless feels uncomfortable. He knows Tolkien is more bothered with what he sees as a serious error of taste than he lets on. Roger has been delighted to read the manuscript about Aslan and the land of Narnia but he can see Tolkien's point. He tried his best to persuade Lewis to drop Father Christmas. His sudden appearance in the story seems to break the magic. Roger knows Lewis took his objection seriously because he clearly liked a children's story of his that he had shown him — indeed, it helped inspire Lewis's very first Narnia story. But his plea made no impression. Lewis remained adamant that Santa should stay.

"The truth is," Tolkien confides, leaning over the table towards Roger, "Jack and I don't always see eye-to-eye about our work. Not all of the 'new Hobbit' is within the range of his sympathy. Mind you, he's enormously encouraging — always has been. He's been wet-eyed at times as the story's progressed. He thinks, you know, there's too much of hobbits and their ways at the beginning." He ends his short speech in a soft voice.

Roger is a little tongue-tied, if the reality be known. Lewis's comments about the new hobbit story rang in his memory — he had positively glowed about Tolkien's sequel. He had said something to the effect that to read *The Hobbit* was really only to paddle in the glorious sea of Tolkien. There was so much more. Roger himself had not heard Tolkien read any of his new story. He had not attended many Inklings, and when he did Dyson had interrupted any suggestion by Tolkien to read a latest chapter. Roger suspected that he was rather hurt by this veto.

The talk then passes to safer, other things — the Merton library, Tolkien's desire to move to a better house slightly closer to Merton College, the Communist advances in China, his plans to finish *The Lord of the Rings* that summer. Tolkien also asks Roger about his wife, June — they had recently married — and how his writing is going.

The two men part, Tolkien heading for Merton, and Green walking slowly up High Street. He thinks back to Lewis's story about the magical world of Narnia.

The first Green had known about it was when, one evening, a few weeks previously, Lewis had mentioned to him that he had been working on a children's book. He added: "I don't know if it's any good. My question is — shall I go on with it? You see, Tolkien doesn't like it. I read the first two chapters and he made it very clear that he didn't approve of the story. May I read you the first chapters? See what you think."

Lewis and Green had walked to his rooms at Magdalen College. There Lewis read to him the first three chapters of what was to become *The Lion, the Witch and the Wardrobe*. As Green listened, a feeling of awe came over him — he distinctly felt that he was listening to one of the great children's books of the world for the first time. He had read such books widely for his thesis and for a study he had written, *Tellers of Tales*, about the tradition of children's literature, a book admired by Lewis. It was as if he had heard *The Wind in the Willows* read to him for the first time by its author.

"Well?" Lewis had asked, studiously drawing at his pipe. "It it really worth going on with?"

"Rather!" replied Green, without hesitation.

Shortly after that meeting Lewis had handed Green a manuscript, the first of a series of Narnian stories he was to read in Lewis's small, reasonably neat handwriting.

Tolkien had moved to the Merton Chair of English Language and Literature back in 1945. This involved special responsibility for Middle English up to A.D. 1500. He had held the Chair in Anglo-Saxon for twenty years. The move reflected his wider interests, particularly the language and literature of the West Midlands. With the new Chair, as was the custom, he became a Fellow of Merton College though he had no responsibility to tutor undergraduates, as his friend Lewis did. Tolkien soon settled into his new college and, when later in the year, a second Merton English Chair became vacant, his immediate wish was that it would go to Lewis. "It ought to be C. S. Lewis," he said at the time, "or perhaps Lord David

Cecil, but one never knows." Tolkien as an elector for the Chair had a considerable sway, but his friend was passed over in favor of F. P. Wilson, Lewis's old English tutor.

The sudden death of Charles Williams in May 1945 had not fully restored the old intimacy between Lewis and Tolkien; while the latter felt Williams's loss keenly he still felt that Lewis was too taken with him. The continuing influence of Williams on Lewis after his death, reinforced by Tolkien's dislike of Lewis's popular theology, stood between them.

With the friendship remaining somewhat cool Tolkien perhaps found it harder to accept Lewis's well-meant criticisms of *The Lord of the Rings* (particularly the poetry in its pages), despite the enormous encouragement his friend exercised. This however did not distract Tolkien from his resolve to place his friend in a Chair — if not the Merton Professorship, then another. Though he considered Lewis's popularizing of theology a flaw in his friend's output he did not sympathize with a general hostility to Lewis in the Oxford hierarchy, reflected in passing over Lewis for the Merton Chair and perhaps in a later failure to give him the Professorship of Poetry in 1951. In fact, he was grateful to his friend as a close ally in the reforms he had accomplished in the syllabus of the Oxford English School. Tolkien was, however, concerned with the speed at which Lewis produced his Narnian Chronicles (it was to be seven in as many years), in what he regarded as a slapdash manner. He had toiled over his *The Lord of the Rings* far longer than that, drawn on by his vision of sub-creation — the making of a consistent secondary world of the imagination. While Lewis seemed at one with him in this view of fantasy, Narnia as a world did not reflect the loving care taken over the creation of Middle-earth. Furthermore, Tolkien, like his friend, had struggled over the need to create fairy stories for an adult readership. Though it was valid to write children's fairy stories, the battle, Tolkien felt, was really to establish heroic fantasy and romance as contemporary adult literature. He had felt that Lewis's *That Hideous Strength* had failed to do this because of the unfortunate influence of Charles Williams upon its plot, and now Lewis had turned to children's writing. Tolkien, however, was wrong if he inferred that Lewis was withdrawing from the battle to establish fantasy for grown-ups. Lewis was in fact following his instincts as a communicator; he did not share

Tolkien's purism. He later explained that he wrote "a children's story because a children's story is the best art-form for something you have to say."

Lewis did essentially agree with Tolkien about fantasy as an adult form of storytelling. Writing about *The Lord of the* Rings in 1955, when the final volume was published, Lewis commented in a letter that he continued unfailingly to be delighted when his belief was justified that the fairy story is actually an adult genre, not a children's one, and that an audience exists that is starved for such books.

In hindsight Lewis's children's writing was clearly not a regression, despite fears Tolkien may have had. The Narnian stories complete a developing process of an imaginative communication of Christian and older, premodern values — what Lewis and Tolkien thought of as Old Western values — that began with *The Pilgrim's Regress*. After that first fiction Lewis's skills dramatically improved in writing his science fiction trilogy, beginning with *Out of the Silent Planet* and ending with the less successful but nevertheless powerful *That Hideous Strength*. Lewis like Tolkien was very interested in the imaginative possibilities of the science fiction genre. Then partly through reading in the 1940s Roger Lancelyn Green's story, "The Wood That Time Forgot" (never published), and partly through having the right pictures in his head, Lewis bounded like Aslan into Narnia. He felt that the genre of children's stories, like science fiction, gave him a better platform for what he wanted to say as a Christian communicator than even his immensely popular broadcast talks. He saw the same limitations with *The Problem of Pain* (1940) and *Miracles* (1947). Though masterly, and continuing today to have appeal and theological significance, these books limited what the primary "imaginative man" in Lewis wished to communicate.

Ironically the writing of the Narnian Chronicles owes a very great deal to Tolkien. He had persistently argued for and demonstrated an allusive approach to Christian communication. His views, as always, deeply influenced his friend. Lewis knew that Tolkien did not really approve of his popular theology. However, after the plain-language broadcast talks, Lewis's theological message gradually demanded more of its readers; *Miracles*, Lewis's best and most representative theological work, is considerably more intellectual than *Mere Christianity* (the published broadcast talks). Lewis argued the points raised in one chapter with a leading and sympathetic contemporary philosopher, Elizabeth Anscombe. This debate confirmed Lewis's view that modern philosophical writing was for an increasingly specialist audience. After this he took a much more indirect approach to Christian communication. He followed in the spirit of Tolkien, even if not in the letter (Tolkien nevertheless continued to disapprove of Lewis's theologizing). This allusiveness applied to further works of lay theology, *The Four Loves, Reflections on the Psalms, A Grief Observed,* and *Letters to Malcolm: Chiefly on Prayer,* as well as to *The Chronicles of Narnia* and a work of fiction that he regarded as one of his best, *Till We Have Faces,* which, like *The Lord of the Rings,* is a convincing fairy tale for adults in a pagan, pre-Christian setting.

One of Tolkien's central criticisms of Lewis's Narnian stories was that they were too allegorical, too literally representative of Christian doctrine. Though Lewis did insert many pointers to what he calls "secondary meanings" in Narnia, his intention was not to write allegory. He saw the Narnian stories as arising out of what he called a "supposal" — his "supposal" was a world of talking animals — that set the frame of the stories. He explained this in a letter shortly before he died: "The Narnian series is not exactly allegory. I'm not saying 'Let us represent in terms of Märchen [fairy tale] the *actual* story of this world.' Rather 'supposing the Narnian world, let us guess what form the activities in the [scheme of things] a Creator, Redeemer or Judge might take there.' This, you see, overlaps with allegory but is not quite the same."

This inventive process, rather than a consciously didactic one, explains the significance of pictures that Lewis formed in his mind. His imaginative works, he tells us, invariably began with unbidden pictures (just as, with Tolkien, stories usually sprang from words, phrases, and names that emerged in his mind). The first Narnian story began with a vivid mental picture of a faun in a snowy wood carrying a parcel — the image had first come to him, he tells us, when he was a young man of about sixteen. A further ingredient was the landscapes of his childhood. These included the Mourne mountains of County Down, the green countryside at their northeastern feet and beyond, with its drumlins and undulating fields and woods, and the wild, bleak moors and rugged coastline of County Antrim. These were Narnia and its environs, just as the West Midlands of Tolkien's childhood was the model for The Shire. Significantly, on an occasion when he longed to visit Northern Ireland but was confined by the illness of an aging Mrs. Moore, he spoke in a letter of Ulster as his "ain countrie," thinking of the hills of County Down and the coastline of County Antrim. In later years, Warren Lewis would share with Walter Hooper, on a vacation in Ireland, his belief that Narnia had to a great extent been based on a distant view of the Mountains of Mourne across County Down from Carlingford, with the coastline nearby.

The Chronicles of Narnia are seven tales that cover almost half of the twentieth century and over two and a half millennia of Narnian history from its creation to its final days. In order of Narnian chronology the titles are: *The Magician's Nephew* (1955); *The Lion, the Witch and the Wardrobe* (1950); *The Horse and his Boy* (1954); *Prince Caspian: The Return to Narnia* (1951); *The Voyage of the Dawn Treader* (1952); *The Silver Chair* (1953); and *The Last Battle* (1956). Many readers prefer to start with *The Lion, the Witch and the Wardrobe* (the first Narnian story Lewis wrote) because of its simplicity, magical power, and for the way it sets up the basic "supposals" from which Lewis created all the stories and the world of Narnia.

Because of the time anomalies, the children who are drawn into Narnia on a number of occasions find themselves at various points in its history, and thus we get a picture of the entire history of Narnia from its creation to its unmaking and the new creation of all worlds.

Narnia's original creation is recounted in *The Magician's Nephew.* Digory Kirke and Polly Plummer, after entering the old and dying world of Charn through a pool in the Wood between the Worlds, find their way by accident into a land of Nothing. Here, gradually, Narnia is created before their eyes by the song of Aslan, the talking lion and ruler of Narnia. (Narnia is a land of talking animals.) Unfortunately Digory brings evil into that paradisiac world in the form of Jadis, destroyer of Charn, whom he had previously awakened there. Jadis goes off to the fringes of Narnia, but reappears in later ages as the White Witch who puts a spell over

Narnia of a winter that never comes to Christmas. The arrival of four evacuee children — Peter, Susan, Edmund, and Lucy Pevensie — through the Wardrobe (told in *The Lion, the Witch and the Wardrobe*) coincides with the return of Aslan and the beginning of the end of the witch's curse. Aslan's death on behalf of Edmund, and his return to life by a deeper law than the one by which Jadis operates her magic, leads to her defeat and death. Narnia's Golden Age follows.

With the return of the Pevensie children to our world, Narnia slowly falls into disorder. The Telmarines, humans led by Caspian the First, occupy the land and silence the talking beasts and trees. (The Telmarines had stumbled by accident into Narnia.) "Old Narnia" only survives under cover as those faithful to Aslan keep the faith alive that he will return. *Prince Caspian* (his story is told in the book of that name), brought up by his wicked Uncle Miraz and Aunt Prunaprismia, who have deposed his father Caspian the Ninth, learns of the myth of Old Narnia and longs for it to be true. He escapes a plot to kill him and joins forces with the old Narnians. In the nick of time, help comes from the four Pevensie children drawn back into Narnia.

He becomes Caspian the Tenth after adventures at sea recounted in *The Voyage of the Dawn Treader*. His son, Prince Rilian, is kidnapped and held in servitude in an underworld for ten years by a witch of the line of Jadis. She plots to take over Narnia using him as a puppet king. As told in the chronicle of *The Silver Chair*, he is rescued by two cousins of the Pevensie children, Eustace Scrubb and Jill Pole, who are brought into Narnia for this task.

After many ages the last King of Narnia, Tirian, and indeed Narnia itself are threatened by a devilish plot which uses a counterfeit Aslan and links up with the Calormene forces (southerners who are a constant threat to Narnia's security). This is Narnia's darkest hour. As told in *The Last Battle*, Tirian prays for help from the sons and daughters of Adam, and Aslan brings Eustace and Jill to his aid. Aslan himself finally intervenes and dissolves the whole world. This turns out to be a beginning rather than an end as the new Narnia is revealed.

The first story, *The Lion, the Witch and the Wardrobe*, was published in 1950. On June 22 that year, at an Inklings meeting at the Eagle and Child pub attended by Roger Lancelyn Green, Lewis passed around the proofs. A month later he had completed the manuscript of *The Horse and His Boy,* the story which follows on from *The Lion, the Witch and the Wardrobe.* The other books were written in quick succession.

Aslan (Turkish for "lion") is the unifying symbol of all the stories. Aslan is intended to represent Christ, but not as an allegorical figure. In Narnia he appears not as a man but, appropriately, as a Narnian talking lion. The symbol of the lion (a traditional image of authority) perhaps owes something to Williams's novel *The Place of the Lion.* In his *The Problem of Pain* Lewis wrote, "I think the lion, when he has ceased to be dangerous, will still be awful." As a child, significantly, Lewis attended St. Mark's (Anglican) Church in Dundela, on the outskirts of Belfast. The traditional symbol of St. Mark is the lion, a fact reinforced by the name of the church's magazine in later years, *The Lion.*

The children who visit Narnia soon discover that Aslan is not a tame lion. In *The Problem of Pain* Lewis had put a value on the taming of animals, a point Evelyn Underhill took issue with, in an otherwise appreciative letter to him in 1941.

Where . . . I do find it impossible to follow you, is in your chapter on animals. "The tame animal is in the deepest sense the only natural animal . . . the beasts are to be understood only in their relation to man and through man to God." This seems to me frankly an intolerable doctrine and a frightful exaggeration of what is involved in the primacy of man. Is the cow which we have turned into a milk machine or the hen we have turned into an egg machine really nearer the mind of God than its wild ancestor? . . . Your own example of the good-man, good-wife, and good-dog in the good homestead is a bit smug and utilitarian, don't you think, over against the wild beauty of God's creative action in the jungle and deep sea? . . . When my cat goes off on her own occasions I'm sure she goes with God — but I do not feel so sure of her theological position when she is sitting on the best chair before the drawing-room fire. Perhaps what it all comes to is this, that I feel your concept of God would be improved by just a touch of wildness. But please do not take this impertinent remark too seriously.

Evelyn Underhill's remarks about a quality of wildness in animals may have caused Lewis to rethink his position somewhat, and perhaps allowed Aslan and the talking animals of Narnia to come bounding into the early draft of the story. Aslan perhaps provided just that touch of wildness (associated with pagan insights) to Lewis's theology.

⟨⌥⟩

As Narnia came into being, *The Lord of the Rings* drew near to its completion, to Tolkien's great satisfaction. It had proved a long, painstaking task. The writing and overall revision for internal coherence was completed by the fall of 1949. Only the extensive appendices remained. Tolkien recalled in a BBC interview: "I remember I actually wept at the denouement. But then of course there was a tremendous lot of revision. I typed the whole of that work out twice and lots of it many times, on a bed in an attic [in Manor Road]. I couldn't afford of course the typing." He sent the typescript to Lewis, who responded: "All the long years you have spent on it are justified." Much of the final writing and revision for consistency was accomplished in the tranquility of the Oratory School in Berkshire, which had moved from its original location in Birmingham. Tolkien stayed there in a master's room for much of the long vacation in the summer of 1949. It was a fitting environment for his task — part of his childhood had been spent in the vicinity of the Oratory School.

Publication by George Allen & Unwin was to be delayed for a number of years for complex reasons. The main reason was Tolkien's wish to publish the still unfinished "The Silmarillion" at the same time. Late in 1949 Tolkien had sent Milton Waldman at William Collins a large manuscript, much of it hand-written, of the unfinished work. In February the next year Waldman expressed an interest in "The Silmarillion," but later Collins changed its mind when the full implications of trying to publish the vast work became clearer. Perhaps the only benefit of this unfortunate delay was that in 1951 Tolkien wrote a ten-thousand-word letter to Waldman explaining "The Silmarillion," a document that is one of the best keys to the work. Eventually, on June 22, 1952, Tolkien offered *The Lord of the Rings* unconditionally to George Allen & Unwin — who were enthusiastic and sent Raynor Unwin, Stanley Unwin's son, to Oxford to pick up the original, and only, manuscript on September 9, 1952. Because of its length it was decided to publish the book in three parts. The first two volumes — *The Fellowship of the Ring* and *The Two Towers* — were published on July 29, 1954, and November 11, 1954, respectively, with the final volume — *The Return of the King* — appearing the next year, on October 20, 1955. Tolkien wearily admitted to his publisher, Stanley Unwin, how much he had given of himself in writing *The Lord of the Rings*. "It is," he said, "written in my life-blood, such as that is, thick or thin; and I can no other." In November 1952 Tolkien signed a contract for the book which specified a share in any profits rather than the usual percentage royalty of sales. This was because the publishers expected the ambitious publication to take a loss! When the first edition eventually appeared it bore the simple dedication "To the Inklings."

In 1952, before he submitted the trilogy to Unwin, Tolkien had taken a vacation in the town of Malvern, in Worcestershire, with his friend George Sayer, who was the English Master at Malvern College. To entertain him in the evening Sayer pulled out an early-model tape recorder. This was new to Tolkien. To cast out any devil that might be lurking in it he asked, no doubt with a twinkle in his eye, if he could record the Lord's Prayer in the ancient Gothic language he loved. When he heard the result he was delighted and requested if he might record some of the poems from *The Lord of the Rings*. The more he recorded, the more his confidence grew. The experience appealed to his taste for the theatrical.

Sayer had met Tolkien before in Malvern, on a hiking vacation with Lewis and his brother Warnie. The brothers liked to hike on the hills and had persuaded Tolkien on that occasion to join them. After Mrs. Moore's death in 1951, they were able to get away from Oxford much more easily. Tolkien, they found, tended to walk slowly, taking in the details of the countryside, whereas the others wished to press on. Sayer remembers that

it was easy to entertain [Tolkien] by day. He and I tramped the Malvern Hills which he had often seen during his boyhood in

Birmingham or from his brother's house on the other side of the Severn River valley. He lived the book as we walked, sometimes comparing parts of the hills with, for instance, the White Mountains of Gondor. We drove to the Black Mountains on the borders of Wales, picked bilberries and climbed through the heather there. We picnicked on bread and cheese and apples, and washed them down with perry, beer or cider. When we saw signs of industrial pollution, he talked of orcs and orcery. At home he helped me to garden. Characteristically what he liked most was to cultivate a very small area, say a square yard, extremely well.

Among the endorsements for *The Lord of the Rings* on the dust jacket was one from Lewis:

If Ariosto rivalled it in invention (in fact he does not) he would still lack its heroic seriousness. No imaginary world has been projected which is at once multifarious and so true to its own inner laws; none so seemingly objective, so disinfected from the taint of an author's merely individual psychology; none so relevant to the actual human situation yet so free from allegory. And what fine shading there is in the variations of style to meet the almost endless diversity of scenes and characters — comic, homely, epic, monstrous, or diabolic.

Both Tolkien and his publisher feared that using Lewis was a risk, especially with his arcane reference to Ariosto, alluding to his *Orlando Furioso,* and they were not surprised at the reaction of some reviewers to the first two volumes. In a letter to Raynor Unwin on September 9, 1954, Tolkien spoke about the remarkable animosity, as he saw it, that Lewis excited "in certain quarters." Lewis, he said, had warned him many years before that his support might do Tolkien as much harm as good. He had not taken his point until now. However, he told his publisher, he wished to be associated with Lewis despite any negative reaction to his endorsement. It was only because of Lewis's friendship and support that he struggled to the end of the labor of writing *The Lord of the Rings.* Tolkien remarked that many reviewers had preferred lampooning Lewis's endorsement or his review in *Time and Tide* to reading the book. The Lewis review began enthusiastically, "This book is like lightning from a clear sky." It was, Lewis added, "the conquest of new territory."

As a work of literature, the merits and demerits of *The Lord of the Rings* have been extensively discussed by scholars and countless readers and continue to this day to divide the critics. Among its admirers was W. H. Auden, whose *New York Times* review of *The Return of the King* on January 22, 1956, begins:

In "The Return of the King," Frodo Baggins fulfills his Quest, the realm of Sauron is ended forever, the Third Age is over and J. R. R. Tolkien's trilogy "The Lord of the Rings" complete. I rarely remember a book about which I have had such violent arguments. Nobody *seems* to have a moderate opinion: either, like myself, people find it a masterpiece of its genre or they cannot abide it, and among the hostile there are some, I must confess, for whose literary judgment I have great respect. A few of these may have been put off by the first forty pages of the first chapter of the first volume in which the daily life of the hobbits is described; this is light comedy and light comedy is not Mr. Tolkien's forte. In most cases, however, the objection must go far deeper. I can only suppose that some people object to Heroic Quests and Imaginary Worlds on principle; such, they feel, cannot be anything but light "escapist" reading. That a man like Mr. Tolkien, the English philologist who teaches at Oxford, should lavish such incredible pains upon a genre which is, for them, trifling by definition, is, therefore, very shocking.

One mark of the quality of *The Lord of the Rings* as literature is its linguistic basis. Tolkien makes use of his invented languages in names, and also in imaginative possibility. Language is the basis of the background mythology. Another mark of its literary quality is Tolkien's success in integrating the wealth of symbolism in his work. Quest, the journey, sacrifice, healing, death, and many other symbolic elements are beautifully realized in the book. The very landscapes through which the travelers pass are symbolic, suggesting moods that correspond to the stage of the journey, and to the phase of the overall story. The terrors of Moria, the archetypal underworld, for example, contrast with the spiritual refreshment of Lórien. Always, these landscapes are fully part of the movement of the book, aesthetically shaped and integrated. Tolkien's greatest achievement, however, might well be the embodiment of living myth in literature, with its varied applicability to its reader. He shared this ability with George MacDonald.

The Lord of the Rings is a heroic romance, telling of the quest to destroy the one, ruling ring of power before it can fall into the hands of its maker, Sauron, the dark lord of the book's title. As a consistent, unified story, it stands independently of the invented mythology and historical chronicles of Middle-earth recorded in "The Silmarillion." Events of the past provide a backdrop and haunting dimension to the story.

The basic storyline of *The Lord of the Rings* begins as Gandalf, the wizard, discovers that the Ring found by the hobbit Bilbo (as told in *The Hobbit*) is in fact the One Ring, controlling the Rings of Power forged in the Second Age in Eregion. Frodo, who inherits the Ring from his uncle Bilbo, flees from the comfort of The Shire with his companions. On his trail are the Black Riders sent from the evil realm of Mordor by Sauron. With the help of the Ranger, Aragorn, they succeed in reaching the security of Rivendell, one of the few Elven kingdoms remaining in Middle-earth. There Elrond of Rivendell holds a great Council where it is decided that the Ring must be destroyed, and that Frodo should be the Ring-bearer. The Company of the Ring is also chosen to help him on the desperate quest. Led by Gandalf, they are the four hobbits Frodo, Sam, Merry, and Pippin; the men Aragorn and Boromir; the elf Legolas; and the dwarf Gimli. The Ring can only be destroyed in the Mountain of Fire, Mount Doom, in Mordor, whence it was made.

Frustrated in their attempt to cross the Misty Mountains in the snow, the Company is led by Gandalf into the underground mines of Moria, once worked by dwarves. Here dwells a dreadful Balrog, a spirit of the underworld from the dawn of creation. Gandalf, in great sacrifice, gives his life fighting the evil spirit to allow the others to escape. The Company is led on by Aragorn, revealed as the secret heir of the ancient Kings of the West. They pass through the blessed Elven realm of Lórien and then down the great River Anduin. The creature Gollum — encountered by

Bilbo long before, and once a hobbit — is by now on their trail, seeking back his lost Ring.

Boromir tries to seize the Ring by force to use against the enemy. A party of orcs attack, killing Boromir as he defends Frodo's hobbit friends, Merry and Pippin. Frodo and his loyal companion Sam have, by now, parted from the rest of the Company, heading east towards their destination, Mordor. The remainder of the Company follow the track of the orcs who have captured Merry and Pippin, going westwards.

The story now follows the progress of Frodo and Sam, and the others remaining in the Company, in parallel.

After the capture of Merry and Pippin by orcs, they are tracked by Aragorn, Legolas the elf, and Gimli the dwarf to the Forest of Fangorn, where the two hobbits are hiding after escaping the orcs. In the Forest, the hobbits meet Treebeard, guardian of the woodland. He is an Ent, a tree creature. The Ents assault and capture Isengard, the stronghold of the traitor, Saruman, like Gandalf a wizard. Here the hobbits are reunited with the others of the Company, as well as Gandalf, returned from the dead.

Joining the forces of Théoden, the aged king of Rohan, most of the Company move towards the ancient city of Minas Tirith, now under threat from Sauron's forces. Aragorn, Legolas, and Gimli, however, pass through the Paths of the Dead to gather the spirits of long-dead warriors bound by a dreadful oath. These they lead southwards to attack the enemy there.

In the parallel story, Frodo and Sam move slowly towards Mordor, now led by the treacherous Gollum, intent on betrayal, yet held back by the rags of his lost nature. Finding the main entrance to Mordor impassible, Frodo accepts Gollum's offer to show them a secret entrance. There he leads them into the giant spider Shelob's Lair. After many perils (including the near death of Frodo) the two make their hopeless way to Mount Doom. At the final moment Frodo cannot throw the Ring into the Cracks of Doom. Gollum bites off the ring finger but falls to his death with the Ring. The quest is over. As Mordor disintegrates, and the wraith of Sauron fades, Frodo and Sam are rescued by eagles and reunited with their friends, where they are hailed as heroes.

Without the destruction of the Ring, the alliance against the dark powers of Mordor would have failed. Though there was no certainty of the success of the quest of Frodo and Sam, the people of Gondor and Rohan, and the other allies, were prepared to fight to the death against the dreadful enemy.

The story ends with the gradual healing of the land, preparing the way for the domination of humankind, now free from the threat of slavery. The fading of the elves is complete as the last ships pass over the sea to the Undying Lands of the West. Joining the elves are the Ring-bearers Bilbo and Frodo. Sam follows later, after a happy life in The Shire, with his beloved Rosie.

The story completed, at last, Tolkien was able to return more fully to his painstaking work on "The Silmarillion." He continued his quiet life as an Oxford Professor, overseeing postgraduates, teaching in the university English School, and giving an occasional public lecture. He traveled to Ireland as an external examiner for the Catholic University and to Belgium for a conference. He enjoyed his domestic life with Edith, and continued to focus upon the inner world of imagination, memory, and language. Nothing much happened to him, outwardly, unlike Lewis — to whom things were always happening.

10

Surprised by Cambridge and Disappointed by Joy

(1954–1963)

Early on the evening of May 17, 1954, Tolkien calls to Edith as he enters his ordinary, tidy house on Sandfield Road in Headington, an Oxford suburb. Edith has just finished playing a complicated piece on the piano despite the arthritis that torments her joints. "I'm going to ring Jack about going over to see him. You know, about this Cambridge business." He has emerged from the jumble of his converted garage where he makes his "office," has his books, and dreams.

He picks up the black Bakelite receiver and dials a short number.

"Sewage Disposal Plant," comes an unmistakable voice at the other end.

"Jack, Ronald Tolkien here. I need to talk to you, urgently. May I come over now?"

"About the Cambridge Chair? Yes, do. I'll ask Warnie to brew some tea."

"I'll be with you in about half an hour."

When Tolkien's taxi pulls up on the drive outside The Kilns, Lewis, who has been waiting, opens the door. There is quite a wind blowing up, and as he climbs out of the taxi Tolkien pulls his coat around him. Because of the heavy sky, night is settling in early and a welcome light falls from within.

"Come in, Tollers. Warnie — our guest has arrived!" As he calls to Warren, Lewis opens the living room door, and a light cloud of smoke drifts out. The room has a snug fugginess that Tolkien knows the brothers like. Pipe fumes battle with occasional gusts of heavy coal smoke from a struggling grate, obviously just replenished. Though late spring, it is cold this evening.

As Tolkien enters and greets Warren, who has risen unsteadily from his armchair with hand outstretched, he notices once again the peeling wallpaper and the dreary furniture. There is the usual smell of alcohol around Lewis's brother. Tolkien hasn't been to The Kilns for a long time. He smiles to himself as he remembers Dyson's dub for The Kilns — "The Midden." But the obvious, settled contentment of the Lewis brothers, after the tense years of Mrs. Moore's final decline, soon pushes thoughts of the décor aside. Though she has been dead over three years now, Tolkien half expects her to call from the kitchen.

"Take a seat, Tollers, while I fetch the tea," invites Warren, smiling. He is one of the most courteous men Tolkien knows. Though portly like Jack, Warnie's facial features are quite different, more rotund. Had Tolkien seen a photograph of their long-dead parents, he might have recognized that Jack resembles their father almost uncannily, with Warren being more like their mother.

The three settle themselves into the armchairs and Tolkien lights his pipe. Warnie hands him a large cup of tea, and another to Lewis, who likes nothing better. Lewis takes a sip and then quickly places the cup back in its saucer. He turns to Tolkien.

"You know, of course, that I had to decline the Cambridge Chair. Can't see how I could leave The Kilns, and I had already encouraged Smithers to apply. I can't go back on that. The invitation was totally unexpected — I hadn't even applied."

"That's what I want to talk to you about, Jack. You see, I can fill in some details which might well make you see things differently."

"I wanted Jack to take it," interrupts Warren. "He should've had a Chair years ago. Damned Oxford keeps on passing him over. It's left to Cambridge to offer him one!"

When Tolkien leaves The Kilns later that evening he is exultant. With a little help from Warren he has persuaded Lewis to write again to Cambridge, even though he had declined the newly created Chair not once, but twice, in the face of the Vice Chancellor's persistence. Fred Paxford, handyman at The Kilns, has offered to drive him home, and Tolkien can hear strains of "Rock of Ages cleft for me" from the direction of his wooden bungalow. The singing gets louder as Paxford approaches the car....

In her lengthy obituary of Lewis for the British Academy, in 1965, Dame Helen Gardner (1908–86), who knew him well, perceptively reflected on why he had been a prophet without honor in his own country.

In the early 1940s, when I returned to Oxford as a tutor, Lewis was by far the most impressive and exciting person in the Faculty of English. He had behind him a major work of literary history; he filled the largest lecture-room available for his lectures; and the Socratic Club, which he founded and over which he presided, for the free discussion of religious and philosophic questions, was one of the most flourishing and influential of undergraduate societies. In spite of this, when the Merton Professorship of English Literature fell vacant in 1946, the electors passed him over and recalled his own old tutor, F. P. Wilson, from London to fill the Chair. In doing so they probably had the support of many, if not a majority, of the Faculty; for by this time a suspicion had arisen that Lewis was so committed to what he himself called "hot-gospelling" that he would have had little time for the needs of what had become a very large undergraduate school and for the problems of organization and supervision presented by the rapidly growing numbers of research students in English Literature. In addition, a good many people thought that shoemakers should stick to their lasts and disliked the thought of a professor of English Literature winning fame as an amateur theologian; and, while undoubtedly there were a good many people in Oxford who disliked Christian apologetics *per se*, there were others who were uneasy at Lewis's particular kind of apologetic, disliking both its method and its manner. These last considerations were probably the strongest, and accounted for the fact that when, in the following year, a second

Chair in English Literature was established his name was again not put forward.

Helen Gardner also mentioned as significant Lewis's failure to gain the Oxford Professorship of Poetry in 1951, despite huge support from his faculty.

Why then was Lewis honored instead by Cambridge, whose English School had attracted his heavy guns on many occasions? Cambridge undoubtedly remained constant to the ethos it had established in the 1920s and 1930s, emphasizing the analytical tools of literary criticism, which involved training in practical criticism. It remained strongly shaped by the psychological and empirical bent bequeathed by I. A. Richards. Lewis's emphasis on learning and wide reading was very different from this, as was his focus upon the reader's open reception of literary texts in which even the traditional literary canon was a secondary consideration. Cambridge on the other hand seemed to give literature an almost religious significance. F. R. Leavis and his followers energetically championed this crusade of analytical and evaluative criticism. Lewis had been invited to give Cambridge lecture series several times in the past on the medieval and Renaissance period, and the English School clearly was weak in its resources here. It was likely to be weaker still after the impending retirement of Stanley Bennett, who was Reader in English. Cambridge decided to create a Chair of Medieval and Renaissance Literature, using funds from Bennett's readership towards the costs. The Chair seemed heaven-sent for Lewis. Some, Bennett among them, undoubtedly felt that teaching this period, and, in particular, Lewis teaching it, would be a healthy corrective to the "Leavisites" — the followers of F. R. Leavis.

As was the custom at both Oxford and Cambridge, the electors for university Chairs were distinguished scholars. On May 10, 1954, the eight of them — including Tolkien and F. P. Wilson, both representing Oxford — assembled at the Old Schools in Cambridge. Other electors included Stanley Bennett, Professor Basil Willey (a specialist in the historical and social background of English Literature), and E. M. W. Tillyard, the affable combatant and coauthor with Lewis of *The Personal Heresy*. The unanimous verdict of the electors was to invite Lewis to take the post, even though he

149

had not applied, and even though he had voiced his skepticism about the whole idea of the Renaissance in his Cambridge lectures. Lewis had been a reluctant convert to theism and Christianity; he was to prove almost equally reluctant to believe in Cambridge.

When the Vice Chancellor, Henry Willink, got a hasty rejection back from Lewis to the invitation, one reason he had not applied became clear. Lewis had encouraged an interested colleague at Magdalen College, the philologist G. V. Smithers, to apply. He gave other reasons for not accepting the invitation — his domestic situation (by which he meant the health of his brother, Warren, who was given to severe bouts of alcoholism) and his declining vitality. At fifty-six, Lewis felt that he had lost a lot of the energy of his earlier years, and he knew that the post would make new demands on him. In fact, Lewis's home life had changed dramatically since Mrs. Moore's death in 1951, giving him a new freedom.

After waiting a day, Willink wrote back to Lewis, urging him to reconsider his decision and giving him a fortnight to do this. By return of post, Lewis again declined the offer, elaborating on his reasons and specially mentioning Warren's "psychological health." He did, however, raise the issue of residency in Cambridge, almost as a plea or a query, but obviously assuming that he had to be resident during term time at least. Willink felt that there was no more he could do. The very day he got Lewis's second refusal, and after talking with Basil Willey, he wrote a letter of invitation to the "second string," Helen Gardner. Unlike Lewis, she felt that she needed to consider the matter for some time and so did not reply immediately.

In the meantime Tolkien had gone to see Lewis. The very day that Willink wrote to Helen Gardner, Tolkien convinced his friend to change his mind, not knowing of Willink's letter. In his persuasive way he managed to disarm all of Lewis's hesitations. In the first place, he pointed out, G. V. Smithers was not eligible, as a philologist, for the post, so there was no issue of conscience. Second, the residency arrangements at Cambridge were flexible — Lewis would only need to be in Cambridge part of the week during term time. While he was away, there were Paxford, and Mrs. Miller (the housekeeper) to keep Warren company. Third, the transfer would do Lewis good. He needed a change of air, and there seemed no likelihood of advancement at Oxford, despite the best efforts of Tolkien and Lewis's other friends. Tolkien, years later, disclosed to Walter Hooper: "No Oxford don was forgiven for writing books outside his field of study — except for detective stories which dons, like everyone else, read when they were down with the flu. But it was considered unforgivable that Lewis wrote international best-sellers and worse still that many were of a religious nature." Like that momentous night in 1931, the persuasion of Tolkien in 1954 tipped the balances. Just as Tolkien was largely responsible for Lewis's conversion to Christianity then, he was the prime mover in his acceptance of the Cambridge Chair now.

Tolkien wrote to the Vice Chancellor the very next day to report the good news and to ask him to reassure Lewis about residency. He also informed Bennett of Lewis's change of heart. Willink told him about the invitation to Helen Gardner — all they could do now was wait for her decision. On May 19 Lewis in turn wrote to Willink expressing his willingness to accept Cambridge's welcome invitation and saying how ridiculous and foolish he felt. Helen Gardner in the meantime had gotten wind of the fact that Lewis had become interested in the post. She declined therefore, she later explained, "partly on account of having heard that Lewis was changing his mind, for it was obvious that this ought to be Lewis's chair." She took up a post instead as Reader in Renaissance English Literature at Oxford (where she eventually, in 1966, became Merton Professor of English Literature). She disputed Lewis's view of the insignificance of the Renaissance, and that its humanism was retrogressive, but this did not distract from her admiration of his scholarship. Lewis's appointment became effective on October 1, 1954, but because of remaining duties at Oxford, he was given a dispensation until January 1, 1955. On January 7, he took up residence in Magdalene College, Cambridge, thus switching his academic home from Magdalen College, Oxford. Lewis was delighted to retain an allegiance to Mary Magdalen, describing the change to Nevill Coghill, "I have exchanged the *impenitent* for the *penitent* Magdalen."

Lewis is most commonly associated in people's minds with Oxford — he was an undergraduate of University College; he was a Fellow of Magdalen College for nearly thirty years; together with Tolkien he helped shape the curriculum of the Oxford Final Honours English School; most of his academic publications were written there; and, of course, he was the center of the Oxford Inklings. He was, however, to be closely associated with Cambridge University for over eight years, from late 1954 until his early retirement due to ill health in 1963. During those years he resided in his Cambridge College on weekdays during term time, while continuing to live at The Kilns. He would publish several important books at Cambridge — *Studies in Words* (1960), *An Experiment in Criticism* (1961), and *The Discarded Image* (1964). Also of significance are the Cambridge publications *Studies in Medieval and Renaissance Literature* (1966), *Selected Literary Essays* (1969) and *Spenser's Images of Life* (1967) — the latter reconstructed from Lewis's extensive lecture notes.

The critic and novelist David Lodge sums up Lewis's position as a historical approach to literature. For him, Lewis's literary criticism

> shows a remarkable range of interest and expertise, but Lewis was probably best known and admired for his work on medieval literature, especially his masterly book on the literature of Courtly Love, *The Allegory of Love: A Study in Medieval Tradition.* . . . C. S. Lewis in many ways represented the "Oxford" tradition of literary criticism at its best: relaxed, knowledgeable, enthusiastic, conservative. Certainly he stood for principles and practice antithetical to those of [Leavis'] Scrutiny group at Cambridge. . . . It is clear that he regarded the study of literature as primarily a historical one, and its justification as the conservation of the past. *De Descriptione Temporum* expresses eloquently, learnedly and wittily this conception of the subject and Lewis's doubts about its viability in the future.

De Descriptione Temporum was the title of Lewis's 1954 inaugural lecture at Cambridge. However, Lewis was not simply a literary historian. His historical work mainly had a double purpose: to shed light on the textual meaning, and to value a historically distant text as a remarkable window into a previous cultural world. His primary focus was always the individual text, his secondary focus the historical context. That world was the fruit of corporate human imagination and power, containing values that we need to take into account. We need transcendent perspectives on the narrow limitations of our own, current world models. In fact, Lewis actively sought to rehabilitate for us the thought and imagination of earlier ages, particularly that of the sixteenth century.

❧

Lewis's inaugural lecture on November 29, 1954 — his fifty-sixth birthday — gave him a platform in which to set out a defense of "Old Western values" that he and Tolkien had championed in their work. It was an ebullient start to his Cambridge career; in contrast, his later Cambridge publications would be more low-key and allusive, through powerfully reinforcing the same values of learning over mere technique and a machine mentality, seen as the hallmark of modernism.

Helen Joy Davidman Gresham (1915–60), who would become Lewis's wife in 1956, described the lecture to a fellow American, Chad Walsh, in a letter dated December 23, 1954, as:

> ... brilliant, intellectually exciting, unexpected, and funny as hell — as you can imagine. The hall was crowded, and there were so many capped and gowned dons in the front rows that they looked like a rookery. Instead of talking in the usual professorial way about the continuity of culture, the value of traditions, etc., he announced that "Old Western Culture," as he called it, was practically dead, leaving only a few scattered survivors like himself. ... How that man loves being in a minority, even a lost-cause minority! Athanasius *contra mundum*, or Don Quixote against the windmills ... He talked blandly of "post-Christian Europe," which I thought rather previous of him. I sometimes wonder what he would do if Christianity really did triumph everywhere; I suppose he would have to invent a new heresy.

The lecture is full of the flavor of Lewis's bold rhetoric:

> Roughly speaking we may say that whereas all history was for our ancestors divided into two periods, the pre-Christian and the Christian, and two only, for us it falls into three — the pre-Christian, the

Christian, and what may reasonably be called the post-Christian.... I am considering them simply as cultural changes. When I do that, it appears to me that the second change is even more radical than the first.

Between Jane Austen and us, but not between her and Shakespeare, Chaucer, Alfred, Virgil, Homer, or the Pharaohs, comes the birth of the machines.... [T]his is parallel to the great changes by which we divide epochs of pre-history. This is on a level with the change from stone to bronze, or from a pastoral to an agricultural economy. It alters Man's place in nature.

Tolkien's tales in their own manner embody the themes of Lewis's lecture. Tolkien's "Old Western" themes can be seen clearly, for instance, in his treatment of the related topics of possession and power. Possession is a unifying theme in his stories, from the desire of Morgoth to have God's power of creation to the temptation of wielding the One Ring. The wrong use of power is often expressed by Tolkien in magic, the mechanical and the technological. Morgoth, Sauron, and Saruman experiment with genetic engineering — the creation of robot-like orcs — and use or encourage the use of machines. The Ring itself is a machine, the result of Sauron's technological skills. Tolkien contrasts this evil magic with art, typified in the Elves, who have no desire for domination. Similarly Lewis saw a machine attitude, or technocracy, as the modern form of magic, seeking to dominate and possess nature, and expressed this theme in *That Hideous Strength*.

In his inaugural lecture Lewis defined the Old West by placing it in contrast to the modern world. The Great Divide lay, he believed, somewhere in the early nineteenth century. It was as much a social and cultural divide as a shift in ideas and beliefs. On the other hand Lewis saw positive values in pre-Christian paganism that prefigured the Christian values he so championed. He warned, in his lecture:

Christians and Pagans had much more in common with each other than either has with a post-Christian. The gap between those who worship different gods is not so wide as that between those who worship and those who do not. . . . A post-Christian man is not a Pagan; you might as well think that a married woman recovers her virginity by divorce. The post-Christian is cut off from the Christian past and therefore doubly from the Pagan past.

Many in Cambridge, not surprisingly, did not like the lecture or the new Professor. They interpreted Lewis's words as a reactionary attempt to restore a lost Christendom and responded immediately. An entire issue of *Twentieth Century,* in February 1955, focused upon disastrous developments at Cambridge, heralded by Lewis's lecture. The editorial proclaimed that its twelve contributors, from a variety of disciplines, agreed "on the importance of free liberal, humane inquiry, which they conceive to be proper not only to a university community but to any group that claims to be civilized." Novelist E. M. Forster, one of the contributors, saw humanism threatened and religion on the march. Humanism's "stronghold in history, the Renaissance, is alleged not to have existed." Now that Lewis had blown the trumpet, they feared, the walls of humanism might fall. Such fears of a crusade against humanism and the Enlightenment were reinforced later in the year with a prominent visit of evangelist Billy Graham to the Cambridge University mission run by the CICCU (Cambridge Inter-Collegiate Christian Union). Graham and Lewis met and (not surprisingly for the Cambridge humanists, if they had known of the meeting) the two men liked each other very much.

After this inaugural lecture, however (apart from a provocative early series of lectures on Milton, whom Lewis was keen to rehabilitate in Cambridge), Lewis took a much more quiet, indirect approach to literary studies, though continuing to press forward with the basic views on humane learning that he shared with Tolkien.

❧

The long-desired security of an academic Chair for Lewis was a high point in the two men's friendship; Lewis's growing relationship at this time with New Yorker Joy Davidman threatened to destroy it. When Joy first met Lewis in 1952, after an animated correspondence, she was effectively separated from her husband, and divorce was in the wind. Lewis was now free of his self-chosen commitment to looking after Mrs. Moore with her death in 1951. Just how electric this situation was as far as Tolkien was concerned may be seen from his marked differences with Lewis's more liberal theology of divorce. These had come out over certain passages in Lewis's wartime broadcast talks, and were part of Tolkien's reason for his unease about his friend's role as a popular and highly influential lay theologian.

The gist of Lewis's statements that upset his friend were in fact quoted positively by Joy Davidman in her book, *Smoke on the Mountain,* in the chapter on the Seventh Commandment, adultery. It bears on the role of the church and the state: "If people do not believe in permanent marriage, it is perhaps better that they should live together unmarried than that they should make vows they do not mean to keep. It is true that by living together without marriage they will be guilty (in Christian eyes) of fornication. But one fault is not mended by adding another: unchastity is not improved by adding perjury." She quotes another, related passage, which suggests that it might be wise to work instead for "two distinct kinds of marriage; one governed by the State with rules enforced on all citizens, the other governed by the Church with rules enforced by it on its own members." There is an important distinction between the legal and moral.

Tolkien composed a long letter setting out reasons that he thought his friend's views were mistaken. The letter was never sent, but it is likely that the friends discussed the main points, and that Lewis was aware of Tolkien's views when he courted and married a divorcee. It is almost certainly the reason that Lewis was reticent about telling him about Joy (so much so that Tolkien didn't learn about the marriage until after the event). As this brief extract makes clear, Tolkien would not even have countenanced a merely civil wedding, one that took place between Joy and Lewis in April 1956. Tolkien argued:

No item of compulsory Christian morals is valid only for Christians. . . . The foundation is that this is the correct way of "running the human machine." Your argument reduces it merely to a way of (perhaps?) getting an extra mileage out of a few selected machines. . . . Toleration of divorce — if a Christian does tolerate it — is toleration of a human abuse. . . .

This was not the only religious, denominational issue that divided the two friends, one a traditional Roman Catholic and one a Protestant, an Anglican. They had markedly different views on cremation, a fact that emerged in an Inklings meeting. Tolkien argued that the body after death remained a temple and must therefore respectfully be buried. For Lewis, the body was discarded at death. There was therefore no objection to cremation. It merely speeded the process of decay. They found that they felt these differences very strongly.

In his darkest moments, Tolkien too brooded on what he jestingly called his friend's "Ulsterior motive." It was a feature that might have slipped out occasionally when Lewis got carried away in the pub, or another drink-heavy occasion, but which he was careful to avoid in his writings — his Protestant background in the north of Ireland. Reflecting on the term "regress" (in the title of Lewis's book, *The Pilgrim's Regress*) after his friend's death, Tolkien speculated that Lewis

> would not re-enter Christianity by a new door but by the old one: at least in the sense that in taking it up again he would also take up again or reawaken the prejudices so sedulously planted in childhood and boyhood. He would become again a Northern Ireland Protestant — though with a difference, certainly: he was no longer a resident; he was learned; he had the wonderful gifts both of imagination and a clear and analytical mind; and above all his faith came of Grace to which he responded heroically, in patience and self-sacrifice — when he was aware of himself.

It is unlikely that Tolkien expressed these views so explicitly to his friend — Lewis hated the Puritania of *The Pilgrim's Regress* to be equated with the land of his childhood he loved, the Ulster he later transposed into the land of Narnia, just as Tolkien had recast the West Midlands of his memory in The Shire.

❦

Joy Davidman was an award-winning poet and novelist who published *Smoke on the Mountain*, a theological study of the Ten Commandments, in 1955. She was short, with piercing brown eyes, neck-length dark hair, and a striking complexion. Ideas were more important to her than social niceties. After seeing a starving young woman throw herself off a building in the despairing days of the Great Depression she became politically aware and turned to the Communist Party. She was Jewish, but grew up in an agnostic household in New York. She later described her worldview as "Life is only an electrochemical reaction. Love, art, and altruism are only sex. The universe is only matter. Matter is only energy. I forget what I said energy is only." She married another writer, Bill Gresham, a Gentile whom she genuinely loved. Bill had been married before and had fought against Franco in the Spanish Civil War. After giving birth to two sons, David in 1944 and Douglas in 1945, she found herself struggling not only with motherhood but also over Bill's unstable drinking and unfaithfulness. She slowly learned to protect her fundamental shyness in a sometimes abrasive outwardness. Joy eventually converted from Marxism to Christianity, partly through reading Lewis. However her ultimate turning point was a strange experience, at a time of extreme crisis in early spring 1946, which she later shared with Lewis, whose own gradual conversion from atheism had been accompanied by similar mystical theophanies:

It is infinite, unique; there are no words, there are no comparisons. Can one scoop up the sea in a teacup? Those who have known God will understand me; the others, I find, can neither listen nor understand. There was a Person with me in that room, directly present to my consciousness — a Person so real that all my precious life was by comparison a mere shadow play. And I myself was more alive than I had ever been; it was like waking from sleep. So intense a life cannot be endured long by flesh and blood; we must ordinarily take our life watered down, diluted as it were, by time and space and matter. My perception of God lasted perhaps half a minute.

Lewis's attraction to Joy was at first merely intellectual. It was on January 10, 1950, that he first received a letter from the then thirty-four-year-old Joy, one of many letters he received from readers. Hers, however, were noticeably different, and they began to correspond regularly. Lewis, then in his early fifties, met her for the first time during the autumn of 1952 — Joy had come to England with her two young boys. She and Bill Gresham had agreed to a trial separation. Warren was present at a second meeting soon after in Magdalen College, and both brothers were taken with her. Warren particularly enjoyed her uninhibited New York nature. He records in his diary that she turned to him, in the presence of three or four men, and "asked in the most natural tone in the world, 'Is there anywhere in this monastic establishment where a lady can relieve herself?'"

After a period back in New York, and her marriage falling apart, Joy Davidman came to live with her sons in London, and eventually in Oxford, near Lewis. She and he were soon on close terms, meeting daily. In retrospect he wrote, "Her mind was lithe and quick and muscular as a leopard. Passion, tenderness and pain were all equally unable to disarm it. It scented the first whiff of cant or slush; then sprang, and knocked you over before you knew what was happening." They married in a civil ceremony at the Oxford Registry Office on April 23, 1956, solely with the purpose of giving her British nationality.

At least this is how Lewis understood the situation. His head did not know his heart at this stage. His friends, those who knew about the arrangement, could see the obvious more clearly. Tolkien, however, heard nothing about the discreet civil wedding. In the fall of 1956 Lewis and Joy learned not only that she had cancer, but that it was inoperable. It was sudden, unexpected news, and Lewis was deeply shocked. Cancer was an old acquaintance. Joy's two boys were then about the same age as the Lewis brothers had been when their mother died; the parallels were haunting. With Thanatos a rival for Joy (as he put it) Lewis's affection for her quickly deepened into exclusive love. On March 21, 1957, a bedside Christian wedding ceremony took place in the hospital where Joy was being treated. Joy came home to The Kilns to die, joined by David and Douglas.

Tolkien remained unaware of what was going on. The very day of the Christian wedding ceremony he wrote to Kathleen Farrer, a friend of Joy's, expressing his belief that she had been very much taken up with "the troubles of poor Jack Lewis." He confessed that he knew little of these, beyond "cautious hints" let drop by Dr. "Humphrey" Havard (who, when treating Joy as her general practitioner, had failed to diagnose her cancer). Whenever Tolkien met up with Lewis the latter understandably took refuge in talk about books, for which Tolkien had never known any anxiety or grief to temper his enthusiasm. Lewis's devotion to Joy, together with his time spent on his Cambridge duties, meant that he and Tolkien now rarely met. As far as we know Tolkien had stopped attending the weekly Inklings in the Eagle and Child around this time.

After prayer for healing, Joy had an unexpected reprieve. Her horridly diseased bones rejuvenated against all medical expectations and by July 1957 she was well enough to get out and about. Throughout this period Lewis continued his work in Cambridge on weekdays during term time. David and Douglas were away at boarding school. The next year Joy and Lewis had a fortnight's vacation in Ireland. The remission was the beginning of the happiest few years of both their lives. Lewis confessed to fellow Inkling Nevill Coghill: "I never expected to have, in my sixties, the happiness that passed me by in my twenties."

According to Warren, the marriage fulfilled "a whole dimension to his nature that had previously been starved and thwarted." It also, for Lewis, put paid to any doubts he had had as a bachelor that God was an invented substitute for love. "For those few years [Joy] and I feasted on love," he recalled in *A Grief Observed*, "every mode of it — solemn and merry, romantic and realistic, sometimes as dramatic as a thunderstorm, sometimes as comfortable and unemphatic as putting on your soft slippers." In that book he recorded in diary form the stages of his profound grief at her death.

The cancer eventually returned, but the Lewises were able to take a trip to Greece in the spring of 1960, the year of her death, a journey much desired by both of them. They were accompanied by Roger and June Lancelyn Green. Soon after, Joy Davidman Lewis and Edith Tolkien found themselves in the same Oxford hospital, Joy for cancer treatment and Edith because of her severe arthritis. It was their first meeting. Tolkien also met Joy for the first (and probably last) time, being introduced to her by Lewis while visiting Edith. Joy underwent cancer surgery on May 20, 1960, and then returned once again to The Kilns to die. She slipped away on July 13, 1960, two months after the Greek vacation.

Edith becoming acquainted with Joy brought somewhat of a reconciliation between Tolkien and Lewis. Since Lewis's marriage the two friends had seldom met. In fact, his relationship with Joy had cast a gloom over the friendship that had never fully dispersed. Edith had never fitted easily into her husband's academic world, and Lewis had, over the years, felt uneasy when visiting Tolkien at home. He related to Tolkien in the Inklings meetings or on other occasions, in pubs or in his college rooms. It is likely that meeting Joy helped Edith to see Lewis in a new light, and Tolkien to come to terms with his friend's "strange marriage." Their former intimacy, however, was never fully regained, and even after Joy's death, Tolkien and Lewis only met infrequently.

Just as much of Lewis's *That Hideous Strength* was influenced particularly by Charles Williams, it could be said that his novel, *Till We Have Faces*, published in 1956, bears the impression of Joy Davidman. She was a skillful novelist, author of *Anya* (1940) and *Weeping Bay* (1950). Lewis likely enough owes his confidence to write the story from a female's perspective to Joy. Like Orual in the novel, Joy, too had an epiphany that turned upside-down her view of the world. On first reading it hardly seems like a work by Lewis at all, though subsequent readings show it full of his themes. It is Lewis's work with the most affinity to his friend Tolkien, because of its setting in a pre-Christian world, where it explores anticipations of the Christian story in ancient myth.

In *Till We Have Faces*, Lewis retold the classical story of Cupid and Psyche from Apuleius's *The Golden Ass*. In Apuleius's story, Psyche is so beautiful that Venus becomes jealous of her. Cupid, sent by Venus to make Psyche fall in love with an ugly creature, instead falls in love with her himself. After hiding her in a mysterious palace he only visits her in the dark, and forbids her to see his face. Out of jealousy, Psyche's sisters tell her that her lover is a monster that one day will devour her. She takes a lamp one night and looks at Cupid's face, but a drop of oil awakens him. In anger, the god leaves her. Psyche seeks her lover throughout the world. Venus sets her various impossible tasks, all of which she accomplishes except the final one, when curiosity makes her open a deadly casket from the underworld. At last, however, she is allowed to marry Cupid.

In his version of the story Lewis essentially followed the classical myth, but retold it through the eyes of Orual, Psyche's half-sister, who seeks to defend her actions before the gods as being the result of deep love for Psyche, not jealousy. Psyche's outstanding beauty contrasts with Orual's ugliness (in later life she wears a veil). In Glome, a country somewhere to the north of the Greeklands, the goddess Ungit, a deformed version of Venus, is worshiped. After a drought and other disasters in Glome a lot falls on the innocent Psyche to be sacrificed on the Grey Mountains to the Shadowbrute or West-wind, the god of the mountain.

Sometime afterwards, Orual, accompanied by a faithful member of the king's guard, Bardia, seeks the bones of Psyche to bury her. Finding no trace of Psyche, Bardia and Orual explore further and find the beautiful and sheltered Valley of the God. Here Psyche is living, wearing rags but alive. She claims to be married to the god of the mountain, whose face she has never seen. Orual, afraid that the "god" is a monster or outlaw, persuades Psyche, against her will, to shine a light on her husband's face while sleeping.

As in the ancient myth, Psyche as a punishment is condemned to wander the earth, undertaking impossible tasks. Orual's account goes on to record the bitter years of her suffering and grief at the loss of Psyche, haunted by the fantasy that she can hear Psyche's weeping. Orual then records a devastating "undeception" she has undergone (as Lewis elsewhere calls the experience). In sudden, painful self-knowledge, she discovers how possessiveness had poisoned her affection for Psyche.

Princess Psyche in Lewis's story is prepared to die for the sake of the people of Glome. Lewis explained in a letter to Clyde S. Kilby (1902–86) that Psyche was intended as an example of the *anima naturaliter Christiana*. Psyche made the best of the limitations of the pagan religion of her upbringing. The pagan insights guided her towards the true God — but within the restrictions of her own imagination and that of her culture. Lewis concluded, in that letter to Kilby, that Psyche in some ways resembled Christ, but not as a symbol of him. She was like every virtuous man or woman in resembling Christ by the nature of their goodness.

An important element in the story, therefore, is Psyche as an ancient anticipation of Christ. Psyche is able to see a glimpse of the true God himself, in all his beauty, and in his legitimate demand for a perfect sacrifice. A further key to this story lies in the theme of the conflict of imagination and reason, so important to Lewis himself throughout his life, and vividly portrayed in his autobiography, *Surprised by Joy*. The final identification of the half-sisters Orual and Psyche in the story represents the harmony and satisfaction of reason and imagination, mind and soul, made fully possible, Lewis believed (following Tolkien), only within Christian belief. The novel explores the depths of insight possible within the limitations of the pagan imagination, which foreshadows the marriage of myth and fact in the Gospels. *Till We Have Faces,* therefore, reveals the imaginative and theological affinity between Lewis and Tolkien, perhaps more than any other book by Lewis. It is ironic that the novel was written at a time when the two friends had grown apart.

❧

Throughout the 1950s Tolkien continued to explore and teach the literature of the West Midlands in the Middle English period. On April 15, 1953, he delivered the W. P. Ker Memorial Lecture at the University of Glasgow on "Sir Gawain and the Green Knight." Later that year, in December, BBC radio broadcast a dramatization of Tolkien's translation of *Sir Gawain and the Green Knight.* In 1955 his poem, "Imram," originally part of "The Notion Club Papers," was published in *Time and Tide.* In "Imram," Gaelic for "voyage," Tolkien altered the story of St. Brendan's famous early medieval voyage to fit his invented mythology. The poem mentions the Lost Road, a "shoreless mountain" (Meneltarma) marking "the foundered land" (Númenor), a mysterious island (Tol Eressëa) with a white Tree (Celeborn), and a beautiful star (Eärendil) marking the old road leading beyond the world. It indicates Tolkien's continuing passion to find a narrative bridge for the contemporary reader to his mythology of "The Silmarillion."

A new phase of his life started with his retirement in 1959, at the age of sixty-seven, from his university duties. He had not given an inaugural lecture for his Merton Chair. Instead, on June 5, 1959, he delivered a "Valedictory Address" as the departing Merton Professor of English Language and Literature. He said, "Philology is the foundation of humane letters." Referred to his birth in South Africa he added: "I have the hatred of *apartheid* in my bones; and most of all I detest the segregation or separation of Language and Literature. I do not care which of them you think White."

In March 1953 Tolkien and Edith had moved to the smaller house on Sandfield Road in Headington — Edith found stairs increasingly difficult in their previous home due to her arthritis. All the children had left home by 1950, with the departure of Priscilla to study. She eventually became a probation officer. With the loss of his college rooms at Merton the storage of his many books became a problem. He decided to convert his garage to a study *cum* office. Philip Norman, an interviewer from *The Sunday Times*, described the house some years afterwards, when the public began to be interested in Tolkien. It was a three-bedroomed house which looked to Norman just like a church rectory. It was near the Oxford United Football Ground, so the street outside was invaded by football fans whenever there were matches playing. "The study in the garage," he observed, "is filled with books and the smell of distinguished dust." Norman also noted that the study contained a new tin clock and an ancient portmanteau, almost buried under some newspapers. Tolkien explained that the faded leather trunk had been given to him by his "half-Spaniard" guardian (Father Francis Morgan). He had only kept it because inside were "all the things I've been going to answer for so many years, I've forgotten what they are." On the window ledge two papers were tacked. One was a map of Middle-earth that showed the routes of the two hobbit quests — Bilbo's and Frodo's. The other was a list of Tolkien's engagements, in his bold handwriting.

During these years George Sayer occasionally visited Oxford. Just as he was about to take a walk with Lewis, Tolkien handed him a manuscript of "The Silmarillion." Lewis and Sayer looked at the papers while having a bread-and-cheese lunch in a nearby pub. Sayer remembered Lewis remarking: "Good Heavens! He seems to have invented not one but three languages complete with their dialects. He must be the cleverest man in Oxford. But we can't keep these. Take them straight back to him while I have another pint."

11

A Farewell to Shadowlands

(1963–1973)

From the entrance of the centuries-old Church of the Holy Trinity in Headington emerge the coffin bearers. It is a silent, still day, and the flame of a single candle on the heavy casket remains motionless even in the transition from inside to outside.

Behind the bearers, their polished shoes crunching the brittle gravel, come the mourners, led by the pale eighteen-year-old Douglas Gresham, Lewis's stepson and the sole family member attending. Out from the church steps Maureen Blake, née Moore, and her husband; Tolkien, looking gray without his usual ornamental waistcoat, and his son Christopher; The Revd. Peter Bide, who had married Jack and Joy Lewis despite the bishop's prohibition; Fred Paxford, unprepared, despite his habitual gloom, for this loss; Dr. "Humphrey" Havard, the "Useless Quack"; Owen Barfield, once described by Lewis as his alter ego; another Inkling, Commander James Dundas-Grant; Austin Farrer, brilliant theologian, and his wife Kathleen, novelist; George Sayer and John Lawlor, former pupils of Lewis's; the current president of Magdalen College, Oxford — the list of friends and colleagues is long.

The quiet passing of Clive Staples Lewis a few days before brings them together on a late November day in 1963. Warren Lewis is noticeably absent — he is at The Kilns nearby, in alcoholic oblivion, unable to face a loss as great as that of his mother when he was a boy, but now lacking a child's strength. He had insisted that the details of the funeral not be released. The word got around anyway, despite Lewis's death on Friday, November 22, being overshadowed by the assassination of John F. Kennedy the very same day.

The candle flame remains upright as the coffin is placed over the opening that awaits it — the grave is under a larch in the corner of the churchyard, Tolkien notes. He has already had a mass said for his beloved friend at St. Aloysius Roman Catholic Church earlier, at which he had served, also attended by Havard and Dundas-Grant. Tolkien feels the tangible shape of his sorrow. He is an old man now, past seventy, and his leaves are falling one by one, like those of the late autumn trees around the mourners. But this loss of his dear friend feels like an axe-blow near his very roots. All of him shakes to the thud of the heavy blade. The fact that he and Lewis have not been on intimate terms some ten years now does not numb the wound, a wound he knows he will not lose, as one loses a falling leaf. "Men must endure their going hence," Warnie had quoted.

Tolkien's thoughts go to the visit he and his son John had made to his friend just a few weeks before. Though ill, Lewis had talked with them about the fifteenth-century *Morte d'Arthur* and whether trees die. There was a copy of Pierre Choderlos de Laclos's decadent prerevolutionary novel of seduction, *Les Liaisons Dangereuses*, in the sitting room, which Lewis was enjoying with a youthful relish. "Wow, what a book!" he had exclaimed. Still no ascetic, Tolkien had thought. He continued to be amazed at his friend's voracious and eclectic reading.

Tolkien looks over to where the young man is standing whom Lewis had protected and made his stepson — people are now giving their condolences to Douglas. As he looks at Douglas he remembers what Lewis had written to him last Christmas, for he had thought about the words many times since — "All my philosophy of history hangs upon a sentence of your own, 'Deeds were done which were not *wholly* in vain.'" The sentence is from *The Fellowship of the Ring*, which had been read to Lewis long ago: "There was sorrow then too, and gathering dark, but great valour, and great deeds that were not wholly vain." Tolkien's heart feels strangely warmed that his friend had drawn comfort from his words at the end of his life.

❧

Lewis died from a combination of "old man's troubles" — afflictions of bladder, prostate, and weakened heart — and indifferent medical care. He was not one to complain about his ailments. He had also identified so closely with Joy's sufferings that he experienced physical manifestations, such as crippling pain, which took their toll. He saw this as the application of Charles Williams's doctrine of "substituted love," based on Christ's suffering for us, in which we literally bear one another's burdens. Warren was with him for the last months of his life, which gave Lewis considerable comfort, after a long period away in Ireland drinking heavily.

Before he died Lewis managed to complete the proof corrections of his last book — *Letters to Malcolm: Chiefly on Prayer*, published January 27, 1964. It was popular theology in the tradition of his *Mere Christianity, The Problem of Pain, Miracles,* and *Reflections of the Psalms* — all of which continued to be in demand by readers around the world — but with a subtle difference. It was more allusive. The book is made up of fictional letters to a fictional person, Malcolm, from a fictional "C. S. Lewis" — an author like Lewis, and writing in his name. This allowed Lewis to explore ideas and to put forward theories about prayer, purgatory, and heaven that were not necessarily what Lewis would have put in a literal text of theology. The subtlety of this approach is easily lost on a reader but not much in it is out of harmony with what Lewis explicitly put forward elsewhere as his understanding of "mere Christianity." The book affirms his belief in heaven as a place in which ordinary human experience now is fulfilled: "I can now communicate with you the vanished fields of my boyhood — they are building-estates today — only imperfectly by words. Perhaps the day is coming when I can take you for a walk through them. . . . Once again, after who knows what aeons of the silence and the dark, the birds will sing out and the waters flow, and lights and shadows move across the hills and the faces of our friends laugh upon us with amazed recognition."

Malcolm, the fictional friend he has known since undergraduate days at Oxford, receives twenty-two letters from "Lewis" on the theme of prayer, and much else, including heaven and the resurrection of the body. Though we only have the "Lewis" side of the correspondence, we are able to piece together much about Malcolm from that. Some critics have felt that Lewis's theological writings lack an experiential depth (or a shyness of spiritual experience). *Letters to Malcolm,* however, reflects on one of the most experiential subjects of the Christian life, prayer, and Lewis handles it with great power. Right from the time of his conversion to theism Lewis believed thoroughly in the reality of the supernatural. Thus the question of petitionary prayer made in time to a God outside of time was a very important one to him. God could, if he wished, change actual events in the light of the prayers of his people. Indeed, Lewis believed that God had answered prayers for Joy's healing when she was dying. He was convinced that this was why she had a reprieve of three years in which her diseased bones mended themselves.

Prayer, for Lewis, was necessary for our understanding of our relation to God the creator. He wrote:

> Now the moment of prayer is for me — or involves for me as its condition — the awareness, the reawakened awareness, that this "real world" and "real self" are very far from being rock-bottom realities. I cannot, in the flesh, leave the stage, either to go behind the scenes or to take my seat in the pit; but I can remember that my apparent self — this clown or hero ... — under his grease-paint is a real person with an off-stage life. The dramatic person could not tread the stage unless he concealed a real person: unless the real and unknown I existed, I would not even make mistakes about the imagined me. And in prayer this real I struggles to speak, for once, from his real being, and to address, for once, not the other actors, but — what shall I call Him? The Author, for He invented us all? The Producer, for He controls all? Or the Audience, for He watches, and will judge, the performance?

We read that Malcolm has kept in touch with "Lewis" over the years and has a wife, Betty, and a son George, who are part of the story-line inferable from passing references or comments in the letters. The quality of the fictional friendship between "Lewis" and Malcolm owes much to the real-life friendships between Lewis and Arthur Greeves, Owen Barfield, and Tolkien, even though Malcolm is clearly not a portrait of any one of them. There are also hints, in the vivid dialectic of the letters, of how informal discussion in meetings of the Inklings may have run. When the book was published two months after Lewis's death, Tolkien obtained a copy and found it of great interest. It was as if his friend was still challenging him, and also irritating him, as a popularizer of Christian belief. In a letter he commented: "I personally found *Letters to Malcolm* a distressing and in parts a horrifying work. I began a commentary on it, but if finished it would not be publishable." He was more receptive to an anthology of quotations from Lewis's work, arranged thematically, sent to him by its compiler, Clyde S. Kilby, an American scholar who had befriended Tolkien and Lewis, and spent the summer of 1966 helping him with his arrangement of the material making up the still-unfinished "The Silmarillion." This anthology, Tolkien told Kilby, "has reminded me of many good things that are scattered throughout Lewis's works, though they sometimes, not always, lose by being taken out of their context." He had also written to Kilby the previous year that he had been reading *Letters to an American Lady*, a collection of Lewis's letters, and finding it "deeply interesting." He confessed: "I still find it difficult to realize that Jack is dead, though it was 4 years ago."

Around this time Tolkien wrote his last story published during his life, *Smith of Wootton Major* (1967). This short story complements his essay "On Fairy Stories" in tracing the relationship between the world of Faery and the primary world we experience. The story seems deceptively simple at first, but, though children can enjoy it, it is not a children's story. Tolkien described it as "an old man's book, already weighted with the presage of 'bereavement.'" It was as if, like Smith in the story with his Elven star, Tolkien expected his imagination to come to an end; it was a time of self-doubt for him. In a review, Tolkien's friend and fellow Inkling, Roger Lancelyn Green, wrote of the small book: "To seek for the meaning is to cut open the ball in search of its bounce." Like *Farmer Giles of Ham*, the story has an undefined medieval setting. The villages of Wootton Major and Minor could have come straight out of the hobbits' Shire. As in Middle-earth, it is possible to walk in and out of the world of Faery (the realm of Elves). The story contains an Elven-king in disguise, Alf, apprentice to the bungling cake-maker Nokes. Nokes has no concept of the reality of Faery, but his sugary cake for the village children, adorned with its crude Fairy Queen doll, can stir the imagination of the humble. A magic Elven star that Nokes finds and puts in the cake is swallowed by Smith, then a child, giving him access to Faery. In the village it is the children who can be susceptible to the "other," the numinous, where their elders are only concerned with eating and drinking. The star eventually reappears and becomes attached to Smith's brow. Smith grows up to be a Master Smith ("he could work iron into wonderful forms that looked as light and delicate as a spray of leaves and blossom, but kept the stern strength of iron") and, insofar as the book has autobiographical elements, may be said to represent Tolkien himself, and his ability to spin tales of elves and faerie.

As in Tolkien's earlier story, *Leaf by Niggle,* glimpses of other worlds transform art and craft in human life, giving them an elven or spiritual quality. The ordinary work of the village smith is seen in a new light, transformed into the sacramental, just as the humble work of the storyteller can suggest a reality beyond the "walls of the world."

During this period of self-doubt, which began soon after Lewis's death, the popularity of his *The Lord of the Rings* exploded, though Tolkien only heard about the phenomenon gradually. In 1965, when he was writing *Smith of Wootton Major,* Ace Books in the United States, using a loophole in copyright law, issued an unauthorized paperback edition of *The Lord of the Rings.* An authorized edition followed, published by Houghton Mifflin, in a blaze of publicity about the injustice of the rogue publication. Tolkien entered the consciousness of a generation of American college students, and soon his celebrity spread across the world. *Frodo Lives* and *Gandalf for President* buttons were seen everywhere. People were told that Tolkien was "hobbit-forming." The world of the Rings was taking root in the new consciousness of the 1960s.

As Tolkien became an international celebrity he felt the impact of fame in a surge of income from *The Lord of the Rings,* and a huge growth in his correspondence. He was forced to take on a part-time secretary, who worked in the converted garage at Sandfield Road. In 1966 he and Edith celebrated their golden wedding anniversary, the occasion being marked by Donald Swann's performance of his cycle of songs, based upon poems from *The Hobbit* and *The Lord of the Rings*. They were sung, to Tolkien's satisfaction, by the opera singer William Elvin. Some of these were elven poems, and Tolkien enjoyed the coincidence of the singer's surname. "A name of good omen!" he remarked.

Tolkien eventually passed through his doubt about his work, especially the unfinished "The Silmarillion," in which he had invested his life. He now believed that his work would not be "wholly in vain."

Edith was approaching eighty and Tolkien was seventy-six by 1968. Her severe arthritis made tending the house difficult. They decided to move to more congenial accommodations, and away from the attention of fans. Their choice was the coastal resort of Bournemouth, on the south-coast, a favorite of the retired. They had taken vacations here, and Edith found it easier to make friends in the town than in Oxford. The wealth from the books eased their situation as they settled into 19 Lakeside Road, a bungalow, that meant no stairs to climb. Tolkien pottered with diverse manuscripts of "The Silmarillion," bewildering in their variety, less troubled by interruptions. By 1971, he and Edith had settled into a comfortable routine which might eventually have led to a more consistent arrangement of the annals and tales of the earlier ages of Middle-earth. However, Edith's health suddenly failed. She was hospitalized with an inflamed gallbladder and died a few days later, on November 29, 1971.

With the loss of Edith, his Lúthien, Tolkien had no reason to stay in Bournemouth. His old college, Merton, offered him an honorary fellowship and some rooms in a house belonging to the college. In March 1972, he gratefully moved into 21 Merton Street, near the college. In the last two years of his life he was able to travel to see friends and family, take vacations, and visit Buckingham Palace to receive a C.B.E. from the Queen. While on a visit to Bournemouth to stay with friends he was taken ill with an acute bleeding gastric ulcer, which led to a chest infection. Four days later, on Sunday, September 2, 1973, he died.

In his final years it must have been clear to Tolkien that he was a celebrity. This bemused and sometimes irritated him, but he seemed glad to respond with energy to numerous letters about details of *The Lord of the Rings,* many relating to the earlier mythology of "The Silmarillion." This fame was in amusing contrast to an Oxford event in 1965, at which the Hollywood actress Ava Gardner was present. This was a lecture ("ludicrously bad," remembered Tolkien) given by the current Professor of Poetry, Robert Graves. Tolkien, unlike much of the world, had not heard of the film star but found her pleasant when introduced to her. As Tolkien emerged from the venue with Graves and Ava Gardner the flashbulbs were devoted to her. Today, most likely, many more people everywhere know of Tolkien than of the actress!

In the early years of the twenty-first century both Tolkien and Lewis are enormously popular throughout the world. Their readerships have grown consistently since their deaths. They were friends whose affinities far exceeded their differences. In their fiction, and in much of their academic scholarship, they stood against what they saw as a tide of modernism taking over their world. They were inspired by but were distinct from an older romantic movement that, in its own way, stood against the Enlightenment, the parent age of what Lewis called the "Age of the Machine." They were British writers and academics anchored in their faith who have been embraced by countless readers of every possible background around the world.

12

The Gift of Friendship

"Who could have deserved it?"

The friendship between Lewis and Tolkien went back to the time when Tolkien moved to Oxford University from his professorship at Leeds in 1925. It ended, if friendships do end in this way, with Lewis's death in November 1963. This friendship of close to forty years perhaps inevitably had its ups and downs, especially with such different temperaments. There was a marked cooling of the friendship, in which it existed on much less intimate terms, after Lewis had met Joy Davidman in the early 1950s. Furthermore, there always remained a side to Lewis to which Tolkien could not accustom himself — Lewis as the popularizer of Christian faith. Tolkien's disapproval obviously had nothing to do with the faith itself — he was a devout Christian himself.

Much of their friendship was played out in the context of the Inklings. Once the Inklings as a reading group came to an end late in 1949, great changes were inevitable in the pattern of their lives. Members of the club had read to each other for sixteen years — Tolkien had read much of *The Lord of the Rings* and perhaps some of *The Hobbit* to them. He had presented parts of his background mythology of the earlier ages of Middle-earth. From time to time he had shared poems. Lewis had read widely from his prodigious output — his space fiction stories, many poems, *The Screwtape Letters*, *The Great Divorce*, *The Problem of Pain*, his translation of Virgil's *The Aeneid*, and the occasional essay. Many times Lewis read to Tolkien outside of the Inklings, or to Tolkien and Williams. Early in 1949, for example, Lewis read at least part of the manuscript of *The Lion, the Witch and the Wardrobe* to Tolkien. Perhaps because Tolkien disliked the Narnian story Lewis seems to have read little to Tolkien after this, though we cannot be certain, because we have to rely upon incidental documentation in letters, and on Warren Lewis's sporadic diaries.

The Inklings was, to all appearances, a small and obscure reading group of a few academics and professional people meeting in the smoky lounge of the humble Eagle and Child pub or in Lewis's unpretentious college rooms. Furthermore, for the early years at least of the friendship, Tolkien and Lewis were little known outside of their academic circles, especially as writers of fiction. Yet they were enormously important to each other, and had obvious affinities that helped each to keep alive his vision of life.

Of fundamental importance is the influence of Tolkien's faith. Lewis was originally an atheist, and Tolkien helped him to find God. He exerted all his persuasive power on his friend, focusing upon the Gospel narratives as demanding both an imaginative and an intellectual response. Lewis responded in both these ways, and over time developed and mastered the skills of a Christian communicator, both in storytelling and in rhetoric. As the years went on, Lewis's fluency in both imaginative and discursive writing increased. Tolkien failed, however, to persuade Lewis to enter what he felt, in the formidable tradition of Cardinal Newman, to be the only valid church — the Roman Catholic.

Tolkien influenced Lewis significantly, also, with his view of a connection between myth and fact which goes back, as Tolkien believed, to the very nature of language; it could be described as a theology of story or even a theology of language. Tolkien had worked out a complex understanding of the relation of story and myth to reality, and how language itself relates to reality. Story and language were, for him, part of one human inventive process — they were "integrally related." Tolkien saw the Gospel narratives — in his view, a story created by God himself in the real events of history — as having been woven into the seamless "web of story." Human storytelling — whether preceding or subsequent to the Gospel events — is joyfully alive with God's presence. The importance of story became equally central to Lewis. He wrote a chapter "On Stories," included in the collection, *Essays Presented to Charles Williams* (1947), which he expanded in his seminal *An Experiment in Criticism* (1961).

Another important feature of Tolkien's impact upon Lewis, also related, is his distinctive doctrine of sub-creation — his belief that the highest function of art is the creation of internally consistent and coherent secondary or other worlds that, because of such an imaginative accuracy, are able to capture some of the depths and splendor of the primary world. A faery story for Tolkien was not a story that simply concerns faery beings. They are in some sense other-worldly, having a geography and history surrounding them. Tolkien's concept of sub-creation was, in fact, the most distinctive feature of his view of art. Though he saw it in terms of inventive fantasy, his view applies more widely. Secondary worlds can take many forms in art, particularly fiction. The metaphorical quality of an invented world, whether set in this or another world, deepens or indeed modifies our very perception of reality, and can quicken our immortal spirit.

The concept of sub-creation provided the basis for Lewis's invention of the planets of Malacandra and Perelandra (one of his most successful creations), and the country of Glome, north of ancient Greece. It inspired, for younger readers, his most popular world, Narnia.

Alongside this, Tolkien must have conveyed to Lewis a vision and understanding of story that is spiritual and even mystical. In such a view, a story has a significance beyond itself — it points to a reality other than itself. Tolkien distinctively said that "all tales may come true" (because of the link between human and divine making). When Lewis told a story about Digory's apple, in *The Magician's Nephew* (the apple that gave life to Digory's mother), Lewis felt that he was doing more than indulging in wish fulfillment. The story for him embodied the possibility that his own mother (and other people's mothers) might one day live again in a fully human, physical-spiritual existence.

Given that Tolkien had such a great impact on his friend, what was Lewis's importance to Tolkien? Tolkien himself answered this question in a letter written nearly two years after his friend's death: "The unpayable debt that I owe to him was not 'influence' as it is ordinarily understood, but sheer encouragement. He was for long my only audience. Only from him did I ever get the idea that my 'stuff' could be more than a private hobby. But for his interest and unceasing eagerness for more I should never have brought *The L. of the R.* to a conclusion...."

It appears that Lewis did not influence Tolkien the same way the latter influenced the former. Rather, Tolkien found a ready listener and appreciator in Lewis. This reading and listening was institutionalized in the Inklings' Thursday night gatherings. Who knows? Had these Thursday meetings continued past 1949, there might exist today a complete telling of the tales of the earlier Ages of Middle-earth, approaching the scale of *The Lord of the Rings.* Sadly, Lewis did not persist in encouraging the completion of "The Silmarillion," especially the great tales such as that of Beren and Lúthien. One reason might have been the gradual growing apart of the two friends in the 1950s.

Lewis illuminated the nature of his friendship with Tolkien when he wrote *The Four Loves* (1960). The four loves he distinguished are affection, friendship, eros, and charity (*agape*, or divine love). He felt that it is vital not to lose sight of the real differences that give each love its valid character, even where one love merges into another (as when friendship between a man and woman becomes erotic, or when one is called upon to care for a dependent family member, and natural affection deepens into self-sacrificial love). Friendship, like his with Tolkien, involved the "What, you too!" factor, the recognition of a shared vision.

Friendship, for Lewis, was therefore the least instinctive, biological, and necessary of our loves. These days it is hardly considered a love, and Lewis sought to rehabilitate it. In his book, he pointed out that the ancients put the highest value upon this love, as in the friendship between David and Jonathan. The ideal climate for friendship was when a few people are absorbed in some common interest. Lovers, Lewis argued, are usually imagined face-to-face; friends are best imagined side by side, their eyes focused on their common interest. Friendship, as the least biological of the loves, refutes heterosexual or homosexual explanations for its existence. Friendship, Lewis reckoned, made good people better and bad people worse. Tolkien largely agreed with Lewis's view of friendship, especially as it was reinforced by the male character of Oxford society in their day, but he was not as generous as Lewis in the breadth of his friendships. He was also a family man, while Lewis was a bachelor for much

of his life, even though he participated willingly in Mrs. Moore's matri-
archy at The Kilns. This gave Tolkien a wider breadth of relationships —
to Edith, and to his children particularly. An important ingredient in the
glue of their friendship, however, was their shared Christian faith, with
its distinct imaginative cast, even though the friendship became firmly
established while Lewis was still a materialist.

There were, in fact, a great number of shared beliefs deriving from their
common faith. In the very foreground of their perspective, the imagination
was of huge importance. They saw it, in Lewis's words, as the "organ of
meaning"; imagination is involved in the way we sense reality as a whole
(whether perceiving individual things like trees, stones, hills, and even
particular people, or the world as a coherent world around us). Imagination is not, like thought, concerned with abstractions from particular
things, experiences, and relationships. Both Lewis and Tolkien as writers,
therefore, valued looking at reality in a symbolic and mythopoeic way.

Fiction, for Lewis and Tolkien, was therefore the creation of meaning
rather than the literal restating of truths. It reflected for them the greater
creativity of God, when he originated and put together his universe and
ourselves. Natural objects and people are not mere facts. Their meaning
comes from their relationship to other objects, events, and persons, and
ultimately from their relationship to God. They have a created unity, and
their meaning and fullness derive from that. Clyde S. Kilby recorded in
his notes of a meeting with Tolkien that he spoke of an idea, shared
with Lewis, "that everything is unique and . . . each thing, however small,
when a subject of attention, of necessity becomes the center of the world
and requires all knowledge of [the] entire world to make an adequate
explanation of it." What is true of things is also true of our own sensations
and experiences. If we focus exclusively on them we lose their meaning —
they point elsewhere to what is not them, to a whole world of people,
things, and places, and, for Lewis and Tolkien, to things beyond "the walls
of the world." If we see a work of literature simply as the expression of its
writer, rather than as a work of communication intended to be understood
by an audience, that piece of literature loses its meaning. We gain rather
than lose by seeing how things refer to other realities than themselves,
an action that requires our imagination. This, for Lewis in particular,

2222

was how knowledge has always progressed. Tolkien and Lewis agreed that good imagining was as vital as good thinking, and each was impoverished without the other.

The desire to write fantasy and other symbolic fiction was fundamental to Lewis and Tolkien. In a letter Lewis confessed:

> The imaginative man in me is older, more continuously operative, and in that sense more basic than either the religious writer or the critic. It was he who made me first attempt (with little success) to be a poet. It was he who, in response to the poetry of others, made me a critic, and, in defence of that response, sometimes a critical controversialist. It was he who after my conversion led me to embody my religious belief in symbolical or mythopoeic forms, ranging from *Screwtape* to a kind of theological science-fiction. And it was, of course, he who has brought me, in the last few years to write a series of Narnian stories for children; not asking what children want and then endeavouring to adapt myself (this was not needed) but because the fairy-tale was the genre best fitted for what I wanted to say.

Similarly, Tolkien wrote a beatitude in his poem, "Mythopeia," to the makers of legend. These storytellers are blessed as they speak of things outside of recorded time; though they have looked at death and even ultimate defeat, they have not flinched and retreated in despair. Instead, they have often sung of victory, and the fire in their voices, caught from legend, has kindled the hearts of their listeners. In so doing, they have lit up both the darkness of the past and the present day with the brightness of suns "as yet by no man seen."

As well as placing this enormous value upon the imagination, Tolkien and Lewis were alike in welcoming a sense of Other-ness — or "other-worldliness." Great stories take us outside of the prison of our own selves and our presuppositions about reality (hence the frequent accusation of escapism). Insofar as stories reflect the divine maker in doing this, they help us face the ultimate Other — God, distinct as creator from all else, including ourselves. The very well of fantasy and imaginative invention is every person's direct knowledge of the Other. According to Lewis, "to construct plausible and moving 'other worlds' you must draw on the only real 'other world' we know, that of the spirit." Imaginative worlds are "regions of the spirit."

For both friends, this all-pervasive sense of the Other is expressed in a quality of awe or dread, called "the numinous." The numinous is a basic human experience charted by the theologian Rudolf Otto (who coined the word) in *The Idea of the Holy* (1923), a book that had a marked influence on Lewis. Both Tolkien and Lewis successfully embodied this quality in their fiction. The primary numinous experience involves a sense of dependence upon that which stands Wholly Other to humanity. This Otherness (or otherworldliness) is unapproachable and awesome. But, at the same time, it fascinates us. The experience of the numinous is captured better by suggestion and allusion than by a theoretical analysis. Many realities captured in imaginative fiction could be described as having some quality of the numinous. Lewis realized this, incorporating the idea into his apologetic for the Christian view of suffering, *The Problem of Pain*, and he cited an event from Kenneth Grahame's tale for children, *The Wind in the Willows* (1908), to illustrate it. It is the event where Mole and Ratty approach Pan on the island:

> "Rat," he found breath to whisper, shaking, "Are you afraid?" "Afraid?" murmured the Rat, his eyes shining with utterable love. "Afraid?" of Him? O, never, never. And yet — and yet — O Mole, I am afraid.

Many elements in Tolkien's fantasies convey the same quality, much of them the effect of his linguistic creativity. His use of Elven names, words, and phrases — beautiful yet foreign — often invokes a numinous atmosphere or tone. The numinous is embodied in his idea of Faery or the Elven-world — an other world in which it is possible for beings such as Elves to live and move and have a history. The world of the Elves is the focus of *The Silmarillion*. Some of the Elves, like Lúthien or Galadriel, powerfully embody the numinous in their preternatural beauty and wisdom.

Lewis and Tolkien distinctively shared the desire to embody a quality of joy in their work. *Sehnsucht*, seen as a yearning or longing that is a pointer to joy, was for Lewis a defining characteristic of fantasy. Joy is a strong feature too in Tolkien, and valued by him, as his essay "On Fairy Stories" makes clear. Joy is a key feature of fairy stories, he believed, related to the happy ending, or *eucatastrophe*, part of the consolation they endow. Joy in the story marks the presence of grace coming from the world outside of the story, and even beyond our world. "It denies (in the face of much evidence, if you will) universal final defeat and in so far is *evangelium*, giving a fleeting glimpse of Joy, Joy beyond the walls of the world, poignant as grief." He added: "In such stories when the sudden 'turn' comes we get a piercing glimpse of joy, and heart's desire, that for a moment passes outside the frame, rends indeed the very web of story, and lets a gleam come through."

In an epilogue to the essay, Tolkien considered the quality of joy further, linking it to the Gospel narratives, which, in his view, have all the qualities of an otherworldly, faery story, while at the same time being actual world history. This double reference — to the world of the story, and to the first-century world — intensifies the quality of joy, identifying, he believed, its objective source.

Lewis explored the quality of longing, both in his personal quest, which led to his Christian conversion, and in his writings. Such longing, thought Lewis, was the key to the human experience of joy, and inspired the writer to create fantasy. The creation of Another World is an attempt to reconcile human beings and the world of nature, to embody the fulfillment of our imaginative longing. Imaginative worlds, wonderlands, or "regions of the spirit" may be found in some science fiction, some poetry, some fairy stories, some novels, some myths, even may be discovered in a phrase or sentence.

For Lewis, joy was a foretaste of ultimate reality, heaven itself, or, in other words, our world as it was meant to be, unspoiled by the fall of humankind, and one day to be remade. "Joy," wrote Lewis, "is the serious business of Heaven." In attempting to imagine heaven, Lewis discovered that joy is "the secret signature of each soul." He speculated that the desire for heaven is part of our essential (and unfulfilled) humanity.

In Tolkien, the quality of joy is linked to the sudden turn in the story, the sense of *eucatastrophe*, or reversing of disaster. It is also connected to the inconsolable longing, or sweet desire in Lewis's sense. Dominating all Tolkien's tales of Middle-earth is a longing to obtain the Undying Lands of the uttermost west. The longing is often pictured as a longing for the sea, which lay to the west of Middle-earth, and over which lay Valinor. In *The Lord of the Rings* Legolas, an elf of the Woodland Realm, grew to long for the sea and the lands beyond. His desire was awakened by his first sight of the sea in southern Gondor.

A further feature of fantasy for both friends was restoration or recovery. Tolkien, like Lewis, believed that, through story, the real world would become a more magical place, full of meaning. We see its patterns and colors in a fresh way. The recovery of a true view of the world applies both to individual things, like hills and stones, and to the cosmic — the depths of space and time itself. For in sub-creation, in Tolkien's view, there is a "survey" of space and time. Reality is captured on a miniature scale. Through stories like *The Lord of the Rings*, a renewed view of things is given, illuminating the homely, the spiritual, the physical, and the moral dimensions of the world.

Tolkien and Lewis rejected what they saw as a restless and continual quest for originality in modern writers. They believed that freshness in stories comes from reawakening what is already there in God's created world, not from creating something out of nothing. In a sense, we are meant to be like children, who are normally not tired of familiar experiences. This behavior of children, the friends thought, is a true view of things, and by dipping into the world of story adults can restore such a sense of freshness and wonder about the world. Lewis explained: "[The child] does not despise real woods because he has read of enchanted woods: the reading makes all real woods a little enchanted." For Tolkien, fairy stories help us to make such a recovery — they bring healing — and "in that sense only a taste for them may make us, or keep us, childish." While valuing the child's sense of wonder, he was committed to creating fairy stories for an adult readership. Significantly, Lewis subtitled his *That Hideous Strength* "a modern fairy-tale for grown-ups."

Both friends had a deep affinity, too, in their preoccupation with pre-Christian paganism — with Balder and Psyche, Kullervo and Aeneas, Eurydice and Sigurd. Most of Tolkien's fiction is set in a pre-Christian world, as was his great model, *Beowulf.* Similarly Lewis explored a pagan world in his classical novel *Till We Have Faces.*

Another quality that both Lewis and Tolkien shared was their rare ability to portray goodness in places and people. As all fiction writers know, it is easier to create convincing bad characters than good. As David C. Downing observes:

> Joyce, Woolf, Waugh, Fitzgerald, Faulkner — not to mention Stephen King or Anne Rice — are adept at portraying evil, twisted, neurotic, or self-absorbed characters. But how often does one find simple, good, decent, or wholesome characters portrayed so often and so successfully in modern literature? At both the grand scale (Aslan, Galadriel) and the simple (Mr. and Mrs. Beaver, the hobbits), Lewis and Tolkien could show you what goodness looks like in the flesh.

They could also portray good, and sometimes paradisiacal, places — such as Perelandra, Aslan's Country, the fringes of Heaven, Tom Bombadil's Cottage, The Shire, Valinor, or Lórien.

There were, of course, important differences between Tolkien and Lewis, but not large enough to overshadow their affinities, even when they troubled the friendship at times. Lewis was much more earthy and less delicate than Tolkien in his view of art, just as he was more emphatic in the force of his personality. Lewis was closer in fact to the radical puritanism of John Bunyan, the tradition he explored so insightfully in his *English Literature in the Sixteenth Century.* Such puritanism had nothing like the ascetic and severe associations it has now. Lewis, in fact, traced the origin of the association of puritanism with moral severity to Calvin, and pointed out that even this severity was not life-denying. Far from it: Calvin refused to separate the secular and the sacred, public and private faith: "This severity," Lewis wrote,

> did not mean that [Calvin's] theology was, in the last resort, more ascetic than that of Rome. It sprang from his refusal to allow the Roman distinction between the life of "religion" and the life of the

world, between the Counsels and the Commandments. Calvin's picture of the fully Christian life was less hostile to pleasure and to the body than [the Roman Catholic Bishop John] Fisher's; but then Calvin demanded that every man should be made to live the fully Christian life.

Lewis, in this old puritan mode himself, similarly refused a distinction between "the life of 'religion' and the life of the world" and promoted "mere Christianity" (a term that was coined by the puritan Richard Baxter).

Tolkien was struck by the comic inappropriateness of a description of Lewis as life-denying in *The Daily Telegraph*, which spoke of the "ascetic Mr. Lewis." "I ask you!" Tolkien retorted in a letter. "He put away three pints in a very short session we had this morning, and said he was 'going short for Lent.'" Tolkien himself was drawn much more to a spiritual view of art, rather than the warts-and-all approach of Lewis. He regarded some of Lewis's work, particularly *The Chronicles of Narnia*, as too allegorical, that is, too conceptually and explicitly loaded with Christian beliefs. Tolkien struggled to have Christian meanings more naturally and harmoniously embedded in his work, giving it an inner radiance. Yet when Lewis explored a pre-Christian world in *Till We Have Faces* he achieved a depth of symbolism rather than allegory that was as great as that which his friend had accomplished in *The Lord of the Rings*, though on a smaller scale, and lacking Tolkien's popular touch. Not surprisingly, Tolkien approved of *Out of the Silent Planet*, which created the world of Malacandra (Mars), complete with elements of an "Old Solar" language, and a concept of *hnau* (or embodied personal being) that continued to intrigue Tolkien for years to come as he worked on his own creations, such as Treebeard and his fellow Ents in *The Lord of the Rings*.

Overall Lewis portrayed God as much more approachable than Tolkien ever did. In *The Lord of the Rings*, the name of God does not appear at all, even though there is a clear and constant sense of a providence shaping events, a providence to whom worship is due. In *The Silmarillion*, however, God is explicitly called Ilúvatar, the All-Father. The reason for such an approach to the divine might well be that Tolkien placed his tales in a pre-Christian setting. His world is certainly alive with God's presence. Lewis's fiction, on the other hand, is much more literally Christ-centered. (The only real exception is his novel, *Till We Have Faces*, with its pre-Christian setting north of Greece.) In Narnia, the creator-lion Aslan is mediator. In *Perelandra*, Lewis's reworking of Milton's *Paradise Lost*, the death of Maleldil (Christ) on our Silent Planet means that the fall of humankind cannot simply repeat itself. Elwin Ransom's surname refers to his sacrificial resistance to evil, in which he suffers a debilitating wound to his heel (a direct allusion to Christ's suffering in his ultimate battle against Satan, as prophesied in Genesis 3:15). In Tolkien's world, in contrast, it is the Ainur, the Valar, angelic beings, who mediate between the Children of Ilúvatar and Ilúvatar himself. Gandalf the wizard is a lesser angelic being whose role in Middle-earth is that of a protector and guardian, who interprets and initiates events that lead to the defeat of darkness due to good providence.

For Tolkien, the essence of art as a spiritual force was tied up with his conception of the elves. Elves were at the center, for him, of the faery story, among the highest achievements of art. He saw such spiritual art as having been verified by the greatest story of all — the Gospel. Tolkien argued: "God is the Lord, of angels, and of man — and of Elves. Legend and history have met and fused."

At the heart of the friends' shared beliefs therefore lay a profoundly religious view of fantasy, and of the literature of "romance" — for them a literature that evoked or captured in some way other worlds of the spirit. Particularly they both shared a theology of romanticism, which stressed the poetic imagination. The term "romantic theologian," Lewis tells us, was invented by Charles Williams. "A romantic theologian," Lewis pointed out,

> does not mean one who is romantic about theology but one who is theological about romance, one who considers the theological implications of those experiences which are called romantic. The belief that the most serious and ecstatic experiences either of human love or of imaginative literature have such theological implications and that they can be healthy and fruitful only if the implications are diligently thought out and severely lived, is the root principle of all his [Williams's] work.

Whereas a key preoccupation of Williams was romantic love, Lewis's focus was on the "theological" dimension of romantic longing and its connection to human joy, while Tolkien reflected deeply on the spiritual implications of fairy tale and myth, particularly the aspect of sub-creation.

In *The Encyclopedia of Fantasy* (1997), John Clute and David Langford point out the subversive nature of fantasy in encouraging a perceptual shift:

> It could be argued that, if fantasy (and debatably the literature of the fantastic as a whole) has a purpose other than to entertain, it is to show readers *how to perceive;* an extension of the argument is that fantasy may try to alter readers' perception of reality.... The best fantasy introduces its readers into a playground of rethought perception, where there are no restrictions other than those of the human imagination.... Most full-fantasy texts have at their core the urge to *change* the reader; that is, full fantasy is by definition a subversive literary form.

Good works of imagination cannot be reduced to "morals" and lessons, although lessons can be derived from them, and the truer the work the greater the applications that can be drawn from it. In terms of a quip Lewis once made, imaginative writers are not to sell their birthright for a pot of message. In a review of Tolkien's *The Lord of the Rings*, Lewis noted that "What shows that we are reading myth, not allegory, is that there are no pointers to a specifically theological, or political, or psychological application. A myth points, for each reader, to the realm he lives in most. It is a master key; use it on what door you like." People may ask: Why use fantasy to make a serious point, when normal, realistic fiction could do the job? Because, Lewis answered, the writer wants to say that

> the real life of men is of that mythical and heroic quality. One can see the principle at work in [Tolkien's] characterisation. Much that in a realistic work would be done by "character delineation" is here done simply by making the character an elf, a dwarf, or a hobbit. The imagined beings have their insides on the outside; they are visible souls. And Man as a whole, Man pitted against the universe, have we

seen him at all till we see that he is like a hero in a fairy tale? . . . The value of the myth is that it takes all the things we know and restores to them the rich significance which has been hidden by "the veil of familiarity." . . . By putting bread, gold, horse, apple, or the very roads into a myth, we do not retreat from reality: we rediscover it.

Lewis saw friendship as belonging to "that luminous, tranquil, rational world of relationships freely chosen." For both himself and for Tolkien, their friendship with each other was chosen freely. Friendship, for Lewis, was not, like affection and erotic love, "connected with our nerves" — it was rather the "least biological" of our natural loves. It was an intensely human love, not "shared with the brutes." Friendship, like the fantasy tale, gave a person a vantage point to see the world in a fresh way. Friendship with Tolkien, he found, shook him fully awake, out of the cold dream of materialism. Though he had other close friends, Lewis would not have been the writer and thinker that he was without his friendship with the highly strung, visionary author of *The Lord of the Rings*. As for Tolkien, he found a friend in Lewis who matched his memories of his schoolboy friends in the T.C.B.S. who now lay inert in the Dead Marshes of World War I. He relied upon Lewis's encouragement, and without him would not have completed his painstaking creation of his epic for England, as he thought of his thousand-page story. Of friendship Lewis eulogized: "This alone, of all the loves, seems to raise you almost to the level of gods or angels." Thinking of the company of friends after a day's walking, he was certainly including Tolkien when he wrote:

> Those are the golden sessions . . . when our slippers are on, our feet spread out towards the blaze and our drinks at our elbows; when the whole world, and something beyond the world, opens itself to our minds as we talk; and no one has any claim on or any responsibility for another, but all are freemen and equals as if we had first met an hour ago, while at the same time an Affection mellowed by the years enfolds us. Life — natural life — has no better gift to give. Who could have deserved it?

Appendix A

A Brief Chronology of
J. R. R. Tolkien and C. S. Lewis

1857	Arthur Reuel Tolkien, father of J. R. R. Tolkien, born in Birmingham, England.
1862	Birth of Florence (Flora) Augusta Hamilton, mother of C. S. Lewis, in Queenstown, County Cork, in the south of Ireland.
1863	Birth of Albert J. Lewis, father of C. S. Lewis, in Cork, in the south of Ireland.
1870	Mabel Suffield, mother of J. R. R. Tolkien, born in Birmingham, her family originally from Evesham, Worcestershire, England.
1889	January 21: Birth of Edith Bratt (Tolkien's future wife) in Gloucester, England.
	Arthur Tolkien sails to South Africa to work for the Bank of Africa.
1890	Arthur Tolkien appointed to an important branch in Bloemfontein, seven hundred miles from Cape Town.
1891	March: Mabel Suffield, who had met Arthur Tolkien in Birmingham, leaves Southampton on the steamer *Roslin Castle* for South Africa to marry him.
1892	January 3: John Ronald Reuel Tolkien born in Bloemfontein.
1894	February 17: Birth of J. R. R. Tolkien's brother Hilary Arthur Reuel Tolkien in Bloemfontein.
1895	April: Mabel Tolkien and her sons sail for England, and stay in the tiny Suffield family villa in Ashfield Road, King's Heath, Birmingham.

1895   June 16: Birth of C. S. Lewis's brother Warren Hamilton Lewis in Belfast.

1896   February 15: Death of Arthur Tolkien in Bloemfontein.

         Summer: the Tolkien family moves to near Sarehole Mill, then about a mile outside the city of Birmingham.

1898   November 29: Clive Staples Lewis born in Belfast.

1900   Tolkien enters King Edward's School, then near New Street Station, Birmingham.

         Mabel Tolkien and her sister May received into Roman Catholic Church.

1901   January 22: Queen Victoria dies.

         About this time Warnie Lewis brings the lid of a biscuit tin into the nursery of the infant Lewis.

1902   Tolkien family moves to Oliver Road, near The Oratory, Birmingham, and meets Father Francis Xavier Morgan.

1903   Tolkien gains a scholarship for King Edward's School and resumes study there in the fall.

         Death of Edith Bratt's mother, Frances.

         Christmas: Tolkien takes his first communion.

1904   April: Mabel Tolkien in hospital with diabetes. The brothers sent to relatives, Tolkien to his Aunt Jane in Hove.

         June: Tolkien family joins up again at the Oratory cottage in Rednal, Worcestershire.

         November 14: Death of Mabel Tolkien from diabetes, aged thirty-four.

1905   Lewis family moves to their new home, "Little Lea," on the outskirts of Belfast.

1907   Edith Bratt takes lodgings at 37 Duchess Road, Birmingham, having finished boarding school.

1908   February 15: Flora Lewis has major surgery for cancer.

         The Tolkien brothers take lodgings at 37 Duchess Road and Tolkien meets the nineteen-year-old Edith.

         August 23: Flora Hamilton Lewis dies of cancer, on her husband's birthday.

	September: Lewis is sent to Wynyard School in Watford, near London.
1909	Fall: Tolkien fails in his attempt to pass Oxford entrance examination; enforced separation from Edith.
	Edith Bratt moves to Cheltenham to stay with elderly family friends. During this time she becomes engaged to a Warwickshire farmer.
1910	Summer: Start of the Tea Club at King Edward's School. About this time Tolkien begins inventing "private" languages.
	Fall: Lewis attends Campbell College near his Belfast home for half a term. Tolkien succeeds in Oxford entrance examination, and is offered an Open Classical Exhibition to Exeter College.
1911	Lewis is sent to Malvern, England, to study. During this time at Malvern he abandons his childhood Christian faith.
	October: Tolkien enters Exeter College, Oxford, to read Classics.
1912	Joseph Wright begins tutoring Tolkien. Tolkien takes up studying Welsh, discovers Finnish, and begins to invent Quenya, a variant of Elvish based on Finnish.
1913	January: Tolkien is reunited with Edith Bratt.
	Summer: Tolkien gains a Second Class for his Honour Moderations and switches course to the English School after getting an "alpha" in comparative philology.
1914	January 8: Edith Bratt is received into the Roman Catholic Church and becomes engaged to Tolkien.
	February: Warren enters the Royal Military Academy at Sandhurst.
	April: Lewis becomes acquainted with Arthur Greeves.
	August 4: Britain declares war on Germany.
	September 19: Lewis commences private study with W. T. Kirkpatrick, "The Great Knock," in Great Bookham Surrey, with whom he remains until April 1917.
1915	Summer: Tolkien gains a First Class in English language and literature. He is commissioned in the Lancashire Fusiliers.
1916	March 22: Tolkien marries Edith.
	Tolkien serves from July to October in the Battle of the Somme, France. Returns to England suffering from "trench fever."

1916	December: Lewis sits for a classical scholarship and is elected to University College, Oxford.
1917	From April 26 until September, Lewis studies at University College, Oxford. He meets "Paddy" Moore.
	November: Lewis reaches the front line in the Somme Valley in France.
	November 16: Tolkien's son John born.
1918	April 15: Lewis is wounded in battle.
	October: With the war almost over Tolkien seeks out possible jobs in Oxford.
	November 11: End of World War I.
1919–23	Lewis resumes his studies at University College, Oxford, where he receives a First Class in Honour Moderations (Greek and Latin literature) in 1920, a First Class in Greats (philosophy and ancient history) in 1922, and a First Class in English in 1923.
1919	March: Lewis's *Spirits in Bondage* published by Heinemann under the name Clive Hamilton.
1920	Lewis establishes a house in Oxford for Mrs. Moore and her daughter Maureen. Lewis lives with the Moores from June 1921. Tolkien has enough students to end his work on the *Oxford English Dictionary*.
	October: Tolkien's second son, Michael, born.
1921	Tolkien takes up a university post at Leeds, initially as Reader in English literature.
1924	October: Tolkien appointed Professor of English Language at Leeds University, aged thirty-two. Lewis begins teaching philosophy at University College, standing in for E. F. Carritt, for one year.
	November: Tolkien's third son, Christopher, born.
1925	May 20: Lewis elected a Fellow of Magdalen College, Oxford, where he serves as tutor in English language and literature for twenty-nine years until leaving for Magdalene College, Cambridge, in 1954.
	October: Tolkien is appointed Rawlinson and Bosworth Professor of Anglo-Saxon at Oxford.
1926	May 11: The first recorded meeting between Tolkien and Lewis.

1928	May 2: Albert Lewis retires with an annual pension from his position as Belfast Corporation County solicitor.
1929	Lewis becomes a theist.
	September: Albert Lewis dies of cancer in Belfast.
	Birth of Tolkien's daughter Priscilla.
Late 1929	Tolkien gives "Lay of Leithien" to Lewis to read, and draws up his "Sketch of the Mythology" to fill out its background. Lewis reads it the night of December 6.
1930s	Tolkien writes first draft of *Farmer Giles of Ham,* based in Oxfordshire and Buckinghamshire. He also works on an Arthurian poem, never finished, "The Fall of Arthur."
1930	May: Warren Lewis decides to edit and arrange the Lewis family papers.
	October: Mrs. Moore, Lewis, and his brother Warren purchase "The Kilns" near Oxford.
1930 or 1931	Tolkien begins to write *The Hobbit.*
1931	Tolkien's reformed English School syllabus is accepted, bringing together "Lang." and "Lit."
	September 19–20: After a long night conversation on Addison's Walk in Oxford with Tolkien and Hugo Dyson, Lewis becomes convinced of the truth of Christian faith.
	September 28: Lewis returns to Christian faith while riding to Whipsnade Zoo in the sidecar of his brother's motorbike.
Late 1932	Lewis reads the incomplete draft of *The Hobbit.*
1933	May 25: Lewis's *The Pilgrim's Regress* published.
	The fall term marks the beginning of Lewis's convening of a circle of friends dubbed the Inklings.
1934	Publication of Tolkien's poem, "The Adventures of Tom Bombadil," in the *Oxford Magazine.*
1936	March 11: Charles Williams receives first letter from Lewis, in appreciation of his novel, *The Place of the Lion.*
	Spring: Lewis and Tolkien discuss writing time and space stories.
	November 25: Tolkien gives the Sir Isaac Gollancz Memorial Lecture to the British Academy on "Beowulf: The Monsters and the Critics."

1936	Publication of Lewis's *The Allegory of Love*.
1937	September 21: *The Hobbit* is published.
	December: Tolkien begins writing *The Lord of the Rings*.
1939	March 8: Tolkien delivers his Andrew Lang lecture, "On Fairy Stories," at the University of St. Andrews, Scotland.
	September 2: Evacuee children arrive at The Kilns.
	September 4: Warren Lewis recalled to active service the day after Britain declares war on Germany.
	September 7: Williams moves with the London branch of Oxford University Press to Oxford.
1940	Lewis begins lecturing on Christianity for the Royal Air Force, which he continues to do until 1941.
	August 27: Maureen Moore marries Leonard J. Blake, director of music at Worksop College, Nottinghamshire.
	October 14: Lewis's *The Problem of Pain* is published. It is dedicated to the Inklings.
1941	August 6: Lewis broadcasts the first of twenty-five talks on BBC radio.
1942	Williams's *The Forgiveness of Sins* is published, dedicated to the Inklings.
	Lewis publishes *The Screwtape Letters,* dedicated to Tolkien.
	Christopher Tolkien leaves to join the Royal Air Force, training to be a fighter pilot in South Africa.
1943	February 18: An honorary Oxford M.A. is awarded to Williams.
1944	January 5: Williams tells Michal, his wife, about a *Time* magazine journalist writing on Lewis. The cover story eventually appears in 1947 and helps to ensure Lewis's popularity in the United States.
	Lewis lectures at Cambridge — the Clark Lectures. These lectures become the important chapter, "New Learning and New Ignorance," in his volume for the *Oxford History of English Literature*.
1945	Germany surrenders on May 8, Japan on September 2. End of World War II.

May 15: Warren Lewis records in his diary the sudden, unexpected death of Williams. "And so vanishes one of the best and nicest men it has ever been my good fortune to meet. May God receive him into His everlasting happiness."

Fall: Tolkien is appointed Merton Professor of English Language and Literature at Oxford University. He publishes "Leaf by Niggle" in the *Dublin Review.*

1947   Lewis publishes *Miracles.*

1949   Fall: Tolkien finishes *The Lord of the Rings.*

October 20: The last Thursday night Inklings literary meeting is recorded in Warren's diary. "No one turned up" the following week. The group continues to meet informally until Lewis's death.

Late 1949   Tolkien sends Milton Waldman of Collins a large manuscript, much of it hand-written, of the unfinished "The Silmarillion."

1950   January 10: Lewis receives a letter from a thirty-four-year-old American writer, Helen Joy Davidman Gresham.

Publication of *The Lion, the Witch and the Wardrobe.*

1951   January 12: Mrs. Moore dies. Since the previous April, she had been confined to a nursing home in Oxford.

Tolkien attends a philological congress in Belgium.

Second edition of *The Hobbit,* revised in the light of the plot of *The Lord of the Rings.*

1952   June 22: Tolkien offers *The Lord of the Rings* to George Allen & Unwin.

Publication of Lewis's *Mere Christianity.*

September: Lewis meets Joy Davidman for the first time.

1953   March: Tolkien and Edith move to Sandfield Road in Headington, an Oxford suburb.

1954   Lewis accepts the Chair of Medieval and Renaissance Literature at Cambridge. He gives his Inaugural Lecture, *De Description Temporum,* on his fifty-sixth birthday.

Publication of the first two volumes of *The Lord of the Rings.* Tolkien dedicates this first edition to the Inklings.

Lewis publishes *English Literature in the Sixteenth Century, Excluding Drama.*

1955   Publication of Lewis's *Surprised by Joy: The Shape of My Early Life.*

            May 20: Tolkien finishes the appendices to *The Lord of the Rings.*

            October 20: Publication of the final volume of *The Lord of the Rings.*

1956   April 23: Lewis enters into a civil marriage with Joy Davidman at the Oxford Registry Office.

            Lewis publishes *The Last Battle,* which is awarded The Carnegie Medal, a prestigious award for children's books. His *Till We Have Faces* is also published this year.

1957   March 21: Lewis's ecclesiastical marriage with Joy Davidman while she is hospitalized.

            September: Joy Davidman's health is improving; by December 10 she is walking again.

1958   March: Tolkien visits Holland.

1959   June 5: Tolkien delivers his "Valedictory Address" in Oxford as Merton Professor of English Language and Literature.

            October: X ray shows return of Joy's cancer.

1960   May: Joy Davidman and Edith Tolkien in hospital together.

            July 13: Joy dies, at the age of forty-five, not long after the couple's return from a vacation in Greece.

1963   June 15: Lewis admitted to Acland Nursing Home following a heart attack.

            September: Warren returns to The Kilns after having been in Ireland for several months.

            Friday, November 22: Lewis dies, at home, one week before his sixty-fifth birthday.

1964   Publication of *Letters to Malcolm: Chiefly on Prayer,* prepared by Lewis for publication before his death.

            Publication of Tolkien's *Tree and Leaf.*

1965   Increasing popularity of Tolkien on American college campuses after an unauthorized paperback edition of *The Lord of the Rings* is issued by Ace, using a loophole in copyright law. The book sparks college campus craze that spreads around the world. *Frodo Lives* and *Gandalf for President* buttons are seen everywhere.

1966	Warren Lewis publishes *Letters of C. S. Lewis.*
	Summer: Professor Clyde S. Kilby aids Tolkien with "The Silmarillion."
1968	June: The Tolkiens move to Bournemouth, bothered by fans, noise, stairs, and their distance from the Oxford city center.
1971	November 29: Death of Edith Tolkien. Tolkien returns to Oxford, to a Merton College flat at 21 Merton Street.
1972	March 28: C.B.E. conferred on Tolkien by the Queen.
1973	April 9: Warren Lewis dies, still mourning his beloved brother.
	Sunday, September 2: Tolkien dies in Bournemouth.
1975	Death of Henry "Hugo" Victor Dyson Dyson.
1977	Publication of *The Silmarillion,* edited by Christopher Tolkien. It goes on to sell more than one million copies in the United States in hardcover.
1984	Death of Michael Tolkien.
1997	December 14: Owen Barfield dies, just short of his hundredth birthday.
2003	Death of John Tolkien.

Appendix B

The Enduring Popularity of J. R. R. Tolkien and C. S. Lewis

What is the secret of the great spell that Tolkien has cast around the globe? As well as the spirituality of his *The Lord of the Rings,* attractive in our postmodern age, he presents a powerful critique of what he saw as the modernist form of magic — the domination of the machine. Unlike the ideas of modernism, this social and mechanical domination is more tenacious, and thus perhaps Tolkien's exploration strikes a deep chord in contemporary readers and film viewers.

Explorations of virtual reality, particularly in film, have opened up the big philosophical and theological questions about the scope of reality. Does it extend beyond what can be measured, and beyond what can be seen, touched, and heard? The denials of modernist thought, which tried to put reality into a closed box, seem increasingly hollow. *The Lord of the Rings* is a fantasy about *actual* reality. Underpinning it is Tolkien's carefully worked-out idea of sub-creation — the creation of a secondary world — in which the human maker imagines God's world after him. For Tolkien, the moral and spiritual world is as real as the physical world — indeed, each is part of one creation, and a successful sub-creation like the world of Middle-earth captures them all in an organic whole. The result is an image of reality that is making a claim to reliable knowledge. The idea of crafting a secondary world, a possible world, applies far beyond fantasy. Any story, even a novel set in the real world, if it is any good at all, creates a possible world. It is then a big metaphor. Metaphors, of course, speak of one thing by another — in the familiar proverb "love is blind," blindness illumines an aspect of love. If Tolkien is correct, the world created by the story is intentionally about something other than itself, shedding insights into the very nature of reality.

Tolkien's popularity might lie in four main factors.

In the first place he is a great storyteller. *The Lord of the Rings* is a powerfully accomplished story, rooted in the central elements of what he called the Faery Story, or the Elven tale. Storytelling is universal, and stories of myth, legend, and popular folk tale contain archetypes or universal elements, like the motifs of the quest and the journey. Tolkien seems to have seen the elements of a good story most articulated in the Gospel narratives. The Bible is the most global book in history, translated into all written languages. Interestingly, *The Lord of the Rings* is fast becoming one of the most globally read books after the Bible. Though rooted in many biblical motifs and themes (like providence, the problem of evil, sacrifice, redemption) Tolkien masterfully sets the events in a pre-Christian world, supposedly, by a giant and imaginative anachronism, northern European in geographical location. Thus his Christian elements are transformed into a shape that is attractive without raising barriers for those who don't share his Christian beliefs.

Second, Tolkien's story is given many dimensions by his extensive creation of another, secondary world. Middle-earth is replete with its own languages, geography, and history. The vividness and depths of this "sub-created" world undoubtedly reinforce the appeal of *The Lord of the Rings*. Like the vastness of the cosmos, Tolkien's richly invented world opens up possibilities, hopes, and dreams. He helps to formulate in his readers a sense of disenchantment with our secular culture. People today have an uneasy sense that there are dimensions to life untapped by our materialist culture, and that most of us are missing these dimensions. Tolkien's underlying archetypes (such as the quest and the journey) perhaps focus the longing of people throughout the world, based upon the aspirations of our common humanity.

In the third place Tolkien intended *The Lord of the Rings* to sound a warning about the consequences of abandoning "Old Western" values, even though he avoided doing this allegorically, as he felt that in allegory the author was seeking to dominate the reader. The story is marked by a realistic portrayal of evil. It seems to belong with several other prophetic twentieth-century novels (including George Orwell's *Animal Farm* and *1984*, William Golding's *The Lord of the Flies,* and C. S. Lewis's *That Hideous Strength*), in reshaping fiction to come to terms with the horror of palpable evil revealed in modern, global warfare. Tolkien's work (like those other books) might perhaps be more relevant to understanding the fears and terrors of our lives than much so-called realistic fiction, which is not so geared to exploring the big questions of humanity. This is a deep irony, given that some critics dismiss Tolkien's fiction as escapist, and as having a simplicity only suitable for adolescent reading — it is not, they say, for grown-ups like themselves.

At the center of Tolkien's portrayal of the New West is the machine as the modern form of magic. He approaches the issue by way of exploring power and possession. Possession is a major theme in his stories. In a letter Tolkien commented, " 'Power' is an ominous and sinister word in all these tales, except as applied to the gods." Morgoth, Sauron, and the wizard Saruman are power-hungry, employing genetic engineering, and using or encouraging the use of machines. Sauron, in fact, is the supreme technocrat; the Ring itself is a product of his technological skill. Tolkien contrasts art with power, expressed in magic. In his stories art is idealized in the Elves, for whom power has no attraction. They do not wish to dominate. Tolkien, like Lewis, saw a machine attitude, or technocracy, as evil magic in modern guise. Like the magician, modern technocrats desire to oppress and possess nature, rather than to work with and shape her like artists treat their materials.

The two central motifs of the stories of Middle-earth, the Silmarils and the Ring, focus the theme of power and possession. The Silmarils, the gems that captured the original and lost light of the world, are wholly good, and the Ring is wholly evil, yet each test those who come into contact with them. The Elven King Thingol tragically falls morally in desiring a Silmaril; Beren has no desire to possess it. Rather he loves the greater treasure, Lúthien, who is better than any possession. Boromir succumbs to the desire of the Ring; Bilbo resists it, as does Galadriel; it has little power over the humble Sam.

In the fourth place Tolkien's popularity may lay in the fact that he presents an attractive spirituality that appeals to a broad readership seeking new meaning and spiritual fulfillment in a greatly secularized world. Tolkien's spirituality was of great importance in his creation of Middle-earth. Central to his fiction is the creation of elves. These are representative of human spirituality and culture, and human spirituality itself has an elven quality. Just like Lewis, Tolkien was deeply inspired by a broad range of spiritual imagery, like trees, angels, the fall of humankind, the power of healing, the personification of wisdom, light and darkness, nature and grace, and the biblical portrayal of heroism and evil.

Tolkien saw a fundamental quality of good fantasy or fairy story as consolation. Here grace — the presence, will, and mind of God — enters story. The story of the incarnation, death, and resurrection of Christ, he argued, has all the features of the best stories, as the result of a divine shaping of real, historical events. The fairy story, he believed, is at the heart of human storytelling, whether of northern Europe or of the classical world, or elsewhere. The concept of faerie had been mutilated, and Tolkien sought to rehabilitate it, as did Lewis, both in his scholarship and in his own storytelling. In his invented mythology of Middle-earth, Tolkien's elves were an extended metaphor of a defining aspect of human nature, its language, making, and culture.

Perhaps the greatest challenge in understanding Tolkien as a writer is his "The Silmarillion." The published version has to be supplemented by the posthumous publications *Unfinished Tales* (1980) and the twelve volumes of *The History of Middle-earth* (meticulously edited by Christopher Tolkien, and published 1983–96) to begin to grasp the scale and ambition of this unfinished work. It may be unprecedented as a literary oeuvre that exists partly by reconstruction, by a kind of collaboration with the reader, with the published *The Silmarillion* as a guide. A fitting analogy might be if Rembrandt had left a series of two or three hundred closely related and carefully worked-out sketches for a project, never completed, of painting all aspects of seventeenth-century life in northern Europe — its buildings, interiors, trades, landscapes, urban and country life, classes of people and professions, sciences, arts, explorations, means of transportation, inventions, and beliefs. In this analogy, the vast, lifelong project tries to capture the very mystery of human life, as a whole comes into being that is larger than the sum of its parts. Though Rembrandt's approach to the presence of the spiritual and the human in the ordinary world was of course very different from Tolkien's, the material of "The Silmarillion" is very much like a collection of closely related sketches that together point to something larger and more splendid.

In his 1936 lecture on *Beowulf*, Tolkien had used an analogy that can be applied as well to the "matter" of Middle-earth, "The Silmarillion." He had compared the *Beowulf* poem to a tower constructed by a man from an ancient ruin he had inherited; the scholars and critics, failing to see the great poem — the tower — as a whole, described it as a mere pile of stones. Just as the "tower" of *Beowulf* needed to be "rebuilt," rediscovered by its critics to grasp its unique power and beauty, so too the purpose and quality of "The Silmarillion" needs to be much more acknowledged. It is not merely a collection of varied pieces, as the reconstruction Christopher Tolkien made in preparing the publication of *The Silmarillion* so vividly shows.

Looking at the "ruins" of *Beowulf* people had said about the stones, "What a muddle!" Others had murmured:

> "He is such an odd fellow! Imagine his using these old stones just to build a nonsensical tower! . . . He had no sense of proportion."
>
> But from the top of that tower the man had been able to look out upon the sea.

Most of the factors that have made Tolkien so enormously popular also apply to Lewis. He did not, however, produce anything as detailed and mentally inhabitable as Middle-earth. In terms of children's literature, however, *The Chronicles of Narnia* have long established themselves as classics of popular culture like *The Wind in the Willows*, *The Hobbit*, *Winnie the Pooh*, *Alice in Wonderland*, or more recently the Harry Potter stories.

In addition to the factors he shared with Tolkien, there are other reasons for Lewis's enduring popularity. For one, he had a highly eclectic imagination. Screwtape, Puddleglum the Marshwiggle, Elwin Ransom the Cambridge don, Aslan the talking lion and creator of Narnia, Sarah Smith of Golder's Green, Mr. Sensible, Redival of ancient Glome, Jane and Mark Studdock of the English Midlands — these are just a few of Lewis's creations. From his teeming mind and imagination sprang stories and powerful rhetoric aimed at persuading people of the truth of Christian faith. For many years an atheist, Lewis didn't become a Christian believer until more than halfway through his life, which meant that he understood from the inside what a materialist universe looked, tasted, and smelled like.

The second reason is obvious — like his friend, he made an enduring contribution to children's literature, in his case with his Narnian Chronicles, which certainly outstrip the sales of his other writings.

Further reasons might also explain Lewis's wide and enduring appeal.

He was a major literary scholar, with works such as *The Allegory of Love, English Literature in the Sixteenth Century,* and *An Experiment in Criticism,* all of which are still in print despite the fact that there are inevitably points of contention, such as his treatment of humanism and Renaissance, and his thesis that the watershed in Western civilization was reached early in the nineteenth century, not in the sixteenth.

He was an outstanding apologist or defender of Christian faith, making the cover of *Time* magazine as early as 1947. Reluctantly he was one of the first, and one of the best, media evangelists. His *Mere Christianity* alone has been cited in the testimonies of many as a major influence in their Christian conversions. His controversial *Miracles* continues to challenge individuals who see no reason for active divine involvement in human experience, over fifty years after it was written.

He was also a popular theologian, able to convey biblical themes convincingly with wit, imagination, and clarity. His theology is embedded in his fictional works like *The Pilgrim's Regress, The Screwtape Letters, The Narnian Chronicles,* and his science-fiction trilogy. It is also found in his *Mere Christianity, Miracles, Reflections on the Psalms, Letters to Malcolm,* and *The Problem of Pain.*

He was, arguably, a mainstream science-fiction author, earning the respect of leaders in the genre such as Arthur C. Clarke and Brian Aldiss. The first two volumes of his Ransom trilogy are particularly celebrated.

He was a novelist who showed a promise that was cut short by illness and his comparatively early death. *Till We Have Faces* is one of his greatest books, a narrative set several hundred years B.C. in an imaginary but realistic country somewhere north of Greece. It has affinities with his friend Tolkien's work, was deeply influenced by his — very different — friend Charles Williams, and was probably shaped in dialogue with Joy Davidman.

He was a thinker who, early in his academic career, was part of a discussion group with young Oxford philosophers that also included Gilbert Ryle. He taught philosophy for a year before entering his teaching career as an English don. His *The Problem of Pain*, *Miracles*, and *The Abolition of Man* are serious philosophical texts, despite being aimed at a general reader.

He was a poet, though a minor one, whose work ranged from lyrics to long (and currently unfashionable) narrative poems. His early ambition was to be a major poet — his first volume was published at the age of twenty-one — but he increasingly found himself out of kilter with modern verse. He was disappointed by his failure to be elected as Oxford Professor of Poetry in 1951. His poetic sensibility, however, inspired all his prose, whether discursive or fictional.

These varied facets of Lewis constantly interrelated in an organic way, making the whole of his personality larger than the sum of all parts. He could have been looking back at the end of his life when he observed in 1940:

The settled happiness and security which we all desire, God withholds from us by the very nature of the world: but joy, pleasure, and merriment, He has, scattered broadcast. We are never safe, but we have plenty of fun, and some ecstacy. It is not hard to see why. The security we crave would teach us to rest our hearts in this world and oppose an obstacle to our return to God: a few moments of happy love, a landscape, a symphony, a merry meeting with our friends, a bathe or a football match, have no such tendency. Our Father refreshes us on the journey with some pleasant inns, but will not encourage us to mistake them for home.

Notes

1 The Formative Years

1–4   The vignette is based on references by Tolkien to the coal trucks in letters and interviews. The railway line still runs close by the back of his house, 86 Westfield Road, but King's Heath Station has gone. The account of Warren's biscuit tin garden and its significance is found in C. S. Lewis's *Surprised by Joy*, 3–4. "He is the opaque centre of all existences . . .": C. S. Lewis, *Miracles*, chapter 11.

1   BBC Radio 4 interview with Denis Gueroult, *Now Read On*, December 16, 1970.

3   *Surprised by Joy*, 4, 11.

4   *The Tolkien Family Album*, 16.

5   From interviews with Tolkien, BBC Radio 4 interview with Denis Gueroult, *Now Read On*, December 16, 1970, and Philip Norman, *Sunday Times*, January 15, 1967.

5   "Long ago": *The Hobbit*, 15.

5   "The Shire is very like": BBC Radio 4 interview with Denis Gueroult, *Now Read On*, December 16, 1970.

6   "There was an old mill": Tolkien interviewed by John Ezard, quoted by him December 28, 1991, in *The Guardian*.

6   Account of the miller and son, and "The Shire": Tolkien, *Letters*, Letter 303 and Letter 213.

6   For an account of his Atlantis dream, see Tolkien, *Letters*, Letter 163 (to W. H. Auden).

8   Tolkien's memories of his mother: Tolkien, *Letters*, Letter 250.

Notes

9   "The New House is almost": *Surprised by Joy*, 6–7.

9   *My life, By Jacks Lewis. Lewis Family Papers.*

11   "The only stimulating": *Surprised by Joy*, 18.

13   Children making up languages: Tolkien, *Letters*, Letter 131.

13   "raptuous words": From *Christ*, Line 104. Letter to Clyde S. Kilby, December 18, 1965. Quoted in Kilby, *Tolkien and The Silmarillion*, 57.

13–14   The boy's account of his real treasure: *Lewis Papers*, vol. 11, 251–55.

15   "That's all spoof": Interview with Philip Norman, *Sunday Times*, January 15, 1967.

15–16   The Dead Marshes: *The Two Towers*, Book IV, chapter 2.

16   "A real taste": Tolkien, "On Fairy-Stories" in *Tree and Leaf*, 41.

16   "Long before I wrote": BBC Radio 4 interview with Denis Gueroult, *Now Read On*, December 16, 1970.

16   "My stories seem to germinate": Interview with Philip Norman, *Sunday Times*, January 15, 1967.

18   "Rather slim, but": The Wade Center Oral History, interview with Maureen Moore.

18   "the frights, the cold": *Surprised by Joy*, 42.

20   "I cannot help recalling": "Valedictory Address," in Tolkien, *The Monsters and the Critics*, 238.

20   "Perhaps, had he remained": Nancy Martsch, "A Tolkien Chronology," in *Proceedings of the J. R. R. Tolkien Centenary Conference*, 293.

21   Tolkien's verse translation of *Beowulf* remained undiscovered until it was found in 1996 in Oxford's Bodleian Library by Dr. Michael D. C. Drout of Wheaton College, Norton, Massachusetts, USA, and is due to be published in the near future.

22   "more and more obsessed": The Wade Center Oral History, interview with Maureen Moore.

22–23   Albert Lewis's reaction to his son's appointment: *Lewis Papers*, vol. 8, 90.

2 Meeting of Minds and Imaginations

24–26   This vignette is based on Lewis's diary entry for Tuesday, May 11, 1926. In a letter to his brother, September 18, 1939, Lewis recounts the sort of atmosphere created by Mrs. Moore in such situations. Note that Lewis's attitude to his adopted mother is far more positive than that of Warren Lewis, as expressed in diary entries. Don is the name given to tutors or Fellows of colleges in Oxford and Cambridge universities, a term derived from the Latin *dominus*, lord, via the Spanish title, Don, as in Don Quixote.

26–27   "If you take your stand": *Experiment in Criticism*, 105–6.

27   "every finite thing or event": *Miracles*, 23.

28   Passionate love of language: Evidenced, for example, in his *A Study in Words* (1960).

29–30   "Barfield . . . made short work": *Surprised by Joy*, 161.

31   Barfield on individual imagination: *Poetic Diction*, 22.

31   Barfield on knowledge: *Poetic Diction*, 22.

31   Lewis elaborates the same point as Barfield's about the poetic condition of meaning in thought in "Bluspels and Flalansferes" in *Selected Literary Essays*, and the chapter "Horrid Red Things" in *Miracles*, a chapter that tries to popularize Barfield's main idea in *Poetic Diction*.

32   Auden referred to the effect that Tolkien: This was during his inaugural lecture delivered as Professor of Poetry at Oxford, June 11, 1956.

32   A postgraduate from Canada: Perhaps a Rhodes scholar. Quoted in Ready, *The Tolkien Relation*, 17.

33   Lewis explained to his father his method of lecture preparation: Undated letter April or May 1925. *Letters of C. S. Lewis*, 9.

33   He explained a distinction made by the contemporary philosopher: There are similarities here with Michael Polanyi's emphasis, in his *Personal Knowledge*, upon indwelling particulars rather than attending to them, and the themes of philosophical debate about human intentionality and reference in language.

34–35   Mabbott's description of the "Wee Teas": see *Oxford Memories*, chapter 13.

35–36   Lewis's reading habits: Helen Gardner, "C. S. Lewis: 1898–1963," 419.

37   "The most exciting room": *The Tolkien Family Album*, 50.

38   Diotima. This is argued by John Bremmer in *The C. S. Lewis Readers'*
            Encyclopedia (ed. Schutz and West). There is also a Diotima in
            Friedrich Hölderin's novel *Hyperion*, associated with unfulfilled
            longing; Lewis had a strong interest in the German romantic
            movement, so he may have known this novel.

38   Barfield on Mrs. Moore and Lewis. *The Independent*, March 7, 1994.

38   For origin of *Lewis Family Papers*, see below, p. 39.

40   "He had to write by snatches": *Exploring the Christian World Mind*.

40   Leonard Blake's memories of Lewis brothers' conversation: The
            Wade Center Oral History interview.

41   Austin Olney on Tolkien's imagination: From Houghton Mifflin
            webpages, *www.houghtonmifflinbooks.com/*

42   A. N. Wilson on Tolkien's verse: *C. S. Lewis: A Biography*, 117.

43   "Early in 1926 the hardest boiled": *Surprised by Joy*, 174. "We
            somehow got on the historical truth": *All My Road Before Me*, 379.

3   A Story-Shaped World

45–46,   The vignettes in this chapter are based upon Lewis's accounts
52–53   in *Surprised by Joy* (174–75 and 184–85) and Warren Lewis's
            diary entry describing the Whipsnade trip (Monday, September 28,
            1931), in *Brothers and Friends*, 100–102. The style of the Whipsnade
            visit was cramped by the late arrival of the car bearing Mrs. Moore
            and the others and the fact that Lewis and Warnie then took it in
            turns to look after the dog, which was not allowed into the zoo.

46   "I never had the experience": *Christian Reflections*, chapter 14.

47   Early meetings with Tolkien: *Letters of C. S. Lewis*, November 22,
            1931.

47   Helen Gardner, "C. S. Lewis 1898–1963." The Final Honour
            School refers to the main part of the undergraduate course, the last
            two years of the three-year study for a B.A. in English.

47   Lewis's ignorance of Tolkien's names: *Letters of C. S. Lewis*, May 25,
            1957.

47–48   "He is the most unmanageable": Letter to Charles Huttar, March 30,
            1962.

48   "C. S. Lewis was one of the only three persons": Letter to Dick Plotz, *Letters of J. R. R. Tolkien*, Letter 276.

48   "I can honestly say": Letter to Tolkien, December 7, 1929, quoted in *The Lays of Beleriand*, 151.

49   "You might like to know": Tolkien had a similarly positive reaction to Barfield's essay, "Legal Fiction," in *Essays Presented to Charles Williams*, ed. C. S. Lewis. See *Letters of C. S. Lewis*, 384.

49   Information on Tolkien's translations of *Beowulf* based on a personal communication from Dr. Michael Drout, of Wheaton College, Norton, Massachusetts, who in 1996 discovered the material. He has published an extended version of Tolkien's 1936 lecture on *Beowulf*, based on the newfound material, and the translations are due to appear in the near future.

49–50   The Wade Center Oral History interview with Professor Dickens, April 17, 1989.

50   "C.S.L. of course had some oddities": *Letters of J. R. R. Tolkien*, August 30, 1964.

50   "He is a very great man": *Letters of C. S. Lewis*, October 29, 1944.

50   "That great but dilatory": *Letters of C. S. Lewis*, January 12, 1950.

51   "In this book I propose to describe": Quoted in Green and Hooper, *C. S. Lewis: A Biography*, 3d edition, 111.

51   "I should like to know": Letter December 22, 1922. *Collected Letters*, vol. 1, 850.

51–52   "Another of the beauties of coming": Letter, January 26, 1930.

52   Lewis reveals to Jenkin his changing outlook: Letter, March 21, 1930. *Collected Letters*, vol. 1, 887.

52   Letter to Barfield, February 1930.

53   "Friendship with Lewis compensates": Quoted in *J. R. R. Tolkien: A Biography*, 148.

55   Balder and Tegner's *Drapa, Surprised by Joy*, 12. My paraphrase is based on Longfellow's poetic translation of Tegner.

56   "The quality which had enchanted me": Preface to *George MacDonald: An Anthology*.

56   "We do not want merely to see beauty": "The Weight of Glory," in *Screwtape Proposes a Toast*, 106–7.

57   "All my waiting and watching for Joy": *Surprised by Joy,* 170.

58   "The heart of Christianity is": "Myth became fact," in *God in the Dock,* 43–44.

4   The Thirties

60   My description of this representative incident is based upon The Tale of Túrin Turambar, found in *The Silmarillion,* and in various versions in *Unfinished Tales* and *The History of Middle-earth.* An unfinished poetic version exists in *The Lays of Beleriand* (from *The History of Middle-earth*).

64   "Most literary criticism is dated": David L. Russell, in "C. S. Lewis," in *British Children's Writers,* vol. 160, 134–49.

64   "To medieval studies in this country": "Grete Clerk," in *Light on C. S. Lewis,* ed. Jocelyn Gibb.

65–66   "Find out what the author actually wrote": *An Experiment in Criticism,* 121.

66   Lewis's confrontations with the Cambridge English School. For a full account, see Brian Barbour, "Lewis and Cambridge," *Modern Philology* 96, no. 4 (May 1999).

68   "I go to Cambridge to lecture once a week": Quoted in Barbour, "Lewis and Cambridge," 453–54.

69   "The Monsters and the Critics" has been republished in *The Monsters and the Critics and Other Essays,* 1983.

74–75   Harry Blamires, "Against the Stream: C. S. Lewis and the Literary Scene," in *Journal of the Irish Christian Study Centre* 1 (1983): 15. Further insight into the presence of Christian belief in Oxford circles in particular at this period is given in "Is there an Oxford 'School' of Writing?: A discussion between Rachel Trickett and David Cecil" (*The Twentieth Century,* June 1955, 559–70).

75   Edmund Crispin's *Swan Song,* 1947, 59–60.

5   The Inklings Begin

77–78   The vignette is constructed from comments made by Inklings on various occasions. The layout of The Eagle and Child has changed from this date — late in the fall of 1937 — due to restructuring, and expansion at the rear. The gift to the barmaid is fictional, but Chad Walsh does record that, around 1948, he asked a barmaid if she knew anything about Lewis, whom she had often served. She replied, "He's just a nice gentleman from Magdalen College" and was simply astonished to learn that he had written a book. I've adapted this, imagining a barmaid, perhaps with young children, overhearing about *The Hobbit* from the Inklings' boisterous conversation (Chad Walsh — The Wade Center Oral History interview).

79   Tolkien describes the Inklings. Letter 298, *Letters of J. R. R. Tolkien*.

79   Letter to Swann, October 14, 1966.

80   "In each of my friends": *The Four Loves*, 58–59.

81   Barfield in America. The event was recorded in Rand Kuhl, "Owen Barfield in Southern California," *Mythlore* 1, no. 4 (1969).

82–83   My account of Havard is based on The Wade Center interview with him, which took place July 26, 1984. See also, "Philia: Jack at Ease," in *C. S. Lewis at the Breakfast Table*, ed. James Como.

83–84   *Owen Barfield on C. S. Lewis*, ed. G. B. Tennyson (Middletown, Conn.: Wesleyan University Press, 1989).

84   The hypothetical exclusion of Dorothy L. Sayers from visiting the Inklings. The all-male character of The Inklings must be seen in its contemporary context. Such a group was typical of its times. This is helpfully brought out in Mabbott's *Oxford Memories*, particularly in his chapter "Co-ed." In contrast, in his Ulster context, Lewis had female friends, such as Jane McNeill, and closer to home, friends such as Ruth Pitter and Joy Davidman; Tolkien too had female friends outside of the Inklings; and Williams had innumerable women friends. Dorothy L. Sayers was a mutual friend of Lewis and Williams. Lewis and Tolkien shared the view of their period that for men deep friendships were only possible with other men. Joy Davidman contradicted this view for Lewis, but he was still assuming it in his chapter on friendship as late as *The Four Loves* (1960).

84   "One must remember that though in one sense": Quoted in Barbara Reynolds, *Dorothy L. Sayers: Her Life and Soul* (London: Hodder & Stoughton, 1993), 188, 356.

85   Lewis describes *The Place of the Lion*. See letter to Arthur Greeves, *They Stand Together*, February 26, 1936, page 479.

86   "A book sometimes crosses one's path": Letter, Wednesday, March 11, 1936, in *C. S. Lewis: Collected Letters*, vol. 2, *The Christian Scholar 1931–1951*, ed. Walter Hooper.

86   "If you had delayed writing": Bodleian Library, MS.Eng. c.6825, fol 48. Letter March 12, 1936. Quoted in Hooper and Green, *C. S. Lewis: A Biography*, 137.

6 Two Journeys There and Back Again

88–89   The vignette is based on several interviews by Tolkien describing the origin of *The Hobbit*. The description of the room is based on memories of their father's study by John and Priscilla Tolkien in *The Tolkien Family Album* (55–56), and the fictional study of Professor Timbermill in J. I. M. Stewart's *Young Pattullo* (New York: W. W. Norton, 1975), 106–8 — Timbermill is based on Tolkien at 20 Northmoor Road.

89   "Reading his fairy tale": Letter 183, February 4, 1933, *They Stand Together*.

89   "He agreed that for what *we* meant": Letter 184, March 25, 1933, *They Stand Together*. The "horns of elfland" alludes to a chapter in G. K. Chesterton's *Orthodoxy*, whose understanding of fantasy and faery tale is akin to that shared by Lewis and Tolkien.

93   Tolkien's like of *The Pilgrim's Regress*. See A. N. Wilson, *C. S. Lewis: A Biography*, 135.

93–94   Allegory as a form. Tolkien's short story, *Leaf by Niggle* (1945), is an allegory, even though he tended to avoid and lack sympathy with the genre.

94   "It is yours by right": Letter 184, March 25, 1933, *They Stand Together*.

94–95   "The rider threw back the cloak": *The Pilgrim's Regress*, book 3, chapter 9.

95   "Learning in Wartime": In *Essay Collection and Other Short Pieces*, chapter 84, 579–86.

95–96   J. I. Packer on *The Pilgrim's Regress*: "Living Truth for a Dying World: The Message of C. S. Lewis," in *The J. I. Packer Collection*, ed. Alister McGrath (Leicester: Inter-Varsity Press, 1999). The story maps a vivid picture of Lewis's intellectual climate of the 1920s and early 1930s.

96   The "dialectic of desire": The preface to the 3d edition, 1943.

97   "Poor Uncle George": From book 1, chapter 3.

97   Lewis's annoyance with his publisher: Letter 194, *They Stand Together*.

7   Space, Time, and the "New Hobbit"

99–100   The setting of Lewis's rooms in Magdalen is based on several descriptions, including those in "Don v. Devil," *Time* magazine, September 8, 1947; John Wain's *Sprightly Running*, 184; and C. S. Lewis's *Arthurian Torso*, quoted below, page 118. The vignette draws largely upon Christopher Tolkien's account of the challenge, set out in *The Lost Road*, 7–10, and in a number of letters: Tolkien's (July 1964, Letter 257; February 1968, Letter 257) and Lewis's (October 21, 1925). It also makes use of published comments of the two men from the period on the nature of story. The reference to Mary Shelley and the others is imaginary, but Tolkien was well-read in science fiction, even though he read little contemporary fiction, other than fantasy. The date of the conversation is a matter of speculation but, following Christopher Tolkien, in his commentary on "The Lost Road," I think that 1936 is more likely than 1937.

101   Elendil and Herendil of Númenor. In *The Lord of the Rings* Tolkien reveals that Elendil and his sons, Isildur (equivalent of Herendil?) and Anárion escape east to Middle-earth when Númenor is engulfed and found the realms of Arnor and Gondor.

102   Tolkien on his influence on Lewis: Letter to Green, July 17, 1971, quoted in Hooper and Green, *C. S. Lewis: A Biography*, 210.

103   The date of "The Dark Tower." Barbara Reynolds casts light on the possible date of writing, in reference to the controversy at the time over the new University Library in Cambridge (the tower of which is referred to in Lewis's story), in *VII: An Anglo-American Literary Review* 18 (2001): 102–7.

103   Tolkien on Númenorian and twentieth-century time: *The Lost Road*, 57.

103–4   *The Ainulindalë*: See J. R. R. Tolkien, *The Silmarillion* (1977); "The Music of the Ainur" in *The Book of Lost Tales, I* (1983); "The Ambarkanta" or "The Shape of the World" in *The Shaping of Middle-earth* (1986); "Ainulindalë" in *The Lost Road* (1987).

104   "Alboin liked the flavour": *The Lost Road*, 57.

104   He "was used to odd words and names": *The Lost Road*, 52–53.

105   "Surveying the last thirty years": *The Lost Road*, 45.

106–7   "The creature, which was still steaming": *Out of the Silent Planet*, chapter 9.

107   "As a philologist": Letter 77, *Letters of J. R. R. Tolkien*.

108   "He lay for hours in contemplation": *Out of the Silent Planet*, chapter 5.

109–10   Tolkien writes of *Out of the Silent Planet* "being read aloud to our local club": Letter 24, February 18, 1938, *Letters of J. R. R. Tolkien*.

110   "When Bilbo, son of Bungo of the family of Baggins": *The Return of the Shadow*, 13.

111   Quotations from Tolkien in the final paragraph. See page 105, above, for the full quotation.

8   World War II and After

112–14   My vignette and the description of the evacuees is based on contemporary accounts and on the testimony of evacuees at The Kilns in *In Search of C. S. Lewis*, edited by Stephen Schofield, and *C. S. Lewis at the BBC*, by Justin Phillips. It is also drawn from Lewis's letters of September 2, 1939, and September 18, 1939, in *Letters of C. S. Lewis*.

114   "This book is about four children": Quoted in Hooper and Green, *C. S. Lewis: A Biography*. This fragment survived, according to Roger Lancelyn Green, on a sheet of paper caught within the manuscript of "The Dark Tower," and which had notes for "Broadcast Talks" on the reverse side. Green wrote the original chapter "Through the Wardrobe" in *C. S. Lewis: A Biography* in which this is reproduced (see page 303 in the third edition). Green played an important role in the birth of the first Narnian story — see chapter 10, below.

115–16   "Physically, Williams was not particularly impressive": From *Charles Williams: A Celebration*, Brian Horne, ed. (Leominster: Gracewing, 1995), 1.

116   T. S. Eliot on Williams: "The significance of Charles Williams," in *The Listener*, December 19, 1946, 894–95.

117   His wife, Michal: Michal was Williams's pet name for his wife, Florence.

118   "Picture to yourself...an upstairs sitting-room": "Introductory," *Arthurian Torso*.

119   Dr. Robert Havard's memories of Williams. From The Wade Center Oral History interview, July 26, 1984.

123–24   For a full account of Lewis's broadcasts and what lay behind them see Justin Phillips, *C. S. Lewis at the BBC* (London: HarperCollins, 2002).

124   Real theologians like Austin Farrer: Letter Whit Sunday 1956. Copy in possession of The Wade Center.

126   Title page of "The Notion Club Papers": *Sauron Defeated*, 148.

126   Insights into the past by members of the Notion Club: The influence of Owen Barfield can be seen in this idea.

126   Despite lack of imaginative affinity between Tolkien and Williams, the intrusion of the destruction of Númenor into modern England is a fine, Williams-like touch, recalling the power of the great snowstorm in the latter's *The Greater Trumps* (1932), created by the wicked use of an ancient Tarot pack, which results in disruption of the cosmic order.

128   "While Lewis attacked": John Wain, *Sprightly Running*, 182.

129   Tolkien's readings and the veto against him. See diary entries of Warren Lewis, April 24, 1947; October 23, 1947; and October 30, 1947, *Brothers and Friends*.

9   A Professor's Wardrobe and Magic Rings

130–32   The opening vignette is drawn from the recollections of Roger Lancelyn Green (1918–87) in Hooper and Green, *C. S. Lewis: A Biography*, 305–8, and The Wade Center Oral History interview with Green, June 12, 1986.

132–33   "It ought to be C. S. Lewis": Letter 105, *Letters of J. R. R. Tolkien*.

134   "A children's story is the best art-form": C. S. Lewis, "On Three Ways of Writing for Children," in *Of This and Other Worlds* (1982), 57.

134   Lewis's view that fairy story is an adult genre. Letter March 3, 1955 (copy in The Wade Center).

135   "The Narnian series is not exactly allegory": Letter September 23, 1963 (copy in The Wade Center).

136   Ulster as Lewis's "ain countrie": letter May 31, 1947. Warren Lewis on Narnia and Ulster, in *Past Watchful Dragons*, Walter Hooper, 81.

138–39   "Where...I do find it impossible": Letter January 13, 1941, *The Letters of Evelyn Underhill*, 301.

139   "I remember I actually wept": BBC Radio 4 interview with Denis Gueroult, *Now Read On*, December 16, 1970.

139   Long letter to Waldman of Collins: Letter 131, *Letters of J. R. R. Tolkien*.

140–41   George Sayer on Tolkien: From Sleevenotes, *J. R. R. Tolkien Reads and Sings His The Hobbit and The Fellowship of the Ring*, Caedmon, TC1477, 1975.

10 Surprised by Cambridge and Disappointed by Joy

146–48   The vignette is loosely based on the letters surrounding Lewis's appointment to Cambridge. See Brian Barbour, "Lewis and Cambridge," *Modern Philology* 96, no. 4 (May 1999): 459–65, and Hooper and Green, *C. S. Lewis: A Biography*, 340–45. Full copies of the correspondence are held in The Wade Center archive. The description of The Kilns in the period between the decline of Mrs. Moore and the renewing time after Lewis's marriage to Joy Davidman owes much to Douglas Gresham, *Lenten Lands*, 53–58, 81–82. Lewis's habit of answering the phone with "This is the Sewage Disposal Plant" was told to Clyde S. Kilby by Tolkien (Notes of Clyde S. Kilby, in The Wade Center). "The Midden" comes from Douglas Gresham, 82. I have supposed that H. V. D. Dyson coined the phrase — it seems such an obvious Dysonism.

148–49   "In the early 1940s": From Helen Gardner, "Clive Staples Lewis 1898–1963," 424–25. Her article was reissued in George Watson, ed., *Critical Thought 1: Critical Essays on C. S. Lewis* (Aldershot: Scolar Press, 1992).

151   "No Oxford don was forgiven": Walter Hooper, *Through Joy and Beyond*, 125. John Wain also comments on the dislike of Lewis's popular writings: "Many of his Oxford acquaintances never forgave him for a book like *The Screwtape Letters*, with its knock-down arguments, its obvious ironies, its journalistic facility."

151   Helen Gardner's decision as "second string" to decline the Cambridge Chair: Gardner, "Clive Staples Lewis 1898–1963," 427–28.

152   David Lodge on Lewis. D. Lodge, ed., *Twentieth Century Literary Criticism: A Reader* (1972).

153   "...Brilliant, intellectually exciting": Letter to Chad Walsh, December 23, 1954.

153–54   "Roughly speaking we may say": From *De Descriptione Temporum*, 1955.

154–55   "Christians and Pagans had much more in common": From *De Descriptione Temporum*, 1955.

156   "No item of compulsory Christian morals": Letter 49, *Letters of J. R. R. Tolkien.*

157   Lewis "would not re-enter Christianity by a new door": Quoted in Wilson, *C. S. Lewis: A Biography*, 135–36.

158   "Life is only an electrochemical reaction": Quoted in Lewis's foreword to Joy Davidman, *Smoke on the Mountain.*

158   "It is infinite, unique; there are no words": From Joy Davidman, "The Longest Way Round," in *These Found the Way: Thirteen Converts to Protestant Christianity*, ed. David Wesley Soper (Philadelphia: Westminster Press, 1951), 23.

164   Tolkien's Valedictory Address. Reproduced in *The Monsters and the Critics and Other Essays.*

164   Description of Tolkien's house on Sandfield Road: Interview by Philip Norman, *Sunday Times*, January 15, 1967.

165   "Good Heavens! He seems to have invented": *Proceedings of the J. R. R. Tolkien Centenary Conference*, 25.

11   A Farewell to Shadowlands

166–68   The vignette is based on Tolkien's letter (Letter 251, *Letters of J. R. R. Tolkien*) and Douglas Gresham's *Lenten Lands*, 158. The visit by Tolkien and his son John to Lewis is recorded by John Tolkien, quoted in Hooper and Green, *C. S. Lewis: A Biography*, 430. Lewis's reading *Les Liaisons Dangereuses* is recorded in James Como, ed., *C. S. Lewis at the Breakfast Table*, 104.

170   "I personally found *Letters to Malcolm*": Letter to David Kolb, S.J., Letter 265 (November 11, 1964), *Letters of J. R. R. Tolkien.*

170   Clyde S. Kilby (1902–86) was chair of the department of English at Wheaton College, and set up The Wade Center as a research and study center based around the writings of Lewis and six other authors whose beliefs and work have affinities: Tolkien, Charles Williams, Owen Barfield, Dorothy L. Sayers, G. K. Chesterton, and George MacDonald.

170   "The anthology has reminded me": April 15, 1968.

170   "I still find it difficult": December 3, 1967.

173   Tolkien and Ava Gardner: Letter 267, *Letters of J. R. R. Tolkien.*

Notes

12   The Gift of Friendship

176–77   "The unpayable debt that I owe": Letter 276, *Letters of J. R. R. Tolkien.*

178   Imagination as the organ of meaning. See "Bluspels and Flalansferes: A Semantic Nightmare" in *Selected Literary Essays.*

178   Tolkien's idea "that everything is unique": From Clyde S. Kilby's Notes, held by The Wade Center.

179   "The imaginative man in me is older": *Letters of C. S. Lewis*, 444.

179–81   "To construct plausible and moving 'other worlds'": "On Stories," in *Of This and Other Worlds*, 35–36.

180   The illustrations of Mole and Rat. *The Problem of Pain*, 6.

181   Tolkien on joy and grace: "On Fairy-Stories," in *The Monsters and the Critics and Other Essays*, 153, 154, 155.

181   Lewis on joy and heaven. See his speculations in chapter 10, "Heaven," in *The Problem of Pain*, and "The Weight of Glory," in *Screwtape Proposes a Toast and Other Pieces.*

182   "[The child] does not despise real woods": "On Three Ways of Writing for Children," in *Of This and Other Worlds*, 65.

183   "Joyce, Woolf, Waugh": Quoted with permission from a personal communication from David C. Downing, December 12, 2002.

183–84   "This severity did not mean that [Calvin's] theology": *English Literature in the Sixteenth Century*, 42.

184   "I ask you! He put away three pints": Letter 56, *Letters of J. R. R. Tolkien.*

184   Treebeard. See *J. R. R. Tolkien: A Biography*, 194. Around winter 1940–41 Tolkien "discovered" Ents, making notes that used Lewis's concept of *hnau* (embodied personal being). He speculated, "Are the Tree-folk...*hnau* that have gone tree-like, or trees that have become *hnau?*"

186   *The Encyclopedia of Fantasy.* The quotations are from the entries on "Perception" and "Fantasy," respectively.

186   Lewis's review of *The Lord of the Rings* was republished in *Of This and Other Worlds.*

187   "Those are the golden sessions": from "Friendship," in *The Four Loves*, chapter 4.

Appendix B   The Enduring Popularity of J. R. R. Tolkien and C. S. Lewis

200   *The Lord of the Rings* belonging with several other writings: This point is made by Tom A. Shippey, "Tolkien as a Post-War Writer," *Scholarship and Fantasy: Proceedings of The Tolkien Phenomenon, May 1992, Turku, Finland,* ed. K. J. Battarbee (Turku, Finland: University of Turku, 1993).

202   "He is such an odd fellow!": "Beowulf: The Monsters and the Critics," in *The Monsters and the Critics and Other Essays,* 7–8.

228   "The settled happiness and security": *The Problem of Pain,* chapter 7.

The Writings of C. S. Lewis and J. R. R. Tolkien

Major writings of C. S. Lewis, in order of first publication

Spirits in Bondage: A Cycle of Lyrics. London: William Heinemann, 1919.

Dymer. London: J. M. Dent, 1926.

The Pilgrim's Regress: An Allegorical Apology for Christianity, Reason and Romanticism. London: J. M. Dent, 1933.

The Allegory of Love: A Study in Medieval Tradition. Oxford: Clarendon Press, 1936.

Out of the Silent Planet. London: John Lane, 1938.

Rehabilitations and Other Essays. London: Oxford University Press, 1938.

The Personal Heresy: A Controversy (with E. M. W. Tillyard). London: Oxford University Press, 1939.

The Problem of Pain. London: Geoffrey Bles, Centenary Press, 1940.

Broadcast Talks. London: Geoffrey Bles, 1942.

A Preface to Paradise Lost. London: Oxford University Press, 1942.

The Screwtape Letters. London: Geoffrey Bles, 1942. Reprinted with an additional letter as *The Screwtape Letters and Screwtape Proposes a Toast*. London: Geoffrey Bles, 1961. Further new material in *The Screwtape Letters with Screwtape Proposes a Toast*. New York: Macmillan, 1982.

The Weight of Glory. Little Books on Religion 189. London: SPCK, 1942.

Christian Behaviour: A Further Series of Broadcast Talks. London: Geoffrey Bles, 1943.

Perelandra. London: John Lane, 1943. Reprinted in paperback as *Voyage to Venus*. London: Pan Books, 1953.

The Abolition of Man: Reflections on Education with Special Reference to the Teaching of English in the Upper Forms of Schools. Riddell Memorial Lectures, fifteenth series. London: Oxford University Press, 1943.

Beyond Personality: The Christian Idea of God. London: Geoffrey Bles, Centenary Press, 1944.

That Hideous Strength: A Modern Fairy Tale for Grown Ups. London: John Lane, 1945. A version abridged by the author was published as *The Tortured Planet*

221

(New York: Avon Books, 1946) and as *That Hideous Strength* (London: Pan Books, 1955).

The Great Divorce: A Dream. London: Geoffrey Bles, Centenary Press, 1946. Originally published as a series in *The Guardian.* Bles inaccurately dated the book as 1945.

George MacDonald: Anthology. Compiled by, and with an introduction by, C. S. Lewis. London: Geoffrey Bles, 1946.

Essays Presented to Charles Williams. Edited by, and with an introduction by, C. S. Lewis. London: Oxford University Press, 1947.

Miracles: A Preliminary Study. London: Geoffrey Bles, 1947. Reprinted, with an expanded version of chapter 3, London: Collins Fontana Books, 1960.

Arthurian Torso: Containing the Posthumous Fragment of the Figure of Arthur by Charles Williams and A Commentary on the Arthurian Poems of Charles Williams by C. S. Lewis. London: Oxford University Press, 1948.

Transposition and Other Addresses. London: Geoffrey Bles, 1949. Published in the United States as *The Weight of Glory and Other Addresses.* New York: Macmillan, 1949.

The Lion, the Witch and the Wardrobe. London: Geoffrey Bles, 1950.

Prince Caspian: The Return to Narnia. London: Geoffrey Bles, 1951.

Mere Christianity. London: Geoffrey Bles, 1952. A revised and expanded version of *Broadcast Talks, Christian Behaviour,* and *Beyond Personality.*

The Voyage of the Dawn Treader. London: Geoffrey Bles, 1952.

The Silver Chair. London: Geoffrey Bles, 1953.

The Horse and His Boy. London: Geoffrey Bles, 1954.

English Literature in the Sixteenth Century Excluding Drama, vol. 3 of *The Oxford History of English Literature* (Oxford: Clarendon Press, 1954). In 1990 the series was renumbered and Lewis's volume was reissued as vol. 4, *Poetry and Prose in the Sixteenth Century.*

The Magician's Nephew. London: Bodley Head, 1955.

Surprised by Joy: The Shape of My Early Life. London: Geoffrey Bles, 1955.

The Last Battle. London: Bodley Head, 1956.

Till We Have Faces: A Myth Retold. London: Geoffrey Bles, 1956.

Reflections on the Psalms. London: Geoffrey Bles, 1958.

The Four Loves. London: Geoffrey Bles, 1960.

Studies in Words. Cambridge: Cambridge University Press, 1960.

The World's Last Night and Other Essays. New York: Harcourt, Brace, 1960.

A Grief Observed (published under the pseudonym "N. W. Clerk"). London: Faber & Faber, 1961.

An Experiment in Criticism. Cambridge: Cambridge University Press, 1961.

They Asked for a Paper: Papers and Addresses. London: Geoffrey Bles, 1962.

Posthumous Writings and Collections

Letters to Malcolm: Chiefly on Prayer. London: Geoffrey Bles, 1964.

The Writings of C. S. Lewis and J. R. R. Tolkien

The Discarded Image: An Introduction to Medieval and Renaissance Literature. Cambridge: Cambridge University Press, 1964.

Poems. Edited by Walter Hooper. London: Geoffrey Bles, 1964.

Studies in Medieval and Renaissance Literature. Edited by Walter Hooper. Cambridge: Cambridge University Press, 1966.

Letters of C. S. Lewis. Edited, with a memoir, by W. H. Lewis. London: Geoffrey Bles, 1966. Revised edition, edited by Walter Hooper, 1988.

Of Other Worlds: Essays and Stories. Edited by Walter Hooper. London: Geoffrey Bles, 1966.

Christian Reflections. Edited by Walter Hooper. London: Geoffrey Bles, 1967.

Spenser's Images of Life. Edited by Alistair Fowler. Cambridge: Cambridge University Press, 1967.

Letters to an American Lady. Edited by Clyde S. Kilby. Grand Rapids, Mich.: Eerdmans, 1967; London: Hodder and Stoughton, 1969.

A Mind Awake: An Anthology of C. S. Lewis. Edited by Clyde S. Kilby. London: Geoffrey Bles, 1968.

Narrative Poems. Edited and with a preface by Walter Hooper. London: Geoffrey Bles, 1969.

Selected Literary Essays. Edited and with a preface by Walter Hooper. Cambridge: Cambridge University Press, 1969.

God in the Dock: Essays on Theology and Ethics. Edited and with a preface by Walter Hooper. Grand Rapids, Mich.: Eerdmans, 1970. British edition: *Undeceptions: Essays on Theology and Ethics* (London: Geoffrey Bles, 1971).

Fern Seeds and Elephants and Other Essays on Christianity. Edited and with a preface by Walter Hooper. London: Collins Fontana Books, 1975.

The Dark Tower and Other Stories. Edited and with a preface by Walter Hooper. London: Collins, 1977.

The Joyful Christian: Readings from C. S. Lewis. Edited by William Griffin. New York: Macmillan, 1977.

They Stand Together: The Letters of C. S. Lewis to Arthur Greeves (1914–1963). Edited by Walter Hooper. London: Collins, 1979.

Of This and Other Worlds. Edited by Walter Hooper. London: Collins Fount, 1982.

The Business of Heaven: Daily Readings from C. S. Lewis. Edited by Walter Hooper. London: Collins Fount, 1984.

Boxen: The Imaginary World of the Young C. S. Lewis. Edited by Walter Hooper. London: Collins, 1985.

Letters to Children. Edited by Lyle W. Dorsett and Marjorie Lamp Mead. London: Collins, 1985.

First and Second Things: Essays on Theology and Ethics. Edited and preface by Walter Hooper. Glasgow: Collins Fount, 1985.

Present Concerns. Edited by Walter Hooper. London: Collins Fount, 1986.

Timeless at Heart. Edited by Walter Hooper. London: Collins Fount, 1987.

Letters: C. S. Lewis and Don Giovanni Calabria: A Study in Friendship. Edited by, and with an introduction by, Martin Moynihan. Glasgow: Collins, 1988. Includes Latin text. First issued as *The Latin Letters of C. S. Lewis,* paperback edition. Westchester, Ill.:, Crossway Books, 1987, without Latin text.

All My Road Before Me: The Diary of C. S. Lewis 1922–27. Edited by Walter Hooper. London: HarperCollins, 1991.

The Collected Poems of C. S. Lewis. Edited by Walter Hooper. London: Harper-Collins, 1994.

The Collected Letters, vol. 1, *Family Letters 1905–1931.* Edited by Walter Hooper. London: HarperCollins, 2000.

C. S. Lewis: Collected Letters, vol. 2, *The Christian Scholar 1931–1951.* Edited by Walter Hooper. London: HarperCollins: 2003.

Major Writings of J. R. R. Tolkien, in order of first publication

A Middle English Vocabulary. Oxford: Clarendon Press, 1922. Prepared for use with Kenneth Sisam's *Fourteenth Century Verse and Prose* (Oxford: Clarendon Press, 1921) and later published with it.

Sir Gawain and the Green Knight. Edited by J. R. R. Tolkien and E. V. Gordon. Oxford: Clarendon Press, 1925 (new edition, revised by Norman Davis, 1967).

The Hobbit, or There and Back Again. London: George Allen & Unwin, 1937.

Farmer Giles of Ham. London: George Allen & Unwin, 1950.

The Fellowship of the Ring: Being the First Part of The Lord of the Rings. London: George Allen & Unwin, 1954.

The Two Towers: Being the Second Part of The Lord of the Rings. London: George Allen & Unwin, 1954.

The Return of the King: Being the Third Part of The Lord of the Rings. London: George Allen & Unwin, 1955.

The Adventures of Tom Bombadil and Other Verses from the Red Book. London: George Allen & Unwin, 1962.

Ancrene Wisse: The English Text of the Ancrene Riwle. Edited by J. R. R. Tolkien. London: Oxford University Press, 1962.

Tree and Leaf. London: George Allen & Unwin, 1964.

The Tolkien Reader. New York: Ballantine Books, 1966.

The Road Goes Ever On: A Song Cycle. Poems by J. R. R. Tolkien, music by Donald Swann. Boston: Houghton Mifflin, 1967 (enlarged edition, 1978).

Smith of Wootton Major. London: George Allen & Unwin, 1967.

Posthumous Writings

Sir Gawain and the Green Knight, Pearl and Sir Orfeo. Translated by J. R. R. Tolkien; edited by Christopher Tolkien. London: George Allen & Unwin, 1975.

The Father Christmas Letters. Edited by Baillie Tolkien. London: George Allen & Unwin, 1976.

The Silmarillion. Edited by Christopher Tolkien. London: George Allen & Unwin, 1977.

Pictures by J. R. R. Tolkien. Edited by Christopher Tolkien. London: George Allen & Unwin, 1979.

Unfinished Tales of Numenor and Middle-earth. Edited by Christopher Tolkien. London: George Allen & Unwin, 1980.

The Letters of J. R. R. Tolkien. Edited by Humphrey Carpenter, with the assistance of Christopher Tolkien. London: George Allen & Unwin, 1981; Boston: Houghton Mifflin, 1981.

Old English Exodus. Text, translation, and commentary by J. R. R. Tolkien; edited by Joan Turville-Petre. Oxford: Clarendon Press, 1981.

Finn and Hengest: The Fragment and the Episode. Edited by Alan Bliss. London: George Allen & Unwin, 1982.

Mr. Bliss. London: George Allen & Unwin, 1982; Boston: Houghton Mifflin, 1983.

The Monsters and the Critics and Other Essays. Edited by Christopher Tolkien. London: George Allen & Unwin, 1983.

The History of Middle-earth. Edited by Christopher Tolkien. Published in twelve volumes between 1983 and 1996, by George Allen & Unwin, Unwin Hyman, and HarperCollins.

Roverandom. Edited by Christina Scull and Wayne G. Hammond. London: HarperCollins, 1998.

Beowulf and the Critics. Edited by Michael D. C. Drout. Tempe, Ariz.: Arizona Center for Medieval and Renaissance Studies, 2002.

Bibliography

Adey, Lionel. C. S. Lewis's "Great War" with Owen Barfield. University of Victoria: Canada, 1978.

———. C. S. Lewis: Writer, Dreamer and Mentor. Grand Rapids, Mich.: Eerdmans, 1998.

Armstrong, Helen, ed. Digging Potatoes, Growing Trees: Twenty-five Years of Speeches at the Tolkien Society's Annual Dinners. Vols. 1 and 2. The Tolkien Society, 1997, 1998.

Arnott, Anne. The Secret Country of C. S. Lewis. London: Hodder, 1974.

Barfield, Owen. Poetic Diction: A Study in Meaning. 2nd ed. London: Faber and Faber, 1962.

Battarbee, K. J., ed. Scholarship and Fantasy: Proceedings of The Tolkien Phenomenon, May 1992, Turku, Finland. Turku, Finland: University of Turku, 1993.

Becker, Alida, ed. The Tolkien Scrapbook. New York: Grosset and Dunlap, 1978.

British Children's Writers. Dictionary of Literary Biography. Detroit: Bruccoli Clark Layman, 1996.

Burson, Scott, and Jerry Walls. C. S. Lewis and Francis Schaeffer. Downers Grove, Ill.: InterVarsity Press, 1998.

Carnell, Corbin S. Bright Shadows of Reality. Grand Rapids, Mich.: Eerdmans, 1974.

Carpenter, Humphrey. The Inklings: C. S. Lewis, J. R. R. Tolkien, Charles Williams and Their Friends. London: George Allen & Unwin, 1978; Boston: Houghton Mifflin, 1979.

———. J. R. R. Tolkien: A Biography. London: George Allen & Unwin, 1977; Boston: Houghton Mifflin, 1977.

Chance, Jane. The Lord of the Rings: The Mythology of Power. Lexington: University Press of Kentucky, 2001.

———. Tolkien the Medievalist. New York: Routledge, 2002.

———. Tolkien's Art: A Mythology for England. Lexington: University Press of Kentucky, 2001.

Christensen, Michael J. C. S. Lewis on Scripture. London: Hodder, 1980.

Christopher, Joe R. *C. S. Lewis.* Boston: G. K. Hall, 1987.

Clute, John, and John Grant. *The Encyclopedia of Fantasy.* London: Orbit, 1997.

Como, James T., ed. *C. S. Lewis at the Breakfast Table and Other Reminiscences.* New York: Macmillan, 1979.

Cunningham, Richard B. *C. S. Lewis, Defender of the Faith.* Philadelphia: Westminster Press, 1967.

Curry, Patrick. *Defending Middle-earth: Tolkien, Myth, and Modernity.* London: HarperCollins, 1997.

Dorsett, Lyle. *Joy and C. S. Lewis.* London: HarperCollins, 1988, 1994.

Downing, David C. *The Most Reluctant Convert: C. S. Lewis's Journey to Faith.* Downers Grove, Ill., and Leicester: InterVarsity Press, 2002.

———. *Planets in Peril: A Critical Study of C. S. Lewis's Ransom Trilogy.* Amherst: University of Massachusetts Press, 1992.

Duncan, John Ryan. *The Magic Never Ends: The Life and Work of C. S. Lewis.* Nashville: W Publishing Group; Milton Keynes: Authentic Publishing, 2002.

Duriez, Colin. "'Art Has Been Verified....' The Friendship of C. S. Lewis and J. R. R. Tolkien," in *Digging Potatoes, Growing Trees: Twenty-five Years of Speeches at the Tolkien Society's Annual Dinners.* Edited by Helen Armstrong. Vol. 2. The Tolkien Society, 1998.

———. *The C. S. Lewis Encyclopedia.* Wheaton, Ill.: Crossway Books, and London: SPCK, 2000.

———. "C. S. Lewis' Theology of Fantasy," in *Behind the Veil of Familiarity: C. S. Lewis (1898–1998).* Edited by Margarita Carretero González and Encarnación Hidalgo Tenorio, Peter Lang: Bern, 2001.

———. "C. S. Lewis' Theology of Fantasy," in *The Pilgrim's Guide.* Edited by David Mills. Grand Rapids, Mich.: Eerdmans, 1998.

———. "In the Library: Composition and Context," in *Reading the Classics with C. S. Lewis.* Edited by Thomas Martin. Grand Rapids, Mich.: Baker Book House, 2000.

———. "J. R. R. Tolkien," in *British Children's Authors 1914–1960*, a volume of the *Dictionary of Literary Biography.* Columbia, S.C.: Bruccoli Clark Layman, 1996.

———. "Sub-creation and Tolkien's Theology of Story," in *Scholarship and Fantasy.* Turku, Finland: University of Turku, 1994.

———. "The Theology of Fantasy in C. S. Lewis and J. R. R. Tolkien," *Themelios* 23, no. 2 (February 1998).

———. *Tolkien and The Lord of the Rings.* London: Azure, 2001. New York: HiddenSpring, 2001.

———. "Tolkien and the Old West," in *Digging Potatoes, Growing Trees: Twenty-five Years of Speeches at the Tolkien Society's Annual Dinners.* Edited by Helen Armstrong. Vol. 2. The Tolkien Society, 1998.

———. "Tolkien and the Other Inklings," in *Proceedings of the J. R. R. Tolkien Centenary Conference: Keble College, Oxford, 1992.* Edited by Patricia Reynolds and Glen H. GoodKnight. Milton Keynes: Tolkien Society; Altadena, Calif.: Mythopoeic Press, 1995.

Edwards, Bruce L. *A Rhetoric of Reading: C. S. Lewis's Defense of Western Literacy.* Provo, Utah: Brigham Young University, 1986.

————, ed. *The Taste of the Pineapple: Essays on C. S. Lewis as Reader, Critic, and Imaginative Writer.* Bowling Green, Ohio: Bowling Green State University Popular Press, 1988.

Evans, Robley. *J. R. R. Tolkien.* New York: Crowell, 1976.

Filmer, Kath. *The Fiction of C. S. Lewis: Mask and Mirror.* New York: Macmillan, 1993.

Flieger, Verlyn. *Splintered Light: Logos and Language in Tolkien's World.* Grand Rapids, Mich.: Eerdmans, 1983.

Fonstad, Karen Wynn. *The Atlas of Middle-earth.* Boston: Houghton Mifflin, 1981.

Ford, Paul F. *Companion to Narnia.* San Francisco: Harper & Row, 1980.

Foster, Robert. *The Complete Guide to Middle-earth: From the Hobbit to the Silmarillion.* London: George Allen & Unwin, 1978; New York: Ballantine Books, 1978.

Fuller, Edmund. *Books with Men behind Them.* New York: Random House, 1962.

Garbowski, Christopher. *Recovery and Transcendence for the Contemporary Mythmaker: The Spiritual Dimension in the Works of J. R. R. Tolkien.* Lublin: Maria Curie-Sklodowska University Press, 2000.

Gardner, Helen. "Clive Staples Lewis 1898–1963." *Proc. British Academy* 51 (1965): 417–28.

Gibb, Jocelyn, ed. *Light on C. S. Lewis.* London: Geoffrey Bles, 1965.

Goffar, Janine. *C. S. Lewis Index: Rumours from the Sculptor's Shop.* Riverside, Calif.: La Sierra University Press, 1995; Solway: Carlisle, 1997.

Green, R. L., and Walter Hooper. *C. S. Lewis: A Biography.* London: Collins, 1974; 3d ed., 2002.

Gresham, Douglas. *Lenten Lands: My Childhood with Joy Davidman and C. S. Lewis.* London: Collins, 1989.

Griffin, William. *Clive Staples Lewis: A Dramatic Life.* San Francisco: Harper & Row, 1986. British edition: *C. S. Lewis: The Authentic Voice.* Tring: Lion, 1988.

Grotta, Daniel. *The Biography of J. R. R. Tolkien: Architect of Middle-earth.* Philadelphia: Running Press, 1978.

Hadfield, Alice Mary. *Charles Williams: An Exploration of His Life and Work.* Oxford: Oxford University Press, 1983.

Hammond, Wayne G., with the assistance of Douglas A. Anderson. *J. R. R. Tolkien: A Descriptive Bibliography.* New Castle, Del.: St. Paul's Bibliographies, Winchester and Oak Knoll Books, 1993.

Hammond, Wayne G., and Christina Scull. *J. R. R. Tolkien, Artist and Illustrator.* London: HarperCollins, 1995.

Harris, Richard. *C. S. Lewis: The Man and His God.* London: Collins Fount, 1987.

Harvey, David. *The Song of Middle-earth: J. R. R. Tolkien's Themes, Symbols and Myths.* London: Allen & Unwin, 1985.

Hillegas, Mark R., ed. *Shadows of Imagination: The Fantasies of C. S. Lewis, J. R. R. Tolkien, and Charles Williams*. Carbondale: Southern Illinois University Press, 1969, new edition, 1979.

Holbrook, David. *The Skeleton in the Wardrobe: C. S. Lewis's Fiction, A Phenomenological Study*. Lewisburg, Pa.: Bucknell University Press; London: Associated University Press, 1991.

Holmer, Paul L. *C. S. Lewis: The Shape of His Faith and Thought*. New York: Harper & Row, 1976; London: Sheldon Press, 1977.

Hooper, Walter. *C. S. Lewis: A Companion and Guide*. London: HarperCollins, 1996.

———. *Past Watchful Dragons*. London: Collins Fount, 1979.

Horne, Brian, ed. *Charles Williams: A Celebration*. Leominster: Gracewing, 1995.

Howard, Thomas. *The Achievement of C. S. Lewis: A Reading of His Fiction*. Wheaton, Ill.: Harold Shaw, 1980.

———. *The Novels of Charles Williams*. London: Oxford University Press, 1983; repr. San Francisco: Ignatius Press, 1991.

Huttar, Charles A., ed. *Imagination and the Spirit: Essays in Literature and the Christian Faith*. Grand Rapids, Mich.: Eerdmans, 1971.

Keefe, Carolyn, ed. *C. S. Lewis: Speaker and Teacher*. London: Hodder, 1974.

Kilby, Clyde S. *The Christian World of C. S. Lewis*. Grand Rapids, Mich.: Eerdmans, 1965, 1996.

———. *Images of Salvation in the Fiction of C. S. Lewis*. Wheaton, Ill.: Harold Shaw, 1978.

———. *Tolkien and the Silmarillion*. Wheaton, Ill.: Harold Shaw, 1976; Lion: Tring, 1977.

Kilby, Clyde S., and Douglas Gilbert. *C. S. Lewis: Images of His World*. Grand Rapids, Mich.: Eerdmans, 1973.

Kilby, Clyde S., and Marjorie Lamp Meade, eds. *Brothers and Friends: The Diaries of Major Warren Hamilton Lewis*. San Francisco: Harper & Row, 1982.

Knight, Gareth. *The Magical World of the Inklings*. Longmead, Dorset: Element Books: 1990.

Kocher, Paul H. *Master of Middle-earth: The Fiction of J. R. R. Tolkien*. Boston: Houghton Mifflin, 1972. British edition: *Master of Middle-earth: The Achievement of J. R. R. Tolkien*. London: Thames and Hudson, 1972.

Lawlor, John, ed. *Patterns of Love and Courtesy: Essays in Memory of C. S. Lewis*. London: Edward Arnold, 1966.

Lindskoog, Kathryn. *C. S. Lewis: Mere Christian*. Glendale, Calif.: Gospel Light, 1973.

———. *The Lion of Judah in NeverNeverLand: God, Man and Nature in C. S. Lewis's Narnia Tales*. Grand Rapids, Mich.: Eerdmans, 1973.

Lobdell, Jared. *A Tolkien Compass*. La Salle, Ill.: Open Court, 1975; New York: Ballantine, 1980.

Lochhead, Marion. *Renaissance of Wonder: The Fantasy Worlds of C. S. Lewis, J. R. R. Tolkien, George MacDonald, E. Nesbit and Others.* Edinburgh: Canongate, 1973; San Francisco: Harper & Row, 1977.

Mabbott, John. *Oxford Memories.* Oxford: Thornton's of Oxford, 1986.

Manlove, C. N. *Christian Fantasy: From 1200 to the Present.* Basingstoke and London: Macmillan, 1992.

————. *C. S. Lewis: His Literary Achievement.* New York: St. Martin's Press, 1987.

————. *Modern Fantasy.* Cambridge: Cambridge University Press, 1975.

Menuge, Angus, ed. *Lightbearer in the Shadowlands: The Evangelistic Vision of C. S. Lewis.* Wheaton, Ill.: Crossway Books, 1997.

Mills, David, ed. *The Pilgrim's Guide: C. S. Lewis and the Art of Witness.* Grand Rapids, Mich.: Eerdmans, 1998.

Montgomery, John Warwick, ed. *Myth, Allegory and Gospel: An Interpretation of J. R. R. Tolkien, C. S. Lewis, G. K. Chesterton and Charles Williams.* Minneapolis: Bethany Fellowship, 1974.

Moseley, Charles. *J. R. R. Tolkien.* Plymouth: Northcote House, 1997.

Myers, Doris, *C. S. Lewis in Context.* Kent, Ohio: Kent State University Press, 1994.

Noel, Ruth S. *The Languages of Tolkien's Middle-earth.* Boston: Houghton Mifflin, 1980.

————. *The Mythology of Middle-earth.* Boston: Houghton Mifflin, 1977; London: Thames and Hudson, 1977.

O'Neill, Timothy R. *The Individuated Hobbit: Jung, Tolkien and the Archetypes of Middle-earth.* Boston: Houghton Mifflin, 1979.

Patrick, James. *The Magdalen Metaphysicals: Idealism and Orthodoxy at Oxford 1901–1945.* Macon, Ga.: Mercer University Press, 1985.

Payne, Leanne. *Real Presence: The Holy Spirit in the Works of C. S. Lewis.* Eastbourne: Monarch Publications, 1989.

Pearce, Joseph, ed. *Tolkien: A Celebration, Collected Writings on a Literary Legacy.* London: Fount, 1999.

Phillips, Justin. *C. S. Lewis at the BBC.* London: HarperCollins, 2002.

Polanyi, Michael. *Personal Knowledge: Towards a Post-Critical Philosophy.* London: Routledge & Kegan Paul, 1958.

Purtill, Richard L. *C. S. Lewis's Case for the Christian Faith.* Harper & Row: 1982.

————. *Lord of the Elves and Eldils: Fantasy and Philosophy in C. S. Lewis and J. R. R. Tolkien.* Grand Rapids, Mich.: Zondervan, 1974.

Ready, William. *The Tolkien Relation.* Chicago: Regnery, 1968.

Reilly, Robert J. *Romantic Religion: A Study of Barfield, Lewis, Williams and Tolkien.* University of Georgia Press: Athens, 1971.

Reynolds, Patricia, and Glen H. GoodKnight, eds. *Proceedings of the J. R. R. Tolkien Centenary Conference: Keble College, Oxford, 1992.* Milton Keynes: Tolkien Society; Altadena, Calif.: Mythopoeic Press, 1995.

Sale, Roger. *Modern Heroism: Essays on D. H. Lawrence, William Empson and J. R. R. Tolkien.* Berkeley and Los Angeles: University of California Press, 1973.

Sayer, George. *Jack: C. S. Lewis and His Times.* London: Macmillan, 1988.

Schakel, Peter J. *Reason and Imagination in C. S. Lewis: A Study of "Till We Have Faces."* Paternoster Press: Exeter, 1984.

Schofield, Stephen, ed. *In Search of C. S. Lewis.* South Plainfield, N.J.: Bridge Publications, 1984.

Schultz, Jeffrey D., and John G. West Jr., eds. *The C. S. Lewis Readers' Encyclopedia.* Grand Rapids, Mich.: Zondervan, 1998.

Shideler, Mary McDermott. *The Theology of Romantic Love: A Study in the Writings of Charles Williams.* Grand Rapids, Mich.: Eerdmans, 1962.

Shippey, T. A. *J. R. R. Tolkien: Author of the Century.* London: HarperCollins, 2000.

———. *The Road to Middle-earth.* London: George Allen & Unwin, 1982; New York: Houghton Mifflin, 1983.

Sibley, Brian. *Shadowlands.* London: Hodder, 1985.

Soper, Donald. *Exploring the Christian World Mind.* London: Vision Press, 1964.

Tennyson, G. B., ed. *Owen Barfield on C. S. Lewis.* Middletown, Conn.: Wesleyan University Press, 1989.

Tolkien, John and Priscilla. *The Tolkien Family Album.* London: Unwin/Hyman, 1992.

Urang, Gunnar. *Shadows of Heaven: Religion and Fantasy in the Writing of C. S. Lewis, Charles Williams and J. R. R. Tolkien.* London: SCM Press, 1970; Philadelphia: United Church Press, 1971.

Vanauken, Sheldon. *A Severe Mercy.* London: Hodder, 1977; New York: Harper & Row, 1979.

Wain, John. *Sprightly Running.* London: Macmillan, 1962.

Walker, Andrew, and James Patrick, eds. *A Christian for All Christians: Essays in Honour of C. S. Lewis.* London: Hodder, 1990.

Walsh, Chad. *C. S. Lewis: Apostle to the Skeptics.* New York: Macmillan, 1949.

———. *The Literary Legacy of C. S. Lewis.* New York: Harcourt Brace Jovanovich, 1979.

Watson, George, ed. *Critical Thought 1: Critical Essays on C. S. Lewis.* Aldershot: Scolar Press, 1992.

White, Michael. *Tolkien: A Biography.* London: Little, Brown, 2001.

White, William L. *The Image of Man in C. S. Lewis.* London: Hodder, 1970.

Williams, Charles, ed. *The Letters of Evelyn Underhill.* London: Longmans, Green, 1943.

Wilson, A. N. *C. S. Lewis: A Biography.* London: Collins, 1990.

Wilson, Colin. *Tree by Tolkien.* London: Covent Garden Press, 1973; Santa Barbara, Calif.: Capra Press, 1974.

Acknowledgments

Extracts and sourcing from the Oral History Project interviews with Maureen Blake née Moore (Lady Dunbar of Hempriggs), Professor A. G. Dickens, Dr. Robert "Humphrey" Havard, and Roger Lancelyn Green used with the kind permission of The Wade Center, Wheaton College, Wheaton, Illinois, USA.

The quotation from the Oral History Interview with Maureen Blake is used with the permission of the copyright owner, The Marion E. Wade Center, Wheaton College, Wheaton, Illinois © 1984 (and may not be further reproduced without written permission from the copyright owner).

The quotation from the Oral History Interview with Professor A. G. Dickens is used with the permission of the copyright owner, The Marion E. Wade Center, Wheaton College, Wheaton, Illinois © 1989 (and may not be further reproduced without written permission from the copyright owner).

The quotation from the Oral History Interview with Dr. Robert Havard is used with the permission of the copyright owner, The Marion E. Wade Center, Wheaton College, Wheaton, Illinois © 1984 (and may not be further reproduced without written permission from the copyright owner).

The quotation from the Oral History Interview with Roger Lancelyn Green is used with the permission of the copyright owner, The Marion E. Wade Center, Wheaton College, Wheaton, Illinois © 1986 (and may not be further reproduced without written permission from the copyright owner).

The quotation from Clyde S. Kilby, unpublished notes, is used with the permission of the copyright owner, The Marion E. Wade Center, Wheaton College, Wheaton, Illinois © 2003.

David C. Downing, quotation from personal communication to Colin Duriez. Used by permission.

Index

Characters and places in the stories of C. S. Lewis and Tolkien are printed in quotation marks. The titles of their works are indexed under "Lewis, Clive Staples" and "Tolkien, John Ronald Reuel"

Ace Books, 171, 196
"Aelfwine," 102, 106
Aeneas, 182
The Aeneid, 174
aesthetes, 50, 53
"Ainur," 103, 185, 213
"Alboin," 101, 103, 104, 105, 213
Aldiss, Brian, 203
Alexander, Samuel, 33, 57
"Alf," 171
Alice in Wonderland, 202
All Hallows Eve, 121
allegory, 48, 63–66, 70, 71, 93–94, 121–23, 135, 138, 141, 184, 186, 203, 212
alliterative meter, 13, 21
Andrew Lang, 72, 130, 194
angels, 61, 103–4, 185, 201
Anglo-Catholicism, 117
Anglo-Saxon, 32
anima naturaliter Christiana, 162
Animal Farm, 200
"Animal Land," 4
Anscombe, Elizabeth, 135
anthroposophism, 29
Anya, 161
The Apolausticks, 12
apologetics, 35, 148, 180
Apuleius, 161
Aquinas, St. Thomas, 82
"Aragorn," 41, 42, 73, 128, 143, 144
archetypes, 85, 199
Ariosto, 141
"Arnor," 102, 213
Arras, 18

Arthur, King, 41, 118, 193
"Arwen," 2, 42
asceticism, 167, 183–84
"Asgard," 44
Ash Wednesday, 74
"Aslan," 104, 134, 136, 137, 138–39, 185
atheism, 8, 27, 43, 53, 158, 175, 203. *See also* materialism
Atlantic, 101, 105, 111, 125
Atlantis, 6, 10, 61, 101–3, 126, 205. *See also* Númenor
Auden, W. H., 31, 32, 40, 74, 89, 142, 205, 207
"Audoin," 101, 103

B.Litt., 30, 130
Bag End, 37
Baggins, Frodo, 73, 90, 102, 142, 143–45, 164, 171, 196
Balder, 47, 55, 58, 93, 182, 209
Balfour, Arthur James, 30
Bank of Africa, 4, 189
Barbour, Brian, 210, 216
"Bardia," 162
Barfield, Owen, 29–31, 33, 38, 49, 52, 66, 75, 81, 83–84, 127, 197, 207, 209, 215. *See also* The "Great War"
Baxter, Richard, 184
BBC. *See* British Broadcasting Corporation
beauty, 3, 29, 53, 55–56, 162–63
"Beaver, Mr. and Mrs.," 183
Belfast, 2–3, 8–9, 38, 138, 190, 191, 193
Belgium, 145, 195
Bell, George, 74

Index

Belloc, Hilaire, 22
Bennett, Henry Stanley, 38, 149, 151
Bennett, J. A. W., 64
"Beren," 10, 17, 41–42, 48, 88, 177, 200
Berkeley, Bishop, 33, 224
Berkshire, 63, 139
Bernagh, 94
Berry, Francis, 75
Bible, 35, 51, 64, 103, 199
Bide, Peter, 166
Bilbo, 90–92, 102, 110, 112, 143, 144, 145, 164, 200, 214
Birmingham and district, 1–2, 5–8, 10, 139, 140–41
   PLACES: Ashfield Road, 5, 189; Corporation Street, 12; Duchess Road, 10, 190; Edgbaston, 7; Gracewell, 5; Handsworth, 10; King Edward's School, 6, 7, 10, 11, 12, 31, 190, 191; King's Heath, 1, 5, 189, 205; Moseley, 6, 7, 20, 223; Oliver Road, 7, 190; Oratory (see Oratory School); Perrott's Folly, 7; Rednal, 7, 8, 190; Sarehole Mill, 5, 190; Stirling Road, 7; Westfield Road, 205
biscuit tin lid, 3, 55, 190, 205
"Black Riders," 110, 111, 143
Blake, Leonard, 40, 166, 194, 208, 227
Blamires, Harry, 66, 73, 74, 210
Bloemfontein, 4, 5, 189, 190
The Bodley Head, 110
Boethius, 94
"Tom Bombadil," 62–63, 120, 183, 193
Bosanquet, Bernard, 27
Boshell, Patricia, 113
Boswell, James, 79
Bournemouth, 172, 197
"Boxen," 4
Bradley, F. H., 27
Bratt, Edith, 10–11, 13, 16–17, 36–37, 43–44, 69, 120, 145, 146, 160–61, 164, 172
Bratt, Frances, 10, 190
Bridges, Robert, 22
The British Academy, 69, 148, 193
British Army, 17, 37, 39, 114, 115, 119, 120
British Broadcasting Corporation, 114, 123–24, 163
Bromsgrove, 8
Buchan, John, 35
Buckinghamshire, 193
Bultitude, Mr., 52
Bunyan, John, 51, 68, 93, 94, 95, 96, 183
Burnt Norton, 74
Burton beer, 76
Byron, Lord, 100

C. S. Lewis Readers' Encyclopedia, 208, 225
Caird, Edward, 27
Calvin, John, 183, 184, 218
Cambridge University, 26, 28–29, 66–69, 146ff.
"Camilla," 103
Campbell College, 11, 191
Campbell, Roy, 129
cancer, 9, 159, 160, 161
Canterbury, 74
Cape Town, 4, 189
Carlingford, 136
Carnegie Medal, 196
Carpenter, Humphrey, 12, 31
Carritt, E. F., 22, 192
Cecil, Lord David, 133, 210
The Celestial City, 71, 96
"Charn," 136
"Chartres" School, 11
Chaucer, Geoffrey, 64, 68, 154
Cheltenham, 10, 13, 191
Cherbourg House, 11
Chesterton, G. K., 86, 212, 217, 223
Chipping Norton, 62
Christ, 51, 54, 57, 59, 78, 138, 163, 168, 185
Christ, 13
Christendom Group, 115
chronological snobbery, 29, 30
Churchill, Winston, 24
CICCU, 155
Clark Lectures (Cambridge), 68, 194
Clarke, Arthur C., 203
The Coalbiters, 43, 46, 47, 81
Coghill, Nevill, 43, 75, 78, 81, 84, 85, 86, 127, 151, 160
Colbourne, Joan, 34
Coleridge, Samuel Taylor, 31
Collins, Williams, 139
Comus, 121
concrete thinking, 31
consciousness, 26, 30, 67, 84, 108, 171
consolation (as literary theme), 42, 73, 124, 181, 201
The Consolation of Philosophy, 94
Cork, 189
Cornwall, 101, 125
cosmic war, 95
County Antrim, 136
County Down, 2, 97, 135, 136
Courtly love, 152
Coventry, 119
Craigie, William, 20
cremation, 157
Crispin, Edmund, 75, 210
Cullen, Mary, 23

Cupid, 161, 162
Cynewulf, 13

"D," 38
Daily Telegraph, 184
Dante Alighieri, 64, 86, 121
Daudel motorcycle, 52
David and Jonathan, 177
Davidman, Helen Joy (Helen Joy Gresham;
    Helen Joy Lewis), 153, 155–56, 157ff.,
    174
de Laclos, Pierre Choderlos, 167
"The Dead Marshes," 16, 187, 206
Descent of the Dove, 74
dialectic of desire, 96, 212
Diary of an Old Soul, 51
Dickens, A. G., 49, 50, 209, 227
Diotima, 38, 208
The Divine Comedy, 64
divorce, 155, 156
"Dolbear," 127
Downing, David C., 183
Drapa, 55, 209
Drout, Michael D. C., 206, 209
Dublin Review, 121, 195
Duke Humphrey library (Bodleian), 35
Dundas-Grant, James, 166, 167
Dundela, 3, 8, 138
Durham, 96
Dying God, 43, 58
Dymer, 27, 28, 37, 42, 43
Dyson, H. V. D. "Hugo," 53–54, 66, 115, 118,
    127, 128, 129

eagles, 101, 144
Eärendil, 12, 163
Early English, 21, 22, 31, 106
Eddison, E. R., 129
"Elendil," 101, 103, 213
Eliot, T. S., 67, 74, 115, 116, 214
"Elrond," 92, 143
elven quality, 201
Elvin, William, 172
Elvish, 49, 107, 191
Empson, William, 35, 224
Encyclopedia of Fantasy, 186, 218
Endicott, Lizzie, 97
English Dialect Dictionary, 12
The Enlightenment, 155, 173
"Ents," 90, 144, 184, 218
an epic for England, 187
epiphany, 2, 3, 46, 52, 161
Errantry, 79
"Errol, Oswin," 101

escape and escapism, 28, 58, 73, 100, 127, 142,
    143, 179, 200, 213
eucatastrophe, 181
Eurydice, 182
evacuees, 112–15, 214
evangelium, 78, 181. *See also* Gospel
Evesham, 4, 10, 36, 62, 189
Exploring the Christian World Mind, 208, 225
Ezard, John, 205

faerie, 72–73, 170–71, 176, 180, 181, 185, 199,
    201
The Faerie Queene, 94
fairy-land, 84
The Family Reunion, 75
"Fangorn," 144
The Fantastic Imagination, 84
fantasy, 28, 41, 58–59, 72, 73, 133–34, 179ff.,
    201
Farrer, Austin, 124, 166, 215
Farrer, Kathleen, 124, 159
Father Christmas, 20, 131
Faulkner, Mrs., 10, 183
faun, 135
fellowship, 12
Fen, Gervase, 75
Field, George, 11, 13
Finnish, 2, 4, 12–13, 16, 19, 20
Fisher, Bishop John, 184
Fletcher, Ronald, 25
Flewett, June, 114
Forster, E. M., 155
Fox, Adam, 75, 78, 81, 127
France, 15, 18, 119
Frankenstein, 100
Frazer, James, 43
Freud, Sigmund, 28, 29
Fry, Donald K., 69

"Galadriel," 180, 183, 200
"Gandalf," 90, 91, 104, 143, 144, 171, 185
Gardner, Ava, 173, 217
Gardner, Dame Helen, 35, 47, 148–49, 150,
    151
Sir Gawain and the Green Knight, 20, 43, 163
general strike, 24
genetic engineering, 154, 200
George Allen & Unwin, 87, 139, 140
Germany, 13, 112, 115, 191, 194
Gilson, R. Q. "Rob," 12, 15, 16
Glasgow, 163
"Glaurung," 60
"Glome," 59, 162, 176, 203
Gloucester, 10, 189

Index

God, 46, 50–52, 57–58
The Golden Ass, 161
Golding, William, 200
"Gollum," 15, 91, 143, 144
"Gondolin," 16, 19, 100
"Gondor," 7, 102, 141, 145, 182, 213
the good reader, 68
goodness, 56, 163, 183
Gordon, E. V., 20
Gordon, George, 21, 22, 25
Gospel, 43, 54, 57–59, 73, 78, 163, 175, 181, 185
Gothic, 4, 12, 32, 140
Grace Abounding to the Chief of Sinners, 51
Graham, Billy, 155
Grahame, Kenneth, 180
Graves, Robert, 22, 173
"The Great Dance," 104
The Great Divide, 59, 154
Great Haywood, 16
The "Great Knock," 14, 191
great storm, 125–26
The "Great War" with Barfield, 29–31, 33
The Greater Trumps, 74, 119, 215
Greece, 160
Green, Roger Lancelyn, 127, 129, 130–32, 134, 138, 160, 170
Green, T. H., 27
Greene, Graham, 74
Greeves, Arthur, 14, 15, 43, 44, 51, 85, 89, 94, 170
Grendel, 69
Gresham, David, 158
Gresham, Douglas, 158, 159, 160, 166, 167, 216, 217
Gresham, Joy. *See* Davidman, Joy
Griffiths, Bede, 127
Grimm, Brothers, 28
Grove, Jennie, 10, 13, 16
The Guardian, 205
Gueroult, Denis, 205, 206, 215

Haggard, H. Rider, 35, 68, 129
Hamilton, Clive (*nom de plume* of C. S. Lewis), 22, 42, 192
Hamlet, 121
happy ending, 181
Hardie, Frank, 34
Harland and Wolfe shipworks, 3
Harrogate, 16
Harry Potter, 202
Havard, Dr. Robert "Humphrey," 75, 82–83, 119, 127, 160, 166, 167
He Came Down from Heaven, 86

heaven, 3, 123, 168, 169, 181, 183, 218
Heinemann, 22, 86, 192
Helen of Troy, 103
Hell, 95, 128
"Herendil," 101, 103, 213
heroic romance, 41, 143
heroism, 59, 71, 118, 201
History in English Words, 30
hnau, 125, 184, 218
"hobbit," 6, 89, 90, 92, 131, 186
"Hobbiton," 6, 110
Hölderin, Friedrich, 208
Holland, 196
Home Guard, 119
Homer, 36, 154
Hooper, Walter, 136
Hopkins, Gerry, 115
Houghton Mifflin, 171, 208, 222, 223, 225
House by the Stable, 128
Household Journal, 8
Hove, 190
Hull, 84
humanism, 151, 155, 203
Humber, 17
Hyperion, 208

Icelandic, 43, 46
The Idea of the Holy, 180
idealism, 27, 29, 43, 57
"Idril," 102
"Ilúvatar," 103, 184, 185
imagination, 21, 29, 30–31, 54, 56, 58, 71, 72, 93, 126, 157, 163, 178–79, 185–86
immortality, 17, 42
Inaugural Lecture, 68, 195
The Independent, 208
the Inklings, 77ff., 125–29, 174–75
intentionality, 207
Ireland, 2, 8, 14, 17, 94, 97, 136, 145, 157, 160, 168

Jenkin, A. K. Hamilton, 52, 68, 209
Johnson, Samuel, 79
Jones, David, 75
Joy. *See sehnsucht*

The Kalevala, 16, 20
Kennedy, J. F., 167
Kierkegaard, Søren, 117
Kilby, Clyde S., 162, 163, 170, 178, 197, 206, 216, 217, 218, 222, 227
The Kilns, 40, 113, 214
"Kirke, Digory," 14, 136, 176
Kirkpatrick, W. T., 14, 30, 97, 191

Index

Knox, Ronald, 82

Kullervo, 16, 182

Lancashire Fusiliers, 13, 191

Lawlor, John, 166, 222

Laxdale Saga, 43

Le Tréport, 18

Leavis, F. R., 67, 68, 149, 152

Lee, Margaret, 25

Leeds, 20, 21, 36, 49, 81, 174, 192

"Legolas," 143, 144, 182

Lenten Lands, 216, 217

Les Liaisons Dangereuses, 167

Lewis, Albert, 8–9, 14, 18, 23, 38, 189, 193, 206

Lewis, Clive Staples "Jack"

  LIFE: childhood, 3–4, 8–10; death of mother, Flora, 9–10; schooldays, 11, 13–15; Oxford undergraduate, 17, 22; war service, 17–18; meets "Paddy," Maureen and Mrs. Janie Moore, 17–18; tutoring in philosophy and appointment as Fellow of Magdalen College, 22–23; meets Tolkien, 24–26; intellectual climate and "Great War" with Barfield, 27–31; tutoring, lecturing and wide reading, 32–36; keeps diary, 37–38; final years of Albert Lewis, 38–39; purchase of The Kilns, 39–40; cracks in his atheism, 42–43; attends The Coalbiters, 43, 46–47; reluctant conversion to theism, 45–46; regular meetings with Tolkien, 47–49; changing physical appearance, 49–50; conversion to Christian faith, 50–55; importance of longing and joy, 55–57; view of myth become fact, 57–59; engages in literary controversy, 66–69; lectures in Cambridge, 68–69; creates the Inklings, 77ff.; discovers Charles Williams, 84–86; challenges Tolkien to write more adult fantasy, 99–100; writes first science-fiction, with Tolkien-inspired hero, 106–10; wartime evacuees arrive at The Kilns, 112–14; seeds of Narnia, 114; friendship deepens with Charles Williams, 115ff.; becomes popular communicator of Christian faith, and Tolkien disapproves, 123–25; the Inklings enlarge, 127–29; reads part of first Narnia story to Tolkien then Roger Lancelyn Green, 131–32; Tolkien's disapproval, 133–35; endorses *The Lord of the Rings,* 141; persuaded by Tolkien to take Cambridge Chair, 146–48, 149–51; inaugural lecture, 153–55; meets Joy Davidman,

155–56, 158; marriage, 159–60; death of Joy, 161; final months and death, 166–68

  WRITINGS – PRINCIPAL BOOKS: *The Abolition of Man,* 96, 204; *The Allegory of Love,* 33, 38, 63–66, 85, 93, 152, 194, 203; *All My Road Before Me,* 37; *Arthurian Torso,* 213; *The Chronicles of Narnia,* 14, 56, 135, 136–39, 184, 202, 203; *The Discarded Image,* 82, 152; *English Literature in the Sixteenth Century,* 64, 66, 68, 183, 195, 203; *Essays Presented to Charles Williams,* 176, 209; *An Experiment in Criticism,* 68, 152, 176, 203; *The Four Loves,* 80, 118, 135, 177; *The Great Divorce,* 46, 62, 118, 121, 124, 174; *A Grief Observed,* 135, 160; *A Horse and His Boy,* 136, 138; *The Last Battle,* 103, 136, 137, 196; *Letters of C. S. Lewis,* 197, 207; *Letters to an American Lady,* 170; *Letters to Malcolm,* 135, 168, 169, 170, 196, 203; *The Lion, the Witch and the Wardrobe,* 114, 136, 137, 138, 195; *The Magician's Nephew,* 104, 136, 176; *Mere Christianity,* 195; *Miracles,* 11, 27, 46, 54, 57, 134, 168, 195, 203, 204; *Out of the Silent Planet,* 62, 75, 87, 106, 109, 126, 134, 184; *Oxford History of English Literature,* 64, 194; *Perelandra,* 59, 62, 102, 104, 124, 176, 183, 185; *The Personal Heresy,* 67, 149; *The Pilgrim's Regress,* 8, 28, 55, 74, 82, 88, 93–98, 100, 134, 157, 193, 203; *Prince Caspian,* 136, 137; *The Problem of Pain,* 56, 123, 127, 128, 134, 138, 168, 174, 180; *Reflections on the Psalms,* 135, 203; *Rehabilitations,* 67; *The Screwtape Letters,* 110, 123, 124, 174, 194, 202, 203; *Selected Literary Essays,* 152; *Spirits in Bondage,* 22, 27, 42, 192; *Studies in Words,* 64, 152; *Surprised by Joy,* 3, 8, 10–11, 14–15, 29, 35, 38, 43–44, 50, 55–57, 73, 94, 96, 98, 163; *That Hideous Strength,* 14, 62, 97, 102, 118, 124, 133–34, 154, 161, 182, 200; *They Stand Together,* 211; *Till We Have Faces,* 56, 62, 118, 135, 161, 163, 183–85, 196, 204; *The Voyage of the "Dawn Treader,"* 56, 136, 137; *Studies in Medieval and Renaissance Literature,* 152

  OTHER WRITINGS: "After Ten Years," 103; "Bluspels and Flalansferes," 207, 218; "The Dark Tower," 103, 213, 214; *De Descriptione Temporum,* 152; "Horrid Red Things," 207; "Learning in Wartime," 95; "My life," 206; "New Learning and New Ignorance," 194; "On Stories," 175, 218; "The Weight of Glory," 56, 123, 209, 218

239

Lewis Family Papers, 9, 13, 22, 38, 39, 193, 206, 208
Lewis, Flora, 8, 9, 189, 190
Lewis, Joy. *See* Davidman, Joy
Lewis, Richard, 8
Lewis, Warren Hamilton "Warnie," 3, 11, 38, 39, 40, 53, 125, 128, 129, 136, 140, 147, 150, 159, 160, 166, 208
lion. *See* "Aslan"
literary canon, 67, 149
literary criticism, 28–29, 64, 67, 149, 152
Little Lea, 9, 11, 14, 94
Lodge, David, 152
Logical Positivism, 15
Loki Bound, 14
Longfellow, Henry, 55
Lord Haw-Haw, 114
The Lord of the Flies, 200
"Lórien," 143, 183
Lowdham, Arry, 127
Lucifer, 104
"Lúthien," 10, 17, 41, 42, 48, 88, 102, 172, 177, 180, 200
Lyme Regis, 36

Mabbott, John, 27, 34, 211
Macauley, Rose, 75
MacDonald, George, 15, 51, 56, 84, 86, 89, 116, 129, 143, 217
machine, 100, 138, 153, 154, 156, 198, 200
Mackinnon, Donald, 115
"MacPhee, Andrew," 14, 97
Magdalene College (Cambridge), 151, 192
magic, 55, 100, 131, 137, 154, 171, 198, 200
"Maiar," 104
"Malacandra," 106, 108, 176, 184
Malaprop, Mrs., 31
"Maleldil," 185
Malvern, 11, 14, 140, 191
Mappa Mundi, 95, 98, 117
Mars, 106, 108, 184. *See also* "Malacandra"
The Martlets, 67
Martsch, Nancy, 20
Mascall, E. L., 115
materialism, 11, 30, 34, 42, 51, 57, 74, 178, 187, 199, 203
McNeill, Jane, 211
"Melian," 42, 48
"Merry," 143, 144
metaphor, 59, 198
Middle Ages, 26, 63, 64, 65
Middle English, 32, 43, 49, 106, 132, 163
Midlands (of England), 2, 4, 5, 63, 90, 93, 132, 136, 157, 163, 203

Milton, John, 67, 68, 121, 155, 185, 224
Miller, Mrs., 150
"Minas Tirith," 7, 144
"Minto," 22, 25, 38, 112, 113, 114. *See also* Moore, Mrs. Janie
"Misty Mountains," 91, 143
modernism, 2, 15, 26, 29, 36, 47, 58, 59, 66, 67, 68, 73, 92, 95, 100, 101, 107, 108, 124, 129, 135, 153, 154, 173, 182, 183, 198, 200, 204, 215
Mole, 180, 218
Moore, Maureen (Dame Dunbar of Hempriggs), 17, 18, 22, 24, 37, 40, 52, 112, 113, 166, 192, 194, 206, 227
Moore, Mrs. Janie, 17, 18, 22, 24, 37–40, 52, 112, 113, 123, 136, 140, 147, 150, 156, 166, 178
Moore, "Paddy," 17, 18, 22, 192
"Mordor," 143, 144
Morgan, Father Francis, 7, 8, 10, 13, 17, 164, 190
"Morgoth," 17, 60, 61, 101, 104, 154, 200
"Moria," 143
Morris, William, 15, 62, 86, 89, 129
Mount Bernenchon, 18
Mourne Mountains, 2, 135–36
Mr. Bliss, 62
Muir, Edwin, 75
Murder in the Cathedral, 74

"Narnia," 2, 56, 97, 114, 131–32, 133–39, 157, 176, 202, 203
naturalism, 11, 27, 43. *See also* materialism
Neave, Aunt Jane, 37
The new criticism, 67
The new psychology, 28
New Statesman, 90
New Testament, 43, 64
The New West, 200
New Year Letter, 74
New York Times, 89, 142
Newman, Cardinal Henry, 6, 7, 20, 175
Nicolson, Marjorie Hope, 109
"Niggle," 121, 122, 123
1984, 200
"Nokes," 171
Norman, Philip, 164
Norse, 12, 14, 93
northernness, 19, 31, 47, 55, 71, 93, 96, 101, 104, 106, 111, 199
"Númenor," 6, 61, 101, 102, 103, 126, 163, 213, 215
the numinous, 171, 180
nymphs, 56, 131

Index

the occult, 118, 119
Old English, 47, 72
"Old Narnia," 137
Old West, 59, 134, 154, 153, 154, 199
Olney, Austin, 41
Onions, Charles Talbut, 20
Oratory School, 6, 7, 10, 139, 190
"orcs," 2, 141, 144, 154
organ of meaning, 178, 218. *See also* imagination
Orlando Furioso, 141
"Orual," 161, 162, 163
Orwell, George, 200
Osiris, 58
other worlds, otherness, 8, 85, 100, 171, 176, 179–81, 185
Otto, Rudolf, 180
OUP. *See* Oxford University Press
Oxford, 27–29, 47, 66–67, 115, 119, 120–21, 123, 148–49, 151–52
   PLACES: Acland Nursing Home, 196; Addison's Walk, 53, 99; Botanic Gardens, 25; The Eagle and Child (The "Bird and Baby"), 75–76, 77–78, 82, 128, 210–11; Eastgate Hotel, 47, 128; Headington, 22, 25, 39, 45, 53, 82, 146, 164, 166, 195; "Hillsboro," Holyoake Road, 24, 37; Holy Trinity Church, 166; The Kilns, 39–40, 112ff., 147, 159, 178, 216; Northmoor Road, 36, 37, 47, 212; Oxford University (*see* Oxford University); Sandfield Road, 146, 164, 172; St. Aloysius's Church, 167
Oxford University: The Bodleian, 35, 206, 212; Exeter College, 12, 43, 84, 191; Final Honour School, 47, 208; Honour Moderations, 192; Keble College, 17; Lady Margaret Hall, 33; Magdalen College, 32, 40, 43, 51, 75, 80, 99, 118, 150, 151; Merton, 25, 130, 132, 148, 172; Pembroke College, 21, 36, 115, 127; University College, 22, 116, 151, 192; Worcester College, 63
Oxford Magazine, 193
Oxford Memories, 211
Oxford University Press, 65, 85, 115, 116, 117
Oxfordshire, 52, 63, 193
"Oyarsa," 109

Packer, J. I., 95
paganism, 71, 78, 135, 139, 154, 162–63, 182–83
Pan, 180
Papworth, Mr., 37, 52
participation, 31
Paxford, Fred, 113, 148, 150, 166

Pearl, 49
perception, 30, 36, 108, 176, 186
Personal Knowledge, 207, 223
Phantastes, 15
Phillips, Justin, 214
philology, 16, 20, 21, 28, 102, 106–7, 110, 164
Philosophers' Teas, 34
Phippy, 37
Pilate, 58
The Pilgrim's Progress, 93, 94, 95
"Pippin," 143, 144
Pitter, Ruth, 211
The Place of the Lion, 74, 84, 85, 99, 116, 118, 138
Plato, 38, 56, 78, 85
Plotz, Dick, 209
Plummer, Polly, 136
Poetic Diction, 29, 30, 49
Poetic Edda, 43
Polanyi, Michael, 207
"Pole, Jill," 114, 137
positivism, 29
possession (as theme), 62, 154, 200
post-Christian, 59, 124, 153, 155
practical criticism, 67, 149
prayer, 46, 160, 168, 169
the pre-Christian, 71, 135, 153–55, 161, 184, 185, 199
Price, Henry, 34
Prichard, H. A., 27
Professorship of Poetry, 133, 149
Protestant, 6, 93, 157, 217
providence, 92, 103, 104, 184, 185, 199
Prudentius, 65
"Psyche," 56, 161–63, 182
"Puddleglum," 113, 202
purgatory, 121, 122, 168
puritanism, 183–84
"Puritania," 96, 97, 157

Quenya, 13, 191
quest, 56, 90–91, 95, 96, 98, 142, 143, 199

RAF. *See* Royal Air Force
"Ransom, Elwin," 67, 106ff., 185
"Rashbold," 127
Ratty, 180
Reading University, 54, 78, 127
Recovery (as theme), 73, 99, 182
Redemption (as theme), 71, 199
"Reepicheep," 56
reluctant convert, 46, 150
Rembrandt, 201, 202
restoration (as theme), 73, 182

Index

Reveille, 22
Richards, I. A., 28–29, 66, 68, 149
Ridler, Anne, 116
"Rilian," 137
The Rivals, 31
"Rivendell," 92, 143
The Rock, 74
"Rohan," 144, 145
Roman Catholicism, 6–8, 10, 53, 93, 157
romanticism, 117, 185
romance (as literary feature), 8, 65, 89, 100, 109, 128, 133, 143, 185
Romance of the Rose, 33, 64
Rome, 119, 183
Roos, 17
Ross, W. David, 27
Royal Air Force, 120, 194
Russell, David L., 64
Russian Revolution, 42
Ryle, Gilbert, 34, 204

sacramentalism, 41, 54, 93, 171
sacrifice (as theme), 41, 42, 108, 142, 143, 157, 163, 199
"Sam," 15, 90, 143, 144, 145, 200
Sandhurst, 14, 39, 191
"Saruman," 144, 154, 200
Sassoon, Siegfried, 22
"Sauron," 101, 104, 142, 143, 144, 154, 200
Sayer, George, 140, 164, 165, 166
Sayers, Dorothy L., 74, 75, 84, 129, 211
science-fiction, 19, 62, 65, 87, 102, 104, 179, 203
"Scrubb, Eustace," 67, 137
Scrutiny, 152
"Scudamour," 103
secondary worlds, 73, 133, 176, 198–99
sehnsucht, 3, 56–57, 180–81
Severn, River, 2, 141
Shakespeare, William, 67, 68, 154
Shanghai, 38, 39
Sheed and Ward, 97
Shelley, Mary, 100, 213
Shelley, Percy Bysshe, 39, 67, 100
Shippey, T. A., 21, 28, 122
"The Shire," 2, 5–6, 63, 90, 91, 111, 120, 183
Shirreffs restaurant, 86
Shotover, 39
Sidmouth, 36, 112
Sierra Leone, 39
"Sigismund Enlightenment," 28
Sigurd, 182
silmarils, 17, 61, 200
The Silver Trumpet, 30

"Sindarin," 13
Sir Isaac Gollancz Memorial Lecture, 193
sixteenth-century, 64, 68
Smith, G. B., 11, 12, 13, 16
Smith of Wootton Major, 170, 171
Smithers, G. V., 147, 150
Smoke on the Mountain, 156, 157
Socrates, 38
Socratic Club, 148
Somerset Light Infantry, 17
The Somme (battle), 15, 17, 64
Soper, David Wesley, 40
South Africa, 4, 120, 164
Spalding, H. N., 115
Spanish Civil War, 158
Spenser, Edmund, 26, 64, 65, 68, 94, 129, 152
St. Albans, 116
St. Andrews University, 72, 194
St. Brendan, 163
St. Paul's Cathedral, 86, 87
Steiner, Rudolf, 29
Stewart, J. I. M., 32, 212
Stoneyhurst College, 119, 120
the "straight road," 95, 102
sub-creation (as literary feature), 72–73, 133, 176, 182, 186, 198. *See* secondary worlds
Suffields (Edith's family), 4, 5, 37, 189: Aunt Beatrice, 7, 10; May, 190
Sunday Times, 164
supposals, 135, 136
Swan Song, 75
Swann, Donald, 79, 172

T.C.B.S., 12, 13, 15, 16, 41, 80, 187; Barrovian Society, 12; Tea Club, 12, 191
Taliesin Through Logres, 75, 118
talking animals, 4, 59, 135, 136, 139
The Tao, 108
Tarot Pack, 119, 215
technocracy, 154, 200
Tegner, Elias, 55, 209
Tellers of Tales, 132
theism, 46, 50–51, 53, 169
Theism and Humanism, 30
"Théoden," 144
These Found the Way, 217
"Thingol," 10, 42, 48, 200
"Thorin," 91, 92
Tillyard, E. M. W., 67, 149
Timbermill, Professor, 212
Time and Tide, 142, 163
Time magazine, 123, 194, 203, 213
time travel, 100, 105, 106, 111, 125
Times Literary Supplement, 90, 92

"Tinidril," 102

"Tinúviel," 102. *See also* Lúthien

"Tirian," 137

"Tol Eressëa," 102, 163

Tolkien, Christopher, 21, 107, 120, 125, 126, 127, 166, 201, 202

Tolkien, Hilary, 1, 4, 6, 20, 36, 51, 62, 189

Tolkien, John Ronald Reuel

    LIFE: childhood, 1–2, 4–6; early schooling, 6–7; death of mother, Mabel Tolkien, 7–8; meets Edith Bratt, 10; at King Edward's School, Birmingham, 11–12; Oxford undergraduate, 12–13; marriage to Edith, 13; war service in the trenches and recovery in England, 15–17; begins "the Silmarillion," 18–19; employment on *Oxford English Dictionary,* 19–20; move to Leeds University as Reader then Professor in English School, 20–21; appointment and move to Oxford as Professor of Anglo-Saxon, 21–22; meets C. S. Lewis, 25–26; shapes the English syllabus, 26; his intellectual context at Oxford, 27–29; lecturing style, 31–32; home life at Northmoor Road, 36–37; relates his scholarly life to imaginative writing, 40–41; The Coalbiters and deepening friendship with Lewis, 43, 46–49; helps persuade Lewis of truth of Christian faith, 53–54; view of myth become fact, 54, 57–59; work on "The Silmarillion" in the thirties, 61–62; British Academy lecture on *Beowulf,* 69–72; Andrew Lang lecture at St. Andrews on fairy stories, 72–73; part in minor revival of Christian writing, 73–75; active in the Inklings, 77–81; very different man from Lewis, 83; begins *The Hobbit* and lets Lewis read it, 88–90; challenged by Lewis to write adult fantasy on time travel, 99–100; his attempt, 100–102; influence on Lewis's writing, 102–4; autobiographical insights in time story, 104–5; represented as "Ransom" in Lewis's space story, 106–9; begins adult sequel to *The Hobbit,* 110–11; household in war-time, 114–15; meetings with Charles Williams, 115; disapproves of Williams's tastes, 118; service in the Home Guard and impact of World War II, 119–20; writes semi-autobiographical allegory, *Leaf by Niggle,* 121–23; disapproves of Lewis as popular theologian, 124; works on "The Notion Club Papers," reflecting the Inklings, 125–27; Dyson exercises veto against reading of *The Lord of the Rings* at the Inklings, 129; disapproves of the first Narnian story, 131–32; hopes to find Lewis an Oxford Chair, 132–33; completes writing *The Lord of the Rings,* 139; complex path to publication, 139–40; records extracts, 140; persuades Lewis to take on Cambridge Chair in English, 146ff.; Lewis's friendship with Joy Davidman threatens their friendship, 155ff.; Tolkien's contrary views on divorce, 156; unaware of Lewis's marriage, 159–60; first meeting with Joy, 160–61; explores and teaches literature of West Midlands, 163; retirement and Valedictory Address, 164; moves to Sandfield Road, 164; impact of Lewis's death, 167; upset by Lewis's posthumous book, *Letters to Malcolm,* 170; self-doubt, 170; *The Lord of the Rings* becomes a phenomenon, 171; golden wedding anniversary, 172; move to Bournemouth, 172; death of Edith, 172; death, 172

    WRITINGS — PRINCIPAL BOOKS: *Book of Lost Tales,* 16; *Farmer Giles of Ham,* 63, 170; *The Fellowship of the Ring,* 89, 140, 167; *History of Middle Earth,* 16; *The Hobbit,* 21, 61, 82, 89ff., 110, 122, 172; *The Lays of Beleriand,* 209, 210; *Leaf by Niggle,* 104, 121, 123, 171, 195; *The Lord of the Rings,* 15, 42, 44, 62, 105, 111, 115, 122, 133, 134, 139ff., 171, 184, 186, 199ff.; *The Monsters and the Critics,* 69, 72, 206; *The Return of the King,* 140, 142; *The Silmarillion,* 16, 61–62, 103–4, 120, 180, 184, 201; *Tree and Leaf,* 196; *The Two Towers,* 125, 140; *Unfinished Tales,* 16, 201

    OTHER WRITINGS: "The Ainulindalë," 61, 103, 104; " The Akallabêth," 61; "Beowulf: The Monsters and the Critics," 21, 31–32, 49, 69ff., 183, 202; "Imram," 163; "The Lay of Leithien," 48, 193; "The Lost Road," 101, 111, 120, 126, 163; "Mythopoeia," 45, 53, 54, 59, 179; "The Notion Club Papers," 125, 126, 127, 163; "On Fairy Stories," 40, 54, 69, 72, 170, 181, 194; "A Secret Vice," 49; "The Silmarillion," 16, 17, 18–19, 41, 48, 61–62, 72, 90, 92, 101–2, 105, 139, 145, 165, 201–2 "Sketch of the Mythology," 193

Tolkien, John, 17, 21, 89, 119, 167, 197, 212, 217
Tolkien, Mabel, 4, 5, 6, 7, 8, 189, 190
Tolkien, Michael, 20, 62, 89, 120, 192, 197
Tolkien, Priscilla, 36, 37, 115, 120, 164, 193, 212
Tolkien and The Silmarillion, 206
Tolkien as a Post-War Writer, 219
Tolkien Family Album, 205, 208, 212
"Tor," 102
"Treebeard," 90, 144, 184, 218
"Tuor," 102
"Túrin," 16, 21, 60, 61, 210
"The Two Lamps," 61, 104
"The Two Trees," 104

Ulster, 2, 42, 50, 51, 96, 97, 100, 136, 157
"Ulsterior motive," 157
Underhill, Evelyn, 138–39
"Undying Lands," 145, 182
"Ungit," 162
Unwin, Stanley, 87, 105, 109, 110, 126, 140, 141

"Valaquenta," 61
"Valar," 61, 103, 104, 185
Valedictory Address, 164, 196
"Valinor," 182, 183
Venus, 161, 162
Vice Chancellor of Cambridge University, 148, 150, 151
Viking Club, 21
Virgil, 154, 174
Volsung Saga, 43

Wain, John, 127, 128–29, 213, 216
Waldman, Milton, 139, 195
Wales, 1, 101, 141
Wallaby Wood, 52
Wallace, William, 27
Walsh, Chad, 123, 153, 210–11
War in Heaven, 74, 117
Wardale, Edith Elizabeth, 22
Warwick, 13, 16, 223

Warwickshire, 5, 11, 37, 105, 191
Watford, 11, 191
Waugh, Evelyn, 74, 75, 183
"The Way to the Other World," 84
Weeping Bay, 161
Weldon, T. H., 34, 43
Wells, H. G., 100
Welsh, 2, 3, 4, 7, 12, 13, 19, 191
"Weston, Edward," 106, 108
Whipsnade Zoo, 52, 53, 193, 208
"White Witch," 136
Wholly Other, 180. *See also* other worlds, otherness
wildness in nature, 139
"Wilfred Trewin Jeremy," 127
Willey, Basil, 149, 150
Williams, Charles, 74, 80, 85ff., 86, 115–19, 121, 127, 128, 133, 168, 185–86
Williams, Florence "Michal," 117, 194, 214
Willink, Henry, 150, 151
Wilson, A. N., 38, 42
Wilson, F. P., 22, 64, 133, 148, 149
Wind in the Willows, 132, 180, 202
Winnie the Pooh, 202
Wiseman, Christopher, 12, 80
Wish fulfillment, 28, 46, 176
wizards, 62, 90, 91, 143, 144, 185, 200
The Wood that Time Forgot, 134
Worcestershire, 4, 7, 105, 140, 189, 190
Worksop College, 194
world models, 153
worldview (*Weltanschauung*), 83–84
Worminghall, 63
Wrenn, C. L., 75, 81, 127
Wright, Joseph, 12, 20, 191
Wynyard School, 191

Yorkshire, 16
Young, Andrew, 75
Young Pattullo, 212
The Younger Edda, 43

The Zeal of Thy House, 75